THE PREDICAMENT OF CHUKOTKA'S INDIGENOUS MOVEMENT

The Predicament of Chukotka's Indigenous Movement is the first ethnography of the Russian North to focus on post-Soviet relations of domination between an indigenous minority and a nonindigenous majority in an urban setting. As Patty Gray investigates indigenous attempts in Chukotka to overcome this domination, she develops an anthropological approach to social movements that captures the "in-between" activity that is more than everyday resistance, but less than a full-blown movement. In the process, this book explores the post-Soviet transition as it occurred in the part of Russia that is America's closest Eurasian neighbor: Chukotka nearly touches Alaska across the Bering Strait. Gray charts the political transformation in Chukotka as its administration sought to represent itself as "democratic" while becoming ever more repressive and demonstrates how the indigenous population in particular suffered under this new form of domination. The "predicament" refers to how the nascent indigenous movement was prepared to address Soviet-style domination and instead was confronted with this "new-Russian" style.

Patty A. Gray is Assistant Professor of cultural anthropology at the University of Alaska, Fairbanks. She was Post-Doctoral Fellow 2000–2003 at the Max Planck Institute for Social Anthropology in Halle, Germany, and Coordinator of the Siberia Project Group at that institute in 2002–2003. She is the recipient of grants from the Fulbright Program, IREX (International Research and Exchanges Board), the MacArthur Foundation, and the Wenner-Gren Foundation for Anthropological Research.

To Anatoly M. Khazanov, with affection

The Predicament of Chukotka's Indigenous Movement

POST-SOVIET ACTIVISM IN THE RUSSIAN FAR NORTH

Patty A. Gray

University of Alaska, Fairbanks

CAMBRIDGE
UNIVERSITY PRESS

PUBLISHED BY THE PRESS SYNDICATE OF THE UNIVERSITY OF CAMBRIDGE
The Pitt Building, Trumpington Street, Cambridge, United Kingdom

CAMBRIDGE UNIVERSITY PRESS
The Edinburgh Building, Cambridge CB2 2RU, UK
40 West 20th Street, New York, NY 10011-4211, USA
477 Williamstown Road, Port Melbourne, VIC 3207, Australia
Ruiz de Alarcón 13, 28014 Madrid, Spain
Dock House, The Waterfront, Cape Town 8001, South Africa

http://www.cambridge.org

First published 2005

Printed in the United States of America

Typefaces Utopia 10/14 pt. and Gill Sans   *System* LATEX 2$_\varepsilon$ [TB]

A catalog record for this book is available from the British Library.

Library of Congress Cataloging in Publication Data
Gray, Patty A. (Patricia Anne), 1960–
The predicament of Chukotka's indigenous movement : post-Soviet activism in the
Russian Far North / Patty A. Gray.
p.   cm.
Includes bibliographical references and index.
ISBN 0-521-82346-3
1. Ethnology – Russia (Federation) – Chukotskii avtonomnyi okrug.   2. Indigenous
peoples – Russia (Federation) – Chukotskii avtonomnyi okrug – Government
relations.   3. Indigenous peoples – Russia (Federation) – Chukotskii avtonomnyi
okrug – Politics and government.   4. Indigenous peoples – Russia (Federation) –
Chukotskii avtonomnyi okrug – Social conditions.   5. Chukotskii avtonomnyi okrug
(Russia) – History.   6. Chukotskii avtonomnyi okrug (Russia) – Politics and
government.   7. Chukotskii avtonomnyi okrug (Russia) – Social life and customs.
8. Soviet Union – History – 1985–1991.   9. Soviet Union – Politics and government –
1985–1991.   10. Russia (Federation) – History – 1991–   11. Russia (Federation) – Politics
and government – 1991–   I. Title.
GN635.C5.G73   2004
305.8′00957′7–dc22   2004040398

ISBN 0 521 82346 3 hardback

CONTENTS

ILLUSTRATIONS AND TABLES

Maps

Figures

Tables

Preface

CHUKOTKA IN THE TWENTY-FIRST CENTURY

A Place on the Edge

Chukotka is a region of Russia located at the intersection of Russia's north and east coasts. A huge territory of 737,700 square kilometers (about two-thirds the size of Alaska), it is situated as far north and east from Moscow as one can physically travel and still be in Russia – any further, and you would tumble into the Bering Sea. Along with Alaska, it divides the Pacific Ocean from the Arctic Ocean, and provided one-half of the land bridge that underlies the most popular theory of the peopling of North America. Chukotka lies on the leading edge of time; that is, the Chukotka Peninsula occupies time zone number 1 in the system of twenty-four time zones that girds the earth. In this sense, each new day of the earth begins when the sun hits the Chukotkan island of Big Diomede. When a sea mammal hunter from Chukotka working in the Bering Sea catches sight of the coast of Alaska, which he is quite likely to do, he is looking at yesterday.

In spite of the close proximity of this region of the Russian Far East to the United States (the Chukotka Peninsula is less than one hundred kilometers from Alaska's Seward Peninsula at its closest point), when the border was closed and tightly guarded during the Soviet period, the distance may as well have been thousands of miles for anyone but the few local indigenous residents who managed to slip back and forth occasionally across the border illegally under the cover of fog (Schweitzer and Golovko 1995). The distance from Chukotka to the Russian capital of Moscow *is* thousands of miles (Chukotka is in fact closer to Washington, D.C.). Thus Chukotka occupies a position on the edge in a multiple sense – it is literally on the border between two continents and figuratively on the edge of two worlds. However, once the Soviet Union collapsed, the border opened and these people who were once so marginalized found themselves for a time occupying a space that was an international crossroads (Fitzhugh and Crowell 1988). A flood of relatives, tourists, environmentalists, and journalists, not to mention anthropologists, began to inundate coastal Chukotka, creating what some described as a carnival atmosphere.

Framing Chukotka's "Dark Decade"

This book focuses on the final decade of the twentieth century in Chukotka, its first decade after Soviet rule. This was a time of drastic changes throughout Russia, during which many suffered from shock and confusion and experienced greater poverty than in the Soviet period. However, it is generally agreed that Chukotkans were among those who suffered most, and this was in large part due to the particular audacity and corruption of its governor, Aleksandr Nazarov, and the patronage system he constructed far from the scrutiny of the Kremlin. One should not give too much credit to a single figure for monopolizing all power and causing all suffering, but it is nevertheless true that many refer to the period of his tenure as a particularly dark time in Chukotkan history.

With rather poetic symmetry, the first decade of the twenty-first century marked a radical shift in local political dynamics in Chukotka, and before launching into the main subject of the 1990s, it makes sense to foreshadow what followed this "dark decade." In 1999, an election was held for Chukotka's single seat in the federal Duma (the lower legislative house), and this seat was captured handily by one of those who are known as Russia's "oligarchs," Roman Arkadevich Abramovich. Abramovich had previously been well-known in Russia as a "Kremlin insider" and the head of one of the country's largest oil and aluminum companies, Sibneft, as well as a close associate of Boris Berezovskii, perhaps the country's most notorious oligarch.[1] The two had been in business together, and later they became deputies in the Duma together. Berezovskii resigned from the Duma in July amid controversy and by the end of 2000 was living in Europe in a kind of exile, leaving Abramovich as Russia's most visible – and most studied by the media – oligarch.[2]

One of Abramovich's first acts as Duma deputy representing Chukotka was to establish a charitable organization called *Polius Nadezhdy* (Pole of Hope). This organization immediately set about investigating, and then solving, many of the most pressing problems plaguing Chukotka's population, such as salary delays and food shortages in villages – acts of charity that in many cases were financed out of Abramovich's own pocket. A program was quickly established to send groups of children on long holidays to camps in the warm Black Sea locales of Annapa, Ivanovo, and Evpatoriya – to the delight of their parents, who felt that they would "get more vitamins" there. Abramovich also established outreach offices in every district center in Chukotka, as well as Anadyr', where any citizen could come and present any problem that needed solving; Abramovich's staff would then investigate the problem and seek a solution with a minimum of red tape. Abramovich himself made two trips to Alaska in 2000 to meet with the many representatives of state government, humanitarian aid organizations, academic institutions, and businesspeople who had been trying for years to cultivate relations with Chukotkans and were utterly exasperated by being thwarted at every turn. One of the purposes of his visits was to discuss joint Alaska–Chukotka projects in all these spheres.

When I arrived for a follow-up visit to Anadyr' in the summer of 2000, I was amazed to hear the name of Abramovich on literally everyone's lips. All of my consultees expressed a palpable sense of optimism that had simply been nonexistent in all my previous visits, and the source of it was purely Abramovich. Rumors had already begun that this do-gooder deputy might register his candidacy for the upcoming gubernatorial election scheduled for December 2000. In spite of this optimism, hardly anyone fully trusted Abramovich. Some maintained a critical attitude toward his activities as a billionaire businessman and suspected he was interested in Chukotka for its oil and gold deposits. Others accused him of fueling the war in Chechnya for his own financial interests. One could find still worse accusations in the Russian media; many of these accusations were undoubtably false, but they did bespeak the fact that Abramovich was a controversial figure. Yet everyone I spoke to in Chukotka, without exception, said that absolutely anyone would be better than Nazarov – that they could not imagine how anyone else could be worse. They said they would vote for Abramovich if he ran, or for any other candidate opposing Nazarov. Even administration bureaucrats who in the past had never dared to breathe a word of criticism of Nazarov in my presence were now opining on aspects of his policy with which they disagreed. For the first time since I had begun my research in Chukotka in 1995, I sensed the possibility of change on the horizon. It was an intoxicating atmosphere that everyone clearly savored.

Abramovich did finally declare his candidacy for the post of governor in mid-October 2000.[3] On 24 October, the Russian federal tax police reportedly summoned Nazarov for questioning on what the Interfax news agency stated was "an entire array of evil deeds"[4] that included the illegal sale of quotas for the catch of marine bioresources, tax evasion to the tune of $20 million, and misdirection of state funds in relation to deliveries of oil products to the North between 1996 and 2000. Interfax also reported that Nazarov rented a dacha in a health complex maintained by the Russian government and paid for by various enterprises and organizations, providing Nazarov a tax-free financial windfall worth 1.5 million rubles in the year 2000 alone. Nevertheless, Nazarov denied all accusations and proceeded to declare his candidacy for governor of Chukotka on 2 November 2000.[5] But on 16 December, a week before the election, Nazarov withdrew his candidacy, handing Abramovich an easy win.

Rumors immediately circulated that Nazarov pulled out in exchange for a promise that Abramovich would appoint him his representative to the Council of the Federation *(Sovet Federatsii)*, Russia's upper legislative body, in which all elected governors in Russia automatically have a seat. Sure enough, on 18 January 2001, Chukotka's regional legislature officially approved Nazarov's appointment to the Council of the Federation. Thus Nazarov maintained a connection to Chukotka. Yet because he was far away in Moscow and out of the public eye, he was immediately forgotten, one might almost say gleefully, by a Chukotka population that now focused all of its attention on its new hope, Governor Abramovich. Whether or not Abramovich would truly pull Chukotka out of its chronic condition of crisis remained to be seen, but as countless Chukotkans said to me, *"Nadezhda umiraet poslednii"* – hope dies last.

Dramatis Personae

In the chapters that follow, I explore the experience of Chukotka's indigenous peoples in the 1990s, drawing upon a variety of sources: my daily interactions with them, my formal and informal interviews with them, things I read about them in newspapers and heard about them on radio and television, and things said about them by nonindigenous Chukotkans. I endeavor to place their experience in the wider context of Russia's changing social and political environment at the time. It is my desire to make this general Chukotkan experience as specific as possible by providing examples from the lives of individuals. However, this is a delicate matter; although much has changed in Chukotka since the departure of Nazarov as governor, given the extent to which political repression was possible in the 1990s, and may again become possible, I am reluctant to leave my consultees and their sometimes radical views too exposed in these pages.

The solution I have devised is to take the wide variety of individual experiences embodied in the consultees I worked with and concentrate them into a few representative *dramatis personae* bearing pseudonyms. Each character is fictional in the sense that there is no single person with exactly these traits and life experiences. However, each is nonfictional in the sense that the words she or he speaks were in fact spoken by someone, and the experiences she or he shares were in fact shared with me by someone. I have endeavored to create a set of characters that more or less represent the social roles that I encountered most often among inhabitants of Anadyr', or in some cases, roles that stood out as particularly striking. Alongside these disguised figures, others will also appear under their own real names. If a person is a public figure on the regional level in Chukotka or the national level in Russia, and his or her views have been published in media sources, then I do not disguise that person's identity with a pseudonym.

One additional character also appears, not in the main text, but in the vignettes sandwiched between the chapters. This is Malina Ivanovna Kevyngevyt, a fictional Chukchi woman. I wanted to show somehow that, although the post-Soviet transformation was a shock for indigenous Chukotkans (as it was for everyone in Russia), this was not the only or even the most significant change for them. Indigenous Chukotkans, like all indigenous peoples of Russia, experienced a long series of transformations in their lives throughout the Soviet period. I created Malina and her life story in order to illustrate this. While the vignettes are written in a novelesque form, they are derived from life-history accounts related to me by consultees, and they even contain direct quotations from my notes and/or taped interviews. I have deliberately tried to retain the sometimes sentimental, romanticized tone in which the stories were related to me. My intention is that the juxtaposition of a single life against the factual material of the book will help to illuminate that material. In turn, I hope to flesh out Malina's exemplary life more fully in the reader's imagination as the material in each chapter is read.

A Note About Terminology

The term "indigenous" is used here as a catch-all translation for several Russian terms: *korennoi* ("native"), *aborigeny* ("aboriginals"), *tuzemnyi* ("indigenous"), and sometimes *mestnyi* ("local"). Nonindigenous residents of Chukotka are most often referred to as *priezzhie*, from the verb *priezzhat'* ("to arrive"), and the gloss used here is "incomers" (cf. Schweitzer 1993). There is some slippage in these terms; *mestnyi* can also refer to a nonindigenous resident who was born in Chukotka and/or who demonstrates a clear commitment to the region and its people. "Incomer" means, most precisely, those who come with a specific purpose in mind and do not intend to stay.

There are several terms for different levels of federal territorial formations within Russia, which I render in translation as follows: territory = *krai*; province = *oblast'*; region = *okrug*; district = *raion*.

ACKNOWLEDGMENTS

SEVERAL GRANTS SUPPORTED the field research on which this book is based. I was able to conduct my 1995–6 dissertation research by virtue of a 1995–6 U.S. Department of Education Fulbright-Hayes Doctoral Dissertation Research Abroad Fellowship and a 1995–6 Individual Advanced Research Opportunities Research Residency for Eurasian Russia from the International Research and Exchanges Board (IREX). In 1998, the National Science Foundation's Arctic Social Sciences program ("Regional Problems and Local Solutions in the Post-Soviet Transition: A Pilot Study to Assess the Problems Faced by Reindeer Herding Communities in the Chukotka Autonomous Okrug," award #OPP-9726308, principal investigator Peter Schweitzer, co-principal investigators Patty A. Gray and Michael Koskey) supported four months of additional research. I returned for three more months of research in the fall of 2000 and another three months in the spring of 2001, and these two trips were supported by the Max Planck Institute for Social Anthropology in Halle, Germany, while I was a post-doctoral Fellow in Chris Hann's research program. Many thanks to Hann for his generosity in allowing me time to complete revisions on the manuscript. Writing of the book manuscript was supported by a Richard Carley Hunt Fellowship from the Wenner-Gren Foundation for Anthropological Research. I am deeply grateful to these foundations for investing their limited resources in me and making this work possible; none of these organizations is responsible for the views expressed in this book.

In Anadyr' I used the facilities of the V. G. Bogoraz-Tan Public Library's Regional Collection *(Kraevedcheskii fond publichnoi biblioteki im. V. G. Bogoraz-Tan)*, with assistance from library director Liubov Belikoneva and librarians Tatiana Emelianova and Tatiana Lukina. In Snezhnoe, I used facilities of the village library with assistance from librarian Ekaterina Kolodienko. In St. Petersburg, I worked in the Russian National Library's Social Science Reading Room and received attentive and professional assistance from bibliographer Nikita Eliseev. I must also thank the administration of the Chukotka Autonomous Region for granting me permission to work in the region.

Although my name alone appears on this book, I most certainly did not accomplish this work alone. The Chukotka Affiliate of the Northeast Interdisciplinary Scientific Research Institute of the Far East Branch of the Russian Academy of Sciences in Anadyr' *(Chukotskii filial Severo-Vostochnyi Kompleksnyi Nauchno-Issledovatel'skii Institute DVO RAN*, known locally as *NITs "Chukotka")* served as my "responsible organization," a liaison between myself and the Chukotka administration, and without such support, this research would not have been possible. Thanks to former director Aleksandr Vladimirovich Galanin and current director Vladimir Savich Krivoshchekov; to Vladimir Mikhailovich Etylin (head of the Laboratory of Traditional Resource Use and Ethnosocial Research), whose support over the years was unflagging even when he was under unpleasant political pressure from the Chukotkan administration; and to Anna Vitoldovna Belikovich, Nadia Ivanovna Vukvukai, and Tamara Vladimirovna Korave for welcome friendship.

I owe a great deal of thanks to the residents of the Village of Snezhnoe, Anadyrskii District, Chukotka, including its state farm director, Anatoly Iakovlevich Tyneru, and its mayor, Anatolii Ilich Matveev. The greatest thanks must go to the villagers themselves, too numerous to list, who responded to me with kindness and cheerful interest. I am especially grateful to the Omrytagin family, whose many members showed me hospitality and friendship.

I had many consultees in Anadyr', where I conducted the bulk of my work, and I am grateful to them all. Thanks especially to Tatiana Achirgina; Zoia Badmaeva; Varya, Denis, and Maksim Litovka; Aleksandr Omrypkir; Viktor Serekov; Gennady Smirnov; Nina Suiata; Svetlana Tagek; Zoia Tagrina; Anton Tynel; Ivan Vukvukai; and Larisa and Valerii Vykvyraktyrgyrgyn.

I reserve my greatest tribute of thanks for my very treasured friend in Anadyr', Margarita Belichenko, her late husband Vladimir, and their daughters Tanya Bardashevich and Natasha Belichenko. I simply could not have accomplished this work without the support of this family.

I am grateful to my graduate advisor at the University of Wisconsin, Anatoly M. Khazanov, whose matter-of-fact confidence in me surprised me at first and later gave me the courage to forge ahead in my work. His ongoing support remains extremely important to me. I am also grateful to the rest of the faculty of the Department of Anthropology at the University of Wisconsin for their guidance and support during my six years as a graduate student there. I am grateful also to my language teachers at Madison – Aleksandr Dolinin, Gary Rosenshield, and especially Judith Kornblatt – who helped me understand Russian ways of seeing. I had many additional advisors along the way, who had no official obligation to me but nevertheless responded openly to my pleas for advice. Chief among these were Mark Beissinger of UW–Madison and Jon Hill and Jane Adams of Southern Illinois University–Carbondale (where I started my graduate work). Peter Schweitzer has provided treasured comradeship and many opportunities to develop professionally, and Debra Schindler, Anna Kerttula, and Michael Fortescue generously shared advice about the logistics of working in Chukotka. Schindler in particular blazed a trail for research in Chukotka with her dissertation, which was a great inspiration to me. I offer particularly affectionate thanks to Nikolai Vakhtin and Igor Krupnik, who offered me advice and reassurance before, during, and after my fieldwork and who have become valued colleagues. These are fine scholars, but first and foremost they are compassionate human beings. Would that all in academia had their priorities in this order.

Two of my colleagues at the Max Planck Institute for Social Anthropology were generous in reading sections of the manuscript and offering their comments, as well as engaging in endless discussions with me that in the end influenced the book. For this I am grateful to Deema Kaneff and Florian Stammler. Thanks also to Barbara Bodenhorn and Tatiana Bulgakova for useful critical readings of the manuscript.

I also wish to acknowledge two Alaskans, Nancy Mendenhall and Jim Campbell, who have for many years worked tirelessly and efficiently to provide humanitarian aid and support for budding social programs in Chukotka. From their position in Alaska, they were able to maintain much closer ongoing contacts with Chukotkans, and they have often provided me with updates about events in Chukotka when I have not been in the field.

Thanks to Jessica Kuper at Cambridge University Press for shepherding my book through the initial stages and to my other editors at Cambridge University Press who oversaw the final stages. Thanks to Edda Schroeter of the Institute of Geography at the Martin Luther University in Halle, Germany, for creating the maps. I received extremely helpful comments from two anonymous reviewers whose suggestions substantially shaped the arguments in the book, and I am tremendously indebted to these fine scholars.

Finally, I cannot overlook the role of my own family. Their support far predates the actual execution of my research and is largely responsible for enabling me to make the journey to Chukotka. For this I will always be indebted to my parents, Myles and Marilyn Gray, and to my then-husband, Phil Brinkman. They know what they did and what it cost.

NOTES ON TRANSLITERATION

THIS BOOK USES a system for the transliteration of Russian words adapted from the Library of Congress system, with slight adjustments. This transliteration system is violated in cases of familiar words and names whose standard transliteration has already been well established in the media. For example, the name of the former president of the Russian Federation is rendered the familiar *Yeltsin*, rather than the more correct *El'tsyn*. Moreover, the Russian soft sign, which is represented in transliteration by an apostrophe ('), is generally omitted for the sake of readability, especially in the case of proper names. This has been done at the request of the publisher.

The Chukchi language, whose written form uses the Cyrillic alphabet, presents special problems. In particular is the prevalence of the hard letter *e* (often as a word initial), which appears only rarely in the Russian language. The unique spelling of many Chukchi words is therefore poorly represented – and in any case, even Cyrillic poorly represents their pronunciation.

Names of ethnic groups in Russian, upon translation to English, are pluralized according to the rules of English grammar (for example, *koriaki* becomes in English "Koriaks," *chukchi* becomes "Chukchis," *eskimosy* becomes "Eskimos"). The singular generally has two forms, masculine and feminine (for example, *koriak/koriachka, chukcha/chukchanka, eskimos/eskimoska*). These forms are actively in use in Chukotka but are ignored here for the sake of readability.

PLATE 0.1. "Victory! 1945, 9 May": life-size mural commemorating World War II on Otke Street in Anadyr'

MAP 1.1. The Russian Federation, Showing the Location of Chukotka

1948

Little Kevyngevyt lay snuggled on a walrus skin next to her mother, who was sewing a pair of sealskin boots for one of her brothers by the light of a whale-oil lamp. The reindeer-skin tent was calm and quiet except for the sound of the sinewy thread being pulled through the tough skin. Suddenly she heard her father's voice call sharply from outside, "Aoow!" Her mother immediately got up and went out of the inner room to peer outside of the tent; then she came back in, filled a ladle with water, and stepped outside again. Kevyngevyt toddled after her and saw her father coming toward them with a freshly killed seal on a sled. She watched as her mother walked over to the seal, bent down, and poured the water into the seal's lifeless mouth.

Kevyngevyt's father looked over and saw the little girl's wide eyes. "Our guest is thirsty after his long ordeal," he said with a smile. "We must honor this fine guest, so he will tell all his kinfolk that we are decent people, and treat visitors properly!" Kevyngevyt looked at the seal; it did not move, and its eyes did not blink. Her mother and father stood looking down at it, and they seemed very pleased.

Later, when the seal had been skinned and its meat divided into many parts, Kevyngevyt's father called his neighbors over and began to give them portions of the meat. Kevyngevyt squatted next to her father as he handed out portion after portion, until less than half of the seal meat was left. This did not seem right; didn't her father kill this seal himself? Why should he not get to keep most of it? Kevyngevyt's father saw her furrowed brow and said, "Little bird, it's always better to keep a little bit less than you give away. If you don't share, the seals will stop coming. They don't like to socialize with stingy people."

1

EPITOMIZING EVENTS

THE SOVIET PERIOD has been widely reported as a time when indigenous peoples in the Russian North were so badly mistreated through the process of "building socialism" that their cultures were nearly destroyed. While the Soviet regime has certainly earned its criticism, it does not follow that the elimination of that regime automatically improved the lives of Russia's indigenous peoples. In the 1990s, Russia was presumably making a "transition" to a democratic, market-oriented society that was supposed to create a new "civil society" that would bring a better life for all. This was of course an oversimplification (seen in the clarity of twenty-twenty hindsight), and many of the changes that took place actually created greater restrictions and hardships for many people, especially indigenous peoples. Rather than simply taking those hardships as given (with a sigh and a sad shake of the head), this book documents them and analyzes the underlying social and political conditions that created them.

The research initially undertaken for this book in 1995–6[1] began with the hypothesis that Chukotka's indigenous peoples were beginning to redress past wrongs through the new phenomenon of indigenous activism in Russia, a phenomenon assisted through the contact of indigenous peoples in Russia with established indigenous advocacy organizations outside of Russia. This has certainly become a fair depiction of the situation taking shape after the turn of the twenty-first century. However, in the 1990s, largely as a result of transformations in political organization in Russia that partially shifted control from the center to the regions and changed the face of the local administration, indigenous activists in Chukotka found themselves in a predicament. They were not fulfilling their original optimistic goal of improving the status of indigenous peoples in relation to the (post-) Soviet state, as well as having their unique rights and interests recognized. This book ethnographically explores why and how this happened, while making reference to wider political processes in Russia and the work of indigenous activists in national and international contexts.

This is not just a book about indigenous activism; it is also an ethnography of a place, Chukotka – a place that has rarely been explored in American scholarly work, and has been presented only through a very partial lens in Russian and Soviet scholarly work. It is an attempt to situate a specific phenomenon – indigenous activism – within a very "thick" description of a specific place and time – Chukotka during the 1990s. The book's focus is further narrowed to emphasize urban Chukotka, specifically its capital city of Anadyr', and when the book does draw upon rural examples, these all come from Chukotka's western tundra region (while nearly all previous work on Chukotka in English has focused on its eastern coastal area, that is, the Chukotka Peninsula). This book is concerned more with characterizing the phenomenon of indigenous activism in this limited place and time than on analyzing in-depth indigenous activism as activism per se. As a matter of course, this work also maps out some of the changes in the regions of post-Soviet Russia outside of Moscow – "beyond the monolith," as one book phrases it (Stavrakis et al. 1997) – and affords a look at the effects of rapid social, political, and economic change.

Gwich'in Niintsyaa and the Raising of Consciousness

When I came upon the scene in Anadyr' in the fall of 1995, it was during a lull in the post-Soviet momentum of reform. At first glance, it seemed to me that there was almost no political awareness among the indigenous population in Chukotka. My first hint that there indeed *was* political awareness came when I learned of an apparently watershed event that took place a month after my arrival. One of my incomer consultees, Anastasia Zinkevich, had long been an environmentalist, and she had recently visited Alaska and returned with a copy of a video she had received from some acquaintances she made in an environmental group there. The video, titled *Gwich'in Niintsyaa*, was made by members of the Gwich'in people of Arctic Village, in the Arctic National Wildlife Refuge of Alaska. The focus of the video was a 1988 gathering of Gwich'in peoples called by their chiefs, the first such gathering in one hundred years. The motivation for the gathering was the news of impending oil development on Gwich'in land, which threatened the fragile calving grounds of the Porcupine caribou herd. The Gwich'in relied heavily on this herd for subsistence and, moreover, the caribou carried significant symbolic meaning for the Gwich'in people. The gathering sparked the Gwich'in people's struggle to defend their land and their rights on it against the state and the large oil companies wishing to develop it.[2]

Anastasia, who was a supporter of indigenous self-determination (uncommon among Chukotkan incomers), thought the video would have relevance for a Chukotkan audience – especially since the governor of Chukotka, Aleksandr Nazarov, was at the time negotiating the sale of oil drilling rights in the region. She suggested to Sofia Rybachenko, a Chukchi who produced Chukchi-language programming for local television, that the video could be broadcast during her program with a Russian-dubbed translation that Anastasia herself would record. Anastasia had some difficulty convincing Sofia, since her first response, after viewing the video, was that local indigenous viewers would be too depressed when they saw how hard life was for indigenous peoples in rural Alaska. Indigenous Chukotkans had been traveling to urban Alaska since 1989 and had brought back stories of the wonderful, comparatively affluent life of Native Alaskans. These stories were in great contrast to the official Soviet version of how life was for indigenous peoples under U.S. rule, perpetuated in part by the popular stories of the Chukchi writer Iurii Rytkheu, and had given indigenous Chukotkans great hope that reform in Russia would bring them a similar kind of life.[3] Sofia was reluctant to burst their bubble, so to speak, with this video, but Anastasia persisted and persuaded Sofia, and her program presented the video.

Immediately after the video aired, the television station was flooded with telephone calls about the video. Indigenous Chukotkans had been deeply moved by it. "These people are just like us! This film is *about* us!" was Anastasia's paraphrase of the viewers' comments. She said that what most impressed viewers was the way the Gwich'in seemed to be unintimidated by anyone or anything, much unlike indigenous Chukotkans. People demanded that the television station show the video again. Anastasia said that no other television program in recent memory had triggered such a response, especially not from indigenous viewers. A few days later I mentioned the video to Marina Peliave, a graduate student at the research institute where I was based. I told her I had heard that a lot of people had called in after seeing it. "Including me," she said, with a curt nod of her head. I asked Marina what had impressed her about the video. She replied that these people, the Gwich'in, realized that they could fight for their rights, and that they did not have to just sit back and tolerate being treated as if they did not matter. This video about indigenous activism in Alaska seemed to have struck a chord of resonance with indigenous Chukotkans like nothing else had before.

This became a general pattern that I observed regarding indigenous activism in Chukotka: a general inertia punctuated by watershed events that consolidated the awareness of more and more indigenous Chukotkans, events that told them they really were being poorly treated and that they might be able to do something about it. The video made indigenous Chukotkans realize not only that their own situation was similar to that of indigenous peoples in another country, but that those people felt justified to fight back publicly, without being deterred by their small numbers in the face of the government and the oil barons. It served to draw a line in the sand that goaded indigenous Chukotkans into a confrontation, if not directly with authorities or opposing groups, then at least with their own consciousness of their marginal position in Chukotkan society. For a generation raised in a Soviet society that constantly told them how much that state had done to advance the standing of every nationality large or small, that told them they were perhaps the most special of all because they had traveled so much farther than anyone else just to "catch up" in their social development and should therefore be the most grateful of all peoples, this awakened consciousness was perhaps revolutionary enough.

Three Events

The indigenous community of Anadyr' was small and close-knit. I attended or heard about countless small, informal indigenous social gatherings, and there were also frequent large-scale gatherings organized on a more or less informal basis by indigenous organizations. This community was not a seamless entity, however. Aside from the occupational and ethnic divisions it reflected (coastal versus tundra peoples, sea mammal hunting versus reindeer herding peoples, Chukchis versus Eskimos versus Evens, and so on), there were also class distinctions – one could clearly distinguish an indigenous working class from an indigenous intelligentsia. Moreover, different segments of indigenous society at times seemed to blend together with analogous segments of nonindigenous society – for example, white-collar indigenous Chukotkans and incomers could be found working side by side in administrative offices. Intermarriage, especially among the female indigenous intelligentsia, meant that indigenous Chukotkans often bore Russian or Ukrainian surnames.

Nevertheless, the sense that Chukotka's indigenous peoples comprised a single community was quite palpable. Since they came from villages all over Chukotka, the indigenous residents of Anadyr' were woven into kinship networks that extended beyond the city, much as Nancy Fogel-Chance has shown for Iñupiat in Anchorage (Fogel-Chance 1993), and Ann Fienup-Riordan for Alaskan Yup'iks in Anchorage (Fienup-Riordan 2000). They continued to identify strongly with their villages of origin, and they waged a kind of friendly competition as each touted the merits of his or her own natal village. However, greater emphasis was placed on integration – in general, I sensed that the Anadyr' indigenous community was proud of its diversity, and the fact that everyone came from a different village merely emphasized their unity as indigenous peoples of Chukotka.

In this chapter, I focus on showing the Anadyr' indigenous community in action as it responded to the changing political situation in Chukotka. The showing of the video *Gwich'in Niintsyaa* was a relatively quiet event. During my year in Chukotka, three other events occurred that I gradually came to recognize as major landmarks in terms of defining indigenous Chukotkans' understanding of their growing disenfranchisement in relation to the dominant nonindigenous population. One involved the closing of an indigenous meeting house, thus effectively shrinking the physical space that indigenous Chukotkans had to call their own; the second involved the closing of an indigenous newspaper, thus shrinking their space to represent themselves in public media; and the third involved the blockage of an indigenous candidate from running in the gubernatorial election under the endorsement of the indigenous peoples' association, thus shrinking the indigenous population's presence in the social space of politics.

These events were not cataclysmic; rather, each unfolded slowly over the course of several weeks or even months. I refer to these three occurrences as "epitomizing events" because, through their gradual unfolding in a limited context, key issues and conflicts emerged that revealed how different social groups in Anadyr', in a broader context, perceived the social space they occupied and the proper way to share that space. These events are not micro phenomena that somehow magically communicate the macro. Rather, they serve to place the key issues of concern to Chukotka's indigenous population in sharp relief. They are somewhat like the "critical events" that Veena Das isolates and analyzes for India in that after these events, "new modes of action came into being which redefined traditional categories" (Das 1995:6).

The impact in Chukotka may have been more subtle, but these events remain, nonetheless, significant. Each of the events had roots tracing back several years prior to my arrival in Chukotka, but they each came to a head during my first research trip from October 1995 to December 1996.

Event One: The Gutted *Iaranga*

When I first arrived in Anadyr' in October 1995, a gaily painted green and yellow two-story house stood at the end of the street I lived on. It was obviously a public building, because tacked to the front of it was the obligatory plaque revealing its name: *Tsentr Narodnoi Kul'tury*, or Center for Folk Culture. It was also obviously different from other public buildings, because while most plaques were very official looking with their shiny black surfaces and gold lettering, this sign was colorfully hand-painted and embellished with capering reindeer figures. Despite its official name, I learned that the building was known affectionately in the indigenous community as the *Iaranga*. *Iaranga* (plural: *iarangi*) is the Chukchi word for the tentlike structure sewn from reindeer skins that virtually all Chukchis used as a dwelling until the 1930s, when Soviet organizers began to implement a program of resettling indigenous Chukotkans into Russian-style wooden houses.

Even in the 1990s, Chukchis in many parts of the region lived in *iarangi* when they were in the tundra, since it was the dwelling best suited to the mobility required by a reindeer pasturing lifestyle. In Soviet parlance, the *iaranga*, along with fur clothing and the Chukchi language, was one of the key traits of the "national" culture of the Chukchi that defined them as Chukchis. It was also a space that Russians considered filthy, intolerably smoky, and ultimately unfit for civilized human habitation. However, to the Chukchis I interviewed, the *iaranga* carried a very different meaning than this. Without exception, indigenous Chukotkans reminisced about the *iaranga* as the warm and comforting family home of their childhood. It was the place where they curled up on soft reindeer skins alongside other family members and shared meals, stories, and songs. It was a structure that always turned out lopsided when anyone else but mom tried to put it together. When indigenous Chukotkans called this run-down little building in Anadyr' the *Iaranga*, they were reappropriating an otherwise very Russian space as something quintessentially indigenous, and evoking the place – the tundra – where they felt most themselves and in control of their lives.

Founded only three years earlier and given its name affectionately by local Chukchi activist and politician Vladimir Etylin (who was at that time chair of the Chukotka Regional Soviet of People's Deputies), the *Iaranga* quickly became a meeting place for members of all the indigenous groups in Anadyr', including Chukchis, Eskimos, Evens, and Lamuts. Sofia described to me at length and with obvious pleasure of recall the kinds of activities that went on within its walls. Sofia was herself a member of a folk theater troupe called *Enmen* (Chukchi for "so it was" a phrase that typically begins Chukchi-language folktales much as "once upon a time" begins English-language ones), which frequently performed in the *Iaranga*. She said that "evenings" *(vecherinki)* were held in the building every Friday night, and these were open to all who wished to come (nonindigenous as well as indigenous) to see performances of indigenous song, dance, and drama. The evenings would start at 7:00 P.M., would sometimes continue until midnight, and were always well attended. "It was simply entertaining for us to go there," said Sofia. There were times when only indigenous Chukotkans would attend in a more intimate gathering; for example, her folk theater performed stories in Chukchi language that interested only those who could understand the language. Indigenous children would come to learn sewing reindeer skins or traditional singing styles. The indigenous sobriety movement also used the building for its seminars.

Although this appeared to be the most sanctified of indigenous spaces within Anadyr', the *Iaranga* was nevertheless a space allotted to the indigenous population by the Russian-dominated administration, and was maintained within given parameters. The Center for Folk Culture was the official branch of the regional Department of Culture that dealt with indigenous traditional culture. Center employees had their offices in the House of Culture, a large and impressive building across from the regional administration building. The *Iaranga* was considered a "city club" where traditional cultural events could be staged, and according to one of the Center's employees, these were originally planned to occur once a month (Timchenko 1995). But by popular demand, the club was used every week, primarily for indigenous evenings. Thus the *Iaranga* became a space where members of the indigenous community could come and interact in their native language.

The building itself had once housed a kindergarten, but it was given over to the Center for Folk Culture when a better space was found for the city's children. The building was apparently in poor condition when it was given to the Center. It stood in a row of identical two-story wooden buildings that served as a kind of buffer zone between a district of newer apartment blocks and an area of crumbling ruins. Directly across the street from the *Iaranga* was another of these wooden buildings with its windows broken out, and beyond that were piles of rubble and mangled wood. By the fall 1995, the building had actually become unsafe. Its users described how the floor would shake when people danced, and everyone began to fear that it might collapse beneath them. Sofia said that the indigenous community had begun to meet there less often because of this (cf. Timchenko 1995).

By February 1996, the dangerous condition of the *Iaranga* was brought up at a session of the regional legislature (the Duma), and a decision was made that the building had to be closed for renovations. Indigenous consultees reported that the administration had agreed to renovate the old building, promising to provide the financing and to complete the work by November 1996. When I returned to Anadyr' in April 1996 after a visit to Moscow and St. Petersburg, I found the *Iaranga* a dark and empty shell. Renovation had clearly been started – siding had been torn off, windows were broken out, and the wooden floor now lay strewn in bits around the outside of the building. But the renovation work had just as clearly been abandoned; day after day I passed the building only to see no activity whatsoever around it and no progress being made.

Marina lamented that the administration now claimed that no more money was available to finance the renovation, which seemed suspicious in light of the fact that plenty of money was found to finance pet projects of the administration, such as the infamous "Days of Chukotka Culture" in Moscow the following November (see Chapter 5), and considering the administration's repeated defensive claims that it was constantly doling out federal funds on indigenous needs. No date was even estimated for the resumption of work on the renovation. Each time I returned to Anadyr' thereafter, the *Iaranga* had disintegrated further. In 1998, I regularly observed young boys on its roof, pulling the building apart and throwing the pieces to the ground. By 2000, it had been reduced to a pile of rubble that was often on fire under a slow, smoldering flame, while passersby gleaned usable wood for their small construction projects.

In the interim, the Center for Folk Culture was moved to "temporary" quarters within the main House of Culture itself. It was given a set of small rooms, with offices for the director and the trained staff, and a main reception area with display cases where the clerical staff worked. The only meeting space was a long, narrow room that served as the Center's entryway. Sofia said that meetings were held less often after the *Iaranga* was gutted. When I pointed out that they had space to meet in the House of Culture, she said nothing, but simply screwed up her face in an expression of displeasure. I asked Lidia Neekyk, a social activist employed in the Anadyr' district administration, if the indigenous community was meeting someplace else now that the *Iaranga* was gutted. She said no, they had simply stopped gathering. When I asked about the space in the House of Culture, she shuddered slightly and said that the House of Culture was big and cold and that indigenous Chukotkans did not like it there. I asked if perhaps the small and intimate House of Culture in Tavaivaam, an indigenous village located walking distance from Anadyr', would be better, and she demurred that it was awfully far away for city folk. She said that there were certainly times when Tavaivaam invited city folk down to their gatherings, and Anadyr' invited village folk up for their gatherings, but the two groups really felt themselves to belong to separate communities. "When we go down there, we feel like we are at someone else's place," she said.

There should be no implication here that the Russian-dominated administration had insidiously conspired to deprive the indigenous community of its only space to gather as an intimate and cohesive community. This was a difficult economic time for everyone, when entropy seemed to be the prevailing force, and no one seemed to have enough money. However, it was abundantly clear that money could be found whenever a project was sufficiently interesting to the administration. Besides financing "Days of Chukotka Culture" in Moscow, the administration ensured that construction proceeded apace during this same time on an impressive new state bank building in downtown Anadyr'. The administration also continued to allocate funds to stage public performances of traditional indigenous song and dance. But the administration systematically neglected the less visible, more keenly felt needs of the indigenous community, such as a meetinghouse, in a way that it never had in the Soviet period. It was deemed sufficient for indigenous Chukotkans to borrow space within Russian space.

Event Two: *Murgin Nutenut*: The Dispossession of "Our Homeland"

In 1933, not long after Chukotka was created as a "national region" within the Russian Soviet Federative Socialist Republic, the first issue of a new, Russian-language regional newspaper, *Sovetskaia Chukotka*, was published. Twenty years later, once the cultural revolution had taken root in the North and a generation of literate indigenous Chukotkans had been trained, a Chukchi-language newspaper was established, called *Sovetken Chukotka*. The paper shared the same offices with the Russian-language newspaper, although it had its own Chukchi editorial staff. One of the first editors of the paper was Lina Tynel, a Chukchi intellectual who later became active in both regional and national politics in the 1970s. Tynel's name also appears as Chukchi-language translator of many works of Russian literature and political propaganda. *Sovetken Chukotka* was in fact nothing more than a Chukchi translation of the Russian-language paper *Sovetskaia Chukotka*, and the two were issued together.

When Etylin became chair of the Chukotka Regional Soviet of People's Deputies in 1990, he developed a vision for *Sovetken Chukotka* to become an independent newspaper. It would be a native-language gazette that published original articles of interest to the indigenous community, rather than just a slavish translation of Russian articles. He devised a plan to assemble a diverse editorial staff capable of putting out a paper in four languages – Chukchi, Eskimo, Even, and Russian – and eventually to cut the paper loose entirely from *Sovet- skaia Chukotka*, with its own budget and separate editorial offices. All newspapers in the Soviet period (and many still today) were state-controlled and state-funded, but Etylin had in mind to make *Sovetken Chukotka* as independent as it could be within that system. He called upon the paper's former editor, Tynel (then living in retirement in Magadan), to return and take up her old position, believing she could best lead the paper through its transition. *Sovetken Chukotka* began its independent status in January 1990. Soon thereafter, by popular demand, a contest was held to pick a new name for the paper, and the winner was *Murgin Nutenut* – Chukchi for "Our Homeland." Beginning in July 1990, the paper began to appear under that name.[4]

The next few years were stormy ones for Chukotka, politically as well as economically, and Etylin was ousted from local government by 1993. Thus he was no longer able to control the fate of *Murgin Nutenut*. Already by 1992, the man who would become his successor as the key figure in Chukotkan politics, Aleksandr Nazarov, had been appointed head of a newly created regional administration by Russian president Boris Yeltsin. Under Etylin's direction, the editorial staff of *Murgin Nutenut* was slated to move into new offices on Otke Street in the main downtown district of Anadyr', in a building located next door to *Sovetskaia Chukotka* (which eventually changed its own name to *Krainii Sever*, or "Far North"). But something happened along the way, and *Murgin Nutenut* never came to occupy those offices. As Etylin was losing his influence, the staff of *Murgin Nutenut* was hustled out of their old space within *Krainii Sever's* offices and up to a set of dingy rooms on Energetik Street at the upper end of town. They were not allowed to take any of their own furniture or equipment with them, but were instead given ancient desks and chairs and antiquated type-writers that the editorial staff said made their wrists ache.

A separate budget was created for *Murgin Nutenut*, as planned, using federal funds from *Goskomsevera* (State Committee of the North) earmarked for the paper. Anastasia Zinkevich estimated the budget of *Krainii Sever* to be about 2 billion (old) rubles[5] for a staff of thirty-five to forty people, while the budget of *Murgin Nutenut* was a few hundred thousand for a staff of five or six people. But since the *Murgin Nutenut* staff was turned out with no real equipment of their own, they were now forced to pay a large sum back to *Krainii Sever* for the use of their computers to lay out the newspaper, and another large sum to use the printing press. This left very little in the budget to pay the staff's salaries. Several indigenous commentators accused the governor of a kind of money laundering scheme: The money the administration paid to *Murgin Nutenut* could be marked in the regional budget as having been spent on the needs of the indigenous population, thus satisfying federal requirements. But in effect the money flowed directly back to be used for nonindigenous needs, and *Murgin Nutenut* staff claimed that during this time *Krainii Sever* was able to make significant capital improvements.

A crisis occurred in 1993, when the administration moved to return the newspaper to the control of the editorial staff of *Krainii Sever*.[6] Activists within the indigenous community rallied and issued a response to the administration protesting the move. They sent a telegram to the Moscow headquarters of the Association of Less-Numerous Peoples of the North reporting the situation, and they managed to have the telegram read on the radio in Chukotka. This was still at the beginning of Nazarov's tenure; the administration backed off on its threat to close the paper.

Meanwhile, the fledgling independent newspaper floundered. The morale of the staff plummeted, and turnover at the newspaper increased; the productivity of those who remained fell. Tynel became so discouraged by the unsatisfactory conditions that she gave up and returned to Magadan. The paper then went through a series of different editors, each of whom eventually gave up in exasperation. The quality of the newspaper began to fall as the staff printed fewer original articles on timely issues and more excerpts from already-published materials. The circulation began to decline, launching a discussion within the indigenous community of what to do about it. Most people said that if only the paper were more interesting and timely, they might again subscribe. Zoia Badmaeva, a member of the Council of Elders of the Chukotka regional indigenous peoples' association, said she continued to subscribe only "out of solidarity."[7]

Nevertheless, most agreed that the paper's editorial staff was working toward laudable goals, such as reporting to readers the truth about life in the remote areas of Chukotka and promoting the preservation of national culture and "the memory of the past of the peoples of Chukotka."[8] They could boast that *Murgin Nutenut* was "the one and only independent multinational newspaper in the Russian Federation that is published in the languages of the Less-Numerous Indigenous Peoples of the Far North."[9] Moreover, the paper seemed to be getting a better handle on its technical operations. The staff members set aside portions of their own salary toward the collective purchase of a computerized printing press for the paper's exclusive use, which they acquired in May 1995. They knew that this would save them the money they had to pay each month to *Krainii Sever*, and that it would finally allow *Murgin Nutenut* to become the independent native-language newspaper it had set out to be so many years before.

This state of affairs only lasted a few months, however. In October 1995, Nazarov, who was by now referred to as governor of Chukotka, issued a resolution declaring the closure of the paper. The editor of *Krainii Sever* came to the office of *Murgin Nutenut*, accompanied by a special commission, and presented papers for the staff to sign that would hand over control of the paper to *Krainii Sever*. The stated reason for this move was that *Murgin Nutenut's* circulation had become too small to justify the expense to the administration of supporting it as a separate paper. The staff refused to sign the papers. The commission returned after hours with the police and a van to confiscate all of the furniture and equipment in the offices. The commission summoned only the paper's accountant, who protested that the commission's actions were blatantly illegal without the presence of the paper's editor. Nevertheless, the offices were emptied, the locks were changed, and a seal was placed on the door. Within minutes, an independent *Murgin Nutenut* had ceased to exist.

Once again, a few indigenous activists responded to this closure of *Murgin Nutenut* by working to rally the indigenous community and spread the word about the improper, and what they considered unfair, manner in which the paper had been shut down. Telegrams were sent to Chukotka's two legislators in Moscow, and letters were sent to UNESCO and to the offices of a few foreign newspapers. A letter was even dispatched to the vice-president of the Inuit Circumpolar Conference in Greenland, carried by a Yup'ik Eskimo girl who was traveling there for a youth camp. In Anadyr', a session of the Duma was already scheduled for mid-October, and in response to an appeal to the Duma written by members of *Murgin Nutenut's* staff, a few Duma deputies sympathetic to indigenous interests tried to defend the paper's special purpose in the indigenous community. They established a commission to look into options for keeping the independent paper operational, but they were ultimately thwarted from taking concrete action.

Meanwhile, a meeting of concerned indigenous Chukotkans was held, at which it was decided to picket *(piketirovat')* in front of the administration building, an action that some referred to as staging a strike *(bastovat')*. Although street protests had already become common in Moscow, they were virtually unheard of in Chukotka. People gathered in the then-functioning *Iaranga* to make placards to carry in the picket line. They recruited the chair of the city-level Association of Less-Numerous Peoples, Viktor Serekov, to write a rousing appeal to be read at the picket, knowing the persuasive way he had with words. They knew it was illegal to hold a rally without permission, so they even secured that from the administration and scheduled the picket for 1:00 P.M. on a day in early November 1995.

At 12:00 noon on the appointed day, the police department mysteriously decided to hold training exercises in the public square across the street from the administration building, and indigenous commentators described arriving to find a "whole army" of police gathered. Both literally and figuratively, the administration seemed to be laying claim to this public space with a show of potential force. By 1:00 P.M., the exercises broke up and only a handful of police officers remained, while only a few protesters had shown up. One of the organizers of the picket recalled that, as she waited for others to show up, she looked up at the statue of Lenin towering above her there and said to him, "You

probably never dreamed of something like this" (that is, that indigenous people would dare to picket right under his nose), after which
she held her sign up toward his face and cried, "Read!"

Eventually a crowd did form, perhaps one hundred people in all,
and Serekov stood up to read his appeal, explaining the legally questionable manner in which *Murgin Nutenut* had been shut down. This
had the desired effect of sparking discussion in the crowd, and a few
more people got up to make speeches. By the end of the protest, the
crowd was chanting "*Na-zar-ov! Na-zar-ov!*" and "*Dai Ga-zet-u! Dai
Ga-zet-u!*" ("Give us a newspaper!"). An indigenous cameraman from
the television station came over and shot some footage of the protest,
and it was the first item on the local news that night. However, the head
of radio news programming, which reached a larger audience than the
television news, had already forbidden any coverage of the closing of
the paper, calling it "fanatical material." Only a brief report about the
picket was given at the end of the radio newscast, and it portrayed the
protesters as Don Quixotes tilting at windmills.

In concrete terms, very little seemed to result from the protest.
All of the members of the *Murgin Nutenut* staff were summarily left
jobless. Within two weeks, *Krainii Sever* had hired a Chukchi editor who had long ago worked on *Sovetken Chukotka* to take over
and edit a new incarnation of *Murgin Nutenut*, now published out
of *Krainii Sever's* offices. On 17 October 1995, within the pages of
Krainii Sever, a publication appeared with the title "*Murgin Nutenut*,
a special supplement to the newspaper *Krainii Sever*." The banner of
this paper had been redesigned to resemble *Krainii Sever's* banner.
It was marked as issue "No. 1," ignoring the paper's previous publication run. Thereafter, twice a month, pages three to six of *Krainii
Sever* were given over to the publication of the new *Murgin Nutenut*
in the form of a pullout section (the old *Murgin Nutenut* had appeared weekly). The new editor cheerily called it "a paper within a
paper" – once again, indigenous Chukotkans were being relegated to
a space within a Russian space. The matter was closed; looking back
on the whole affair, Sofia waved her arm disgustedly and growled, "Oh,
they just crossed themselves and said 'Thank God we got that taken
care of!'"

Since *Krainii Sever* hired only one full-time staff person to write and edit the entire paper, and that person was a Chukchi speaker, the "supplement" carried no articles in Eskimo or Even, as the old *Murgin Nutenut* had. A few articles eventually appeared in Even, but they were written by a Russian linguist living in St. Petersburg who was an Even language specialist. Indigenous consultees greeted with bitter laughter the suggestion that this incarnation of *Murgin Nutenut* could in any way be taken as a "national" newspaper reflecting the indigenous community. From their perspective, *Krainii Sever* simply stole *Murgin Nutenut's* name along with all of its equipment.

I decided to play devil's advocate and ask my consultees a provocative question: Why in fact is there a need for *any* native-language newspaper, when virtually all literate indigenous Chukotkans are fluent in Russian and could just as well get their news by reading *Krainii Sever*? Without fail, my interlocutors answered vehemently that they had a consciousness as a people, and along with that, they had a right to have their own newspaper in their own native language. The point was not merely to provide a source of news, but rather to provide a locus of identity; *Murgin Nutenut* was a treasured community trust for the indigenous people, *created by* the indigenous people. Having it in the control of the incomer community seemed almost sacrilegious. From their point of view, the administration's aim was not to achieve an economy of scale while still supporting a native-language newspaper, but simply to keep indigenous peoples from having an independent voice. This experience of having their forty-year-old native-language newspaper first fall more fully into their control and then wrenched forcefully from them consolidated in the indigenous community a new awareness of the stakes that would be involved in making sure it continued to have a space to exist in Chukotka.

Event Three: Local Democracy and Political Intrigue

In 1996, Russian president Boris Yeltsin ordered that all of his appointed heads of administration (of which Nazarov was one) should stand for election in all of Russia's eighty-nine regions by the end of the year.[10]

Elections were held throughout the fall, and Chukotka scheduled its own election for 22 December 1996. Aspiring candidates had to form an "initiative group," gather signatures from no less than 2 percent of registered voters, and file declarative papers by a 7 November deadline. Nazarov, the incumbent, was the first to register his candidacy officially, long before the deadline and before anyone else registered. He was eventually followed by a handful of other hopefuls. As current head of administration, Nazarov controlled all media outlets, and by October enthusiastic promotions of Nazarov's candidacy began to appear in the newspaper, as well as on local radio and television broadcasts. Individuals as well as organizations throughout Chukotka began to volunteer their official endorsements.

Meanwhile, rumors began circulating within the indigenous community that Etylin might make a comeback to local politics and declare his candidacy. Many took for granted that if he did declare, he would receive the endorsement of the Association of Indigenous Less-Numerous Peoples of Chukotka. People began to wonder about when Etylin might form his "initiative group" to begin collecting the requisite signatures to register his candidacy. They believed he would first declare his intent to run before the Presidium of the Association.

On 24 September 1996, the Presidium of the Association held a meeting to discuss the upcoming election for head of administration. The only people who showed up were the Association's president, Aleksandr Omrypkir; a member of the Council of Elders of the Association, Zoia Badmaeva (who had happened to encounter a certain ethnographer on the street on the way to the meeting and urged her to come along); and Etylin himself. A reporter from the Chukchi-language radio staff also appeared, but no other Presidium members came. After passing a half hour in pleasant chitchat while waiting for others to arrive, Omrypkir made a couple of calls to track down the missing members of the Presidium. They offered various excuses for their absence, and the meeting was rescheduled for the next day.

The next day, the same thing happened: A few people showed up, including Etylin, but not enough Presidium members to constitute a quorum. The meeting was again rescheduled for 7 October, but Etylin was unable to attend that meeting – he had already purchased a ticket to Alaska in order to attend a seminar there on indigenous self-determination. The Presidium met in his absence, found they had a quorum, and took a major step of historic importance. The Presidium of the Association of Indigenous Less-Numerous Peoples of Chukotka issued an official resolution endorsing the candidacy of the incumbent, Nazarov, for head of administration of Chukotka. This was almost a month in advance of the deadline for registering candidates, so it was as yet unknown who else might enter the race. On 12 October, at the top of the front page of the regional newspaper *Krainii Sever*, an article appeared announcing the Association's endorsement of Nazarov.[11]

A few days later, on 18 October, the city-level Association of Indigenous Less-Numerous Peoples in Anadyr' held a special "gathering of the electorate" in the city's movie theater.[12] About fifty people attended. The main item on the agenda was a discussion of the Presidium's decision to endorse the candidacy of Nazarov, and this was to be followed by a vote of the assembled body on whether to support the decision or not. After Serekov read the Presidium's resolution, he turned the floor over to the chair of the regional Association, Omrypkir. Omrypkir began by talking about Russia's current path. He said that some people still feared (or perhaps hoped, he suggested) that the Communists could again seize power, but that he did not consider that a possibility (this was certainly a jibe at Etylin, who was known to be sympathetic to a kind of reformed Communism). "You cannot close your eyes to the fact that Russia has made her choice," he chided, "the choice was for the market, and like it or not, that is where we are going." Thus, he reasoned, it was in the best interest of Chukotka to retain in power a governor who had been steadily holding to the path of democracy. But even more than this, he said, the Presidium had made its decision for Nazarov in order to defend the indigenous Chukotkans working in the administration. "These people took responsibility on themselves, and they have a real impact on our fate," he said. "They are our representatives, and for me it is more important to defend them."

Omrypkir then fielded a few questions, until Tatiana Achirgina, an internationally known Eskimo activist, asked about the formalities of the Presidium vote. "I'll give you a report," replied Omrypkir, and he carefully explained that although eleven members had been elected to the Presidium four years earlier, for various reasons only seven remained. Only five of these were present at the Presidium meeting at which the decision was made, but those five constituted a quorum. Of those, three voted to support Nazarov, one voted against, and one abstained. This sparked a general murmur among the assembled crowd, and several expressed their incredulity that a vote could be taken with only five members present, and that only three Presidium members out of a proper cohort of eleven had made this decision on behalf of the indigenous community.

At this point, the assembly took on more of the character of a town meeting, and several attendees made short speeches from where they sat in the auditorium. Nikita Suslov, a cultural worker in the Tavaivaam House of Culture, declared that he would just as soon abstain from any vote of confidence in Nazarov, because the governor simply ignored the indigenous villages of Chukotka. "His first priority should be to solve our problems here, after all it is *our* autonomy [that is, the autonomous status of Chukotka exists for the benefit of the indigenous peoples], so we have the right to live here and observe our own laws, customs, and traditions." Boris Etuve, a well-known folk dancer, stood up and with characteristic humor said that politics is politics and he'd just as soon stick with Nazarov, a known quantity. Badmaeva, the Council of Elders member, opined that having so few members present at the Presidium's vote hardly seemed democratic. She proposed that they do more than simply vote for or against the decision, and consider advancing a candidate of their own. "Look," she said, "Vladimir Mikhailovich Etylin is sitting right here. If he agrees, I think he should run."

Etylin had indeed been sitting quietly in the audience throughout the meeting, and he made no move to speak at this point. Serekov accepted this proposal, but kept the floor open for discussion. At that point Achirgina again stood up, this time in the aisle so as to better address the crowd. Achirgina was also a member of the Presidium, but was one of the two absent from the meeting in question. She now asserted that if she had been able to attend, she would have voted against supporting Nazarov. Then she said that this election for the head of administration would be a good political school for the indigenous people of Chukotka, and that they should indeed nominate their own people to run. She reasoned that they should run for office simply for the sake of participating in the process directly. "We may lose," she said passionately, "but we should speak for ourselves, so we can say that we tried to help our own people." She went on to agree with Badmaeva's proposal to consider Etylin as a candidate.

After a few minutes of discussion, during which some suggested there might even be other candidates worthy of consideration that they did not even know about, Badmaeva again stood up to speak. She expressed agreement with Achirgina's words, and then said that previously Omrypkir had always invited her to the meetings of the Presidium.[13] Badmaeva said that for this particular meeting on 7 October, when the decision was made to endorse Nazarov, "for unknown reasons Aleksandr Aleksandrovich [Omrypkir] simply did not find me and gave me no advance warning." As she continued to speak, Badmaeva's voice began to noticeably quaver with anger. She said moreover that on 16 October, she heard on the radio that the Council of Elders supported the nomination of Nazarov for head of administration. "Such was never the case. The Council of Elders did not take part in the discussion of these questions. It seems to me that perhaps not everything was done honestly."

After this, Serekov finally prevailed upon Etylin to stand before the group and respond to the proposal that he be nominated to run for the head of administration. Etylin stepped into the aisle and said that he did harbor the desire to run, and would have liked to have discussed it with the Presidium. He talked about how the Presidium had failed to attain a quorum twice when he was present, and then did manage to attain a quorum at a time when he could not be present. "It seems to me that not everything is quite in place from a moral point of view," he said. At the very least, the Presidium should have waited until a few more candidates had registered or expressed their desire to run. As for his own candidacy, he thanked those who supported him, but he just was not confident he wanted to embroil himself given the coloring that politics had taken on in the region. But he would consider it.

Omrypkir leapt to his feet after this, obviously livid, and said that this was a very sharp accusation and he had a right to respond. He said the facts were simply that "for concrete reasons," certain Presidium members had been unable to come to the first two Presidium meetings, and they scheduled the meeting for when they could attend. "Therefore I repudiate this accusation that it was somehow dirty," he said between his teeth. "I don't even understand such an accusation." A great deal of discussion followed this, and the hall several times dissolved into arguing and sometimes shouting. Finally Serekov brought the meeting back to the two concrete proposals at hand. In the end, the assembled body voted not to approve the Presidium's decision to endorse Nazarov for head of administration, and not to endorse *any* candidate until the deadline for registration had passed. The matter was closed.

Within a few days, Etylin declared his intention to register for the election for head of administration. His initiative group was led by Achirgina and Badmaeva. Badmaeva appeared in a radio interview shortly before the registration deadline, urging people to sign the group's petitions for Etylin. She said the rules allowed for people to sign the petitions of more than one candidate; some people did not realize this and were refusing to sign. I later heard from Nikita Suslov that the problem was more complex: Etylin's people were going into workplaces and finding that if a workplace's manager had already signed a petition for Nazarov, the employees feared losing their jobs if they signed a petition for another candidate. It seemed the odds were against Etylin being able to register at all, much less win the election. However, the initiative group did succeed in gathering the required number of signatures, and Etylin did register in time. In the end, Nazarov won the election handily with 63 percent of the vote, but the results were nonetheless surprising: Etylin came in second with 23 percent of the vote, and three other candidates divided up the remaining 14 percent. Given that indigenous Chukotkans comprised no more than 18 percent of the population at the time, it is clear that either indigenous Chukotkans came out in droves to vote and/or an indigenous/nonindigenous coalition had formed in opposition to Nazarov.

The unfolding of this event of political intrigue demonstrates the extent to which, on the one hand, indigenous Chukotkans saw themselves as being enfranchised in the Russian political system as citizens of Russia, and on the other hand, the extent to which they were alienated from it as indigenous peoples. Politics in the Soviet era had been an entirely different matter – the role of indigenous Chukotkans had always been tightly scripted for them, an idea that I will take up in the next chapter. The Russian governor was trying to continue in this vein; indigenous Chukotkans were free to have a role in government as long as he was clearly the one who granted them the space to do it and defined the terms. In the case of the election for governor, the script was supposed to show that the indigenous Chukotkans had come in as his allies. Nazarov had most likely arranged the details with the president of the indigenous association in exchange for the promise of favors to him and to those indigenous Chukotkans who already held appointments within the administration apparatus. Shortly afterword the Association president was himself appointed to an administration post as local head of the federal agency *Goskomsevera*. But those who wanted their own indigenous candidate in the governor's race had upset the process by trying to re-enter the picture in a role not scripted for them. They recognized that indigenous Chukotkans who were appointed to positions within the administration had no empowering mandate from an indigenous constituency and no freedom to act independently, and thus they had nothing to gain from trying to protect indigenous Chukotkans, as Omrypkir had suggested.

Conclusion

In all three of the events described in this chapter, the message to indigenous Chukotkans was clear: They were a low priority as far as the Russian-dominated administration was concerned. It was not considered important for indigenous Chukotkans to control spaces of their own in Chukotka society; it was sufficient to accommodate them within Russian spaces – a room in the Russian House of Culture, a page inside the Russian newspaper, a token appointment within the administrative apparatus. It was becoming clearer to indigenous Chukotkans that the attention paid to their concerns in the past had been a farce, done for appearances only, and masked by rhetoric of Soviet respect and concern for indigenous Chukotkans. When the post-Soviet federal

government could no longer enforce the propping up of indigenous institutions as a matter of policy and ideology, nonindigenous residents
in positions of power in Chukotka were quick to drop all pretenses,
with no regard for the consequences to indigenous Chukotkans.

As everyone in Chukotka scrambled to make the best of the pro-
found social, economic, and political change sweeping their world, indigenous Chukotkans were left with the fewest resources to draw upon
in their own defense. Moreover, no matter what they did, regardless
of whatever successes they could count in their struggles, indigenous
Chukotkans ultimately remained within Russian space and would so
remain at least as long as Russians were the dominant population.
The self-contained *Iaranga* was nevertheless a Russian building; the
independent native-language newspaper *Murgin Nutenut* had nevertheless been dependent on support from the Russian administration;
and in the local election, indigenous Chukotkans were nevertheless
competing for positions within the Russian-dominated political system. However, what indigenous Chukotkans were attempting in these
first tentative forays into the Russian version of the democratic process
was to break out of the Soviet mold of *managed* participation in the social life of the region and its political process, and this new, uncharted
territory. While it might be hard to see a coherent social movement in
all of this, indigenous activists were clearly trying to redefine social
space. Indigenous Chukotkans had always been a part of the social and political life of the country, but there had always been a
centrally defined template to follow, and their role had always been
carefully scripted by the dominant Russian population. What indigenous Chukotkans had begun to do was toss out the script and ten-
tatively start to ad lib. For the most part, they were doing this reac-
tively instead of proactively, but at least they were exploring a new
collective response.

In the following chapters, I explore the underlying social and political dynamics that gave rise to the three epitomizing events described
in this chapter. I start in Chapter 2 with an overview of the indigenous movement in Chukotka within the context of indigenous activism
at the international level and on the national level in Russia (based
in Moscow), looking as well at some of the devices that Chukotka's

regional administration used to defuse the local indigenous movement. Chapter 3 explores some more general theoretical issues surrounding social movements and resistance, particularly as they relate to the unique situation in Chukotka. Chapter 4 delves into some of the keys issues of the Soviet-era history of Chukotka that are most relevant to shaping indigenous activism in the region, which necessarily means the emphasis here is on indigenous Chukotkan intellectuals. Chapter 5 brings us back to the more recent past, with a descriptive overview of life in Chukotka in the last decade of the twentieth century. Chapters 6 and 7 conclude the book with a more detailed examination of local political dynamics in Chukotka in the 1990s, and socioeconomic conditions during that decade, respectively.

1956

Kevyngevyt trudged up the pebbly beach toward the little wooden apartment house where her family now lived. How stiff and straight it looked, and hard somehow, not at all like the soft and round *iaranga* she had been used to all her life before this. But she didn't mind; she liked looking out the windows toward the sea and watching the Chukchi hunters in their big whaleboats. From inside she could watch the Russian chair of the collective stride about the village in his heavy black boots without him seeing her.

Kevyngevyt shuffled through the front door to find the house full of people, all Chukchi workers from the collective. It was lunchtime, and their homes were situated far up the hill – too far to climb up and back down and have time to relax over a meal – so Kevyngevyt's mother was feeding them, as she often did. She did not invite them; they just showed up at the door and sat down at her table, and she never refused them a hot meal. When the last worker had gone back to work, Kevyngevyt looked up at her mother working to clear away the dishes, and she said, "Oi! Mama! Aren't you tired?" and her mother answered, "Little one, what does that have to do with anything?"

Kevyngevyt instantly felt the sting of shame. She had already gotten so used to the way Russians entertained – acting like they were happy to see you when you dropped by, but getting impatient if you stayed too long. For just a moment she had forgotten what her mother had reminded her of so many times: The Law of the North demanded that all guests be quietly welcomed, fed, and allowed to stay as long as they wished, even if hours turned into days and days into weeks – even if the guests behaved badly. When someone asked for space to dwell, you gave it. To begrudge a guest of one's hospitality was the greatest shame of all.

2

STARTING A MOVEMENT IN CHUKOTKA

A "Global Indigenous Culture"?

IT IS UNDENIABLE that since the advent of *glasnost'* ("openness") in the Soviet Union, and especially since the collapse of the Soviet Union itself, indigenous peoples in Russia have had the opportunity to become politically active in a way they could not in the past. This period of increased openness in the 1980s allowed indigenous peoples in the Soviet Union to begin to communicate more freely with their counterparts in the rest of the world and to share new ideas about indigenous rights within the Soviet Union. Such open and critical activism was not possible in the pre-*glasnost'* Soviet Union, when recognized public voluntary organizations independent of the Communist Party were virtually nonexistent, at least none that could in any way be seen as openly defying the authority of the state (Sedaitis and Butterfield 1991:1).

By contrast, a transnational indigenous movement had been taking shape elsewhere in the world since the 1970s, and much of the initiative grew out of the North. George Manuel, a Shuswap from British

Columbia and the charismatic leader of the National Indian Brotherhood of Canada in the 1970s and 1980s, pursued the idea for the creation of a world council of indigenous peoples after his experiences visiting New Zealand and Australia in 1971 and several European human rights organizations in 1972 (McFarlane 1993:160; Sanders 1980:4). The National Indian Brotherhood endorsed this idea in 1972, and in 1975 an international conference was held in British Columbia with representatives from countries in North, Central, and South America; Scandinavia (including Greenland); as well as Australia and New Zealand. The World Council of Indigenous Peoples was formed as a result, and it acquired officially recognized status as a nongovernmental organization (NGO) at the United Nations.[1] A declaration drafted at the international conference included the following statement:

> We are the Indigenous Peoples, we who have a consciousness of culture and peoplehood on the edge of each country's borders and marginal to each country's citizenship (Sanders 1980:8).

This unified activity on the part of indigenous peoples has come to be called a "Fourth World"[2] movement, and has been described as "a social force that has unleashed a rising tide of political consciousness among aboriginal peoples – estimated to number about 200 million worldwide – locked into states they can never hope to control" (Young 1992:235). By working together, the leaders of indigenous groups based in different countries began to transform indigenous activism into a global phenomenon. They seemed to be content with no less than the creation of a panindigenous identity that traverses the boundaries of the nation-state, as representatives of groups as diverse as !Kung San and Saami worked together to produce the Universal Declaration on the Rights of Indigenous Peoples, a document that presses for greater autonomy and sovereignty for indigenous peoples within the states that have surrounded them (Fliert 1994; Hodgson 2002; Venne 1998).[3] According to Maivan Lâm, who has testified before the United Nations Working Group on Indigenous Populations, "Indeed, it can be said that a world-wide culture of indigenous peoples' resistance is emerging, and growing" (Lâm 2000:48).

It was only by the late 1980s that indigenous peoples in Russia were technically free to tap into that "global indigenous culture." A plethora of published material bears witness to the growing political conscious-ness among the indigenous peoples of Russia in the late 1980s. Much of it indicates awareness of a potential panindigenous identity among the Peoples of the Russian North in particular. The speeches of indige-nous political representatives in the national legislatures of both the Soviet Union and the Russian Soviet Republic addressed the unique problems of the less-numerous peoples of the North as a group.[4] The writings of indigenous intellectuals, published in newspapers and magazines, decried the poor conditions of indigenous peoples living in the North and called for change.[5] These were echoed by the writ-ings of a few concerned ethnographers who could, "for the first time in their careers, explicitly associate themselves with the welfare of 'their peoples' in opposition to state interests and in support of the indige-nous intelligentsia" (Slezkine 1994:371–2). In particular, a watershed article published in the national Soviet newspaper *Kommunist* by the late ethnographer Aleksandr Pika and Boris Prokhorov stirred great in-terest as it described conditions in the North that contradicted all of the success stories that had been told about the indigenous peoples.[6] All of this had the makings of a national social movement that would spread to the regions of Russia from which these central leaders origi-nally hailed. Indeed, Nikolai Vakhtin (1994:70–2) gives examples of local grassroots protests in the late 1980s, and concludes, "Undoubtedly, their membership and participation in the movement are sure to grow" (ibid. 73).

This new activism led in March 1990 to the organization of a national-level ("all-Russia" or *vse-rossiiskii*) Congress of Peoples of the North in Moscow. The fact that this congress was held inside the Kremlin with the blessing of the Party leadership (Slezkine 1994:378) and that USSR president Mikhail Gorbachev made an appearance at the opening session reflects the very progressive mood of the Soviet state at that time. At the same time, it indicates that this congress was not part of a grassroots movement, but rather a top-down, state-sanctioned event. At this congress, an Association of Less-Numerous Peoples of the North was established, with the Nivkh writer Vladimir

Sangi, who originated the idea as early as 1988, elected the founding president (Pika and Prokhorov 1988).[7]

The issues of concern to the indigenous peoples of the Russian North were reflected in the charter of the new Association, which declared the Association to be "a political organization uniting the small peoples of the North to take an active part in the development of the economy" (IWGIA 1990). Article Three of the charter describes the general goals of the Association as follows:

> The Association defends the interests of the small peoples and helps them to implement their political, social, economic and cultural rights, preserve their cultural character and maintain their traditional way of life as well as be in control of the preservation of natural resources in the territories they inhabit.[8]

A program was also outlined at the congress, and it reveals the key areas of concern to national indigenous leaders. Chief among them were rights to the use of land, prevention of further environmental degradation of land, and indigenous participation in economic development in the North. All of this was seen as closely tied to indigenous culture; the program specifically mentions the "preservation of [the small peoples'] cultural character, which is inextricably bound up with the recreation of traditional ways of life, and exploitation of nature's resources on the territories they inhabit" (IWGIA 1990:53). The program also acknowledged the need for international cooperation; the final clause reads as follows:

> The Association will base its activities not solely on Soviet but also international experience, in order to bring Soviet legislation on national relations in agreement with the Universal Declaration on Human Rights and other international documents (IWGIA 1990:56).

Established indigenous advocacy organizations – the Nordic Saami Council, the Inuit Circumpolar Conference, and the International Work Group for Indigenous Affairs (IWGIA) – showed their solidarity with the indigenous peoples of Russia by sending observers to the founding congress of the Association. The event was surrounded by a barrage of international attention.[9] Commensurate with the new international recognition of Russia's indigenous peoples, their representatives began to attend the annual sessions in Geneva of the United Nations Working Group on Indigenous Populations. Activists in Russia working on behalf of the indigenous peoples (which included many nonindigenous individuals, such as Pika) began appropriating the norms and rhetoric of the "Fourth World" movement, and even began to campaign for Russian ratification of the International Labor Organization's Convention 169, "Concerning Indigenous and Tribal Peoples in Independent Countries."[10]

A number of recent studies have examined issues surrounding indigenous rights activism specifically in regions of the circumpolar Arctic.[11] It is tempting here, in comparing indigenous politics in the Russian North with indigenous politics in the rest of the circumpolar Arctic, to assume there is one set of common problems for indigenous peoples throughout this region. Indeed, the rhetoric of activists is often quite similar, with common issues on the agenda: rights to land, control of resources, desire for autonomy and self-government, and preservation of culture and "traditional" economies. Indigenous activists in Russia and in the rest of the circumpolar Arctic have actively sought one another out in order to work together on these issues. There seems to be some poetic symmetry to this, as if, with the addition of Russia's indigenous peoples to the common struggle for rights, the last link has been added that will "close the circle" of the circumpolar North in terms of indigenous politics.

Mark Nuttall sums up best what it is that all circumpolar Arctic communities legitimately *do* have in common:

> ... by and large, they are remote. They are sparsely populated, peripheral and marginal, in the sense that they are geographically and economically distant from urban and industrial centers and markets. Small communities are predominantly indigenous... and are struggling to escape from situations of dependency and underdevelopment by acquiring a degree of political autonomy and economic self-sufficiency (Nuttall 1998:22).

However, strong caveats are in order here. Without resorting to "Bongo-Bongoism" – that is, claiming that the situation in the Russian Arctic is so exceptional that it cannot be subsumed within the comparative context – I would nevertheless argue that the rest of the circumpolar

Arctic states have much more in common with one another historically and in terms of legal structures than any of them has in common
with Russia. It is important to take these fundamental differences into
account when making comparisons.

One of the key differences concerns the divergent ways in which
Arctic indigenous peoples have experienced colonization and the
historically divergent ideologies and philosophies of the states in
which Arctic indigenous peoples find themselves enclosed. Most studies of colonialism assume the experience of the colonized to involve Christian missionization, European enculturation, and a close
encounter with the "post-enlightenment West" (cf. Comaroff and
Comaroff 1992), but this cannot necessarily be taken for granted
throughout the Russian North. Only in western Russia does this profile
have some relevance, and even here, one must consider how colonial
principles played out in the context of the Soviet state. In the twentieth
century, missionization in the Russian North involved indoctrination
in scientific atheism, and enculturation involved a Russia that had
maintained a somewhat schizophrenic relationship to Enlightenment
Europe since the time of Peter the Great (Leatherbarrow and Offord
1987; Walicki 1979).

Another difference to consider, particularly when examining
national-level indigenous activism in Russia, is the fact that – unlike
many other Arctic indigenous activists – most of the indigenous activists who arose in Russia in the late 1980s were not only Moscow-based
intellectuals, but had enjoyed elite positions prior to *glasnost'* by virtue
of their positions in the Soviet Writers' Union or in the Communist
Party. For them it was a more or less natural move to become involved
in the worldwide indigenous movement. These Moscow-centered indigenous activists had a political agenda, and put much effort both
into drafting legislation in Russia that clarified the status of indigenous peoples as well as lobbying the Russian legislature to pass that
legislation – actions that, while important, had only marginal impact
(if any) on the lives of indigenous peoples actually living in the North.

These elite leaders could claim some successes at the national level,
in terms of their struggle for greater recognition within the Russian legal
framework. Indigenous advocates succeeded in getting President Boris

Yeltsin to issue a special decree in 1992 calling for attention to the legal rights of indigenous peoples, and this led to clauses being added to several new laws (on matters such as land, wildlife, and education) mentioning the special rights of indigenous peoples.[12] Two clauses were also added to the 1993 Russian Constitution regarding indigenous peoples.[13] A working group of activists and ethnographers from the Institute of Ethnology and Anthropology of the Russian Academy of Sciences in Moscow created and promoted a draft law titled "Foundations of the Legal Status of Indigenous Peoples of the Russian North" (Sokolova et al. 1995), but although the Russian legislature approved the law (after much lobbying by indigenous advocates), Yeltsin repeatedly refused to sign it. The legislature was later able to pass a broader law that included all indigenous less-numerous peoples of the Russian Federation, a designation that encompasses minority groups that in many cases have very little in common with the indigenous peoples living in the North.[14] In spite of the compromises, indigenous advocates considered this law a qualified success, even if the Russian legal system remained murky and poorly enforced.

Ironically, rather than actually leading indigenous peoples all across Russia, the high-profile indigenous activists in Moscow seemed to have greater impact *outside* Russia. They were most effective in drumming up a heightened consciousness abroad (especially among transnational NGOs) of the fact that there actually *are* indigenous peoples in Russia and that their fate is indeed remarkably similar to the fate of other indigenous peoples around the world, that is, that they were abused and disenfranchised by the dominant majority. The activists were far less effective in drumming up a similarly heightened consciousness among indigenous peoples in the far-flung regions of Russia beyond Moscow. In fact, recognizing the logistical obstacles that prevailed at the time, they did not even try. When I interviewed Association president Eremei Aipin in 1996, he openly admitted that it was far too much for him to monitor what all of the local indigenous associations were doing in the many regions where indigenous peoples resided. He considered it his primary responsibility to focus on making progress at the federal level. Besides, the poor communications infrastructure in the country, and his organization's tiny budget, made it almost impossible for him to maintain regular contact with the regions. It took all their resources to hold a national congress once every three years and bring regional delegates together to elect officers of the national Association.

Moreover, the Association was experiencing internal conflicts. In 1993, the leadership split – some expressed dissatisfaction with the leadership of Vladimir Sangi and asked him to step down. Sangi refused to relinquish control of the Association of the Less-Numerous Peoples of the North, and so a group of leaders in essence formed a new organization with a slightly different name – the Association of Less-Numerous Peoples of the North, Siberia, and the Far East – and elected Aipin president. This new Association appears to have maintained the assets and the following of the original Association, leaving Sangi with an organization primarily in name only.

This rather grim state of affairs for the national Association in Moscow would not last long; by the end of the decade, the Association had successfully tapped into the resources of transnational organizations and with large infusions of grant money from Canada, Denmark, and Norway, it created a website[15] and began to implement development programs throughout the Russian North. However, in the middle of the decade, such eventualities could barely be imagined, neither by myself nor seemingly by the leadership of the Association.

The State of the Movement in Chukotka

The locally published sources that I had read, dating from 1989 to about 1993, gave the impression that an indigenous movement was indeed growing in Chukotka. Magazine and newspaper articles told the story of how the Association of Indigenous Less-Numerous Peoples of Chukotka and Kolyma[16] was created in 1990 (even before the national Association had been officially established), and how a regional conference was held in Anadyr' in January 1990 that brought delegates from each village in Chukotka (Grichenkovaia and Ivkev 1990; Tymnetuvge 1990). A well-known Chukchi intellectual, Aleksandr Aleksandrovich Omrypkir, was elected president of the new Association. The regional

Association had a charter similar to that of the national Association, with an accompanying program divided into four general areas of concern: 1) strengthening of political rights; 2) social reorientation of the economy; 3) spiritual development and revival of national culture; and 4) protection of health.[17] District, town, and village chapters of the regional Association were established throughout Chukotka, and an aura of excitement and optimism had surrounded what seemed to be the growth of a movement throughout Chukotka.

On the basis of the background information I had been collecting, I had the impression that I would find a consolidated, active, and independent indigenous social movement in Chukotka. When I arrived in Anadyr' to begin my research in 1995, I started in what seemed the most logical place: with the president of the Association, Omrypkir. I imagined I would find him amidst a buzz of activity in the Association's offices – I assumed it would be a central gathering place for discussion and exchange of information among indigenous Chukotkans. Instead, I found what to me seemed like baffling inactivity – Omrypkir sat alone in a tiny, rather desolate office. He seemed exceptionally intelligent and well informed about the problems of Chukotka's indigenous peoples, particularly from a legal perspective, and he seemed to fit the role of a quintessential intellectual leader perfectly. But the Association held no regular meetings, it sent out no periodical newsletter, and there was no evidence of active participation by a constituent membership. It had the office, it had a tiny budget given by the administration, and it had a reputation as being the one organization that represented the views of all indigenous peoples in Chukotka, but very few of those indigenous peoples were involved in its day-to-day functioning. Yet aside from the Association, none of my consultees could indicate to me any locus of an indigenous movement. When I asked them who the indigenous leaders were in Chukotka, aside from Omrypkir, they were likely to point out only the few indigenous peoples working as bureaucrats in an array of administrative organs in the capital.

I was surprised to find so little evidence of the indigenous movement I had expected, and for the first few weeks I felt perplexed as I sought to reconcile the information in the written sources with what I was observing on the ground. The national leaders and their activities were virtually unknown in Chukotka to all but educated, urban indigenous peoples. The national Association in Moscow sporadically published a newspaper (*Slovo Narodov Severa*, "Word of the Peoples of the North"), which Aipin had told me was distributed to the regions. Yet in spite of repeated inquiries, I could not find a single Chukotkan who had ever heard of it, let alone seen a copy, even among urban intellectuals in Anadyr'. In the course of the three months I spent in the village of Snezhnoe, I learned that there had been a village Association there; but when I tracked down the woman who had been its chair, she seemed bemused that I wanted to talk about it, and said the Association had not held a meeting for several years.

I interviewed Omrypkir again in 1996 and I asked him why there seemed to be so little activity – why did he not hold regular meetings, why did he publish no newsletter? He blamed the current financial crisis that had gripped all of Russia. Fundraising was a perennial problem, he said. They used to collect dues from members, but now people were not even getting their salaries paid on a regular basis, so the last thing they had money for was dues. The Association was an officially registered social organization in Chukotka, which entitled it to be included in the regional budget, and Omrypkir even received a small salary from the regional administration at first.[18] Nevertheless, Omrypkir lamented that the Association did not have enough ready cash to buy the paper, envelopes, and stamps it would take to send out any kind of newsletter to the local chapters of the Chukotka Association in the district centers and villages in order to maintain communication. A regional conference of the Association had been held in 1992, but since then it had not been able to afford to hold another one, although the Association's charter stipulates that it must convene such a conference every two years, during which it must hold elections. Omrypkir had thus remained president by default.

The state of the economy had obviously caused particular hardships for the indigenous population in Chukotka; nevertheless, I felt there had to be more to why the Association seemed so inactive. Why, for example, was the indigenous community of Anadyr' so little involved with the Association, when it was right in its midst? Anadyr' had an indigenous population of about fifteen hundred in 1996 (out of a total population of about thirteen thousand), and there was no financial barrier to communication within the tiny city.[19] Anadyr's indigenous community did maintain strong personal ties through telephoning one another and visiting one another's homes, and they had native-language radio and television programs as well as a native-language newspaper to serve as a locus of indigenous identity and communication, although these all had limitations. The indigenous inhabitants of Anadyr' were highly visible in society by virtue of their colorful performances of indigenous song and dance in traditional costume. By all appearances, this was fertile ground on which the Association could have promoted the full agenda of the indigenous rights movement as it was articulated in the documents of both the regional and national associations. Enthusiastic and optimistic reports in local papers provided some evidence that indigenous peoples had tried to promote this agenda in the early 1990s. So why in 1995–6 did it seem that effort had fizzled out?

Civil Soviet Society

Because the Association appeared during the period of *glasnost'*, it might seem logical to think of it as a new phenomenon of a new era, a sign of an incipient civil society forming in the soon-to-be-defunct Soviet Union. There are two problems with this view. First is the implicit assumption that there was no civil society whatsoever in the Soviet Union – since it was supposedly totalitarian to the bitter end, it presumably consisted of only the state and the individual (Wedel 1998:83). This idea has come under some criticism,[20] and Chris Hann and Elizabeth Dunn (1996) have suggested that part of the problem is the narrowly defined and ethnocentric usage of the term "civil society." But even supposing we take as given that the Soviet Union had no civil society as it is defined in the West, this begs the question: How did the Soviet state fill the space of social programming that the West ideologically believes should be undertaken by voluntary associations and NGOs?

Here we find a paradox, for if the Soviet Union lacked civil society, it certainly had no lack of social and political activism. Here I am not referring to dissident activity that the state considered subversive, but rather the activity of highly visible pro-Soviet political and social activists. Ironically, the stated agendas of these activists are remarkably similar to the agendas found in the mission statements of present-day Western NGOs, if the word "socialism" is substituted for "democracy," and "Soviet society" for "civil society." Countless examples of this kind of activism could be found throughout the Soviet Union, amounting to a kind of "movement mentality" – it was as though the presence of social movements, spontaneously emerging to address social problems, was considered the norm. This was perhaps driven in part by the Leninist spirit of maintaining society in a perpetual attitude of revolution. Part of it surely grew out of Joseph Stalin's culture of terror – people feared they could be shot for things like not volunteering to overfill the plan, and many felt it was a matter of sheer survival to appear to be more enthusiastically activist than the next person. When Stalin died, the terror was gradually forgotten, but the compulsion toward activism seems to have lingered and taken on a life of its own.

What I have conspicuously omitted so far is the role of the Communist Party in virtually every visible social movement or organization in the Soviet Union. Indeed, all manifestations of Soviet social activism – including indigenous activism in Chukotka – always required the endorsement of the local branch of the Communist Party, and quite often were mandated and initiated by the Party. In a sense, this perpetual activism was scripted by the Party, in both subtle and nonsubtle ways. The "activists" who were the leaders of sanctioned social movements were virtually always Communist Party members, and they understood the script and the role they were expected to perform. Caroline Humphrey (1994) deftly characterizes this phenomenon in her examination of the Mongolian Bogd Khan. Humphrey proposes the term "evocative transcript" to refer to "the social reproduction of texts that circulate as the reiteration of previous texts" (Humphrey 1994:22). Everyone knew the texts, and knew when and how they were expected to reproduce them, and the most successful performances came with certain rewards.

Western sovietologists asserted that the Communist Party *was* the state in the Soviet Union, so saying the Party or Party members initiated a social movement or founded a social organization would thus seem to be saying the state itself initiated it. But the Party *was* the state and *was not* at the same time; locally, it could also function as a detachable agent of the state that could masquerade as a cheerleader for social and political activism among "the people." Moreover, while from the outside it may seem obvious that the Communist Party was synonymous with a state that sought to repress its population, from the inside it was possible to buy into the notion that the Communist Party was an activist organization working for the betterment of society, and to see oneself as a partner with it. In this sense, awareness of the script can become deeply subverted, while attention is drawn to the positive aspects of one's social involvement. Tina Rosenberg, in her book *The Haunted Land* (1996), found this to be true of the dozens of subjects of Communist regimes she interviewed in Czechoslovakia, Poland, and East Germany. Even Stasi informers sometimes saw themselves as agents for positive change. My environmentalist consultee, Anastasia Zinkevich, told me of her own positive experiences dealing with Communist Party members. She described them as always being the most responsible and conscientious members of society, and even the best environmentalists. My point is that there was a space for citizen action in the Soviet Union for those willing to accept the limitations placed on that action, and many Soviet citizens made the most of this space. Those who wished to participate accepted the ways in which the Party channeled their activism as a given component of the social system.

This leads us to the second problem with the view that the Association was a sign of incipient civil society. Rather than representing a new kind of activism, it actually makes far more sense to think of the Association as properly belonging to this very genre of Soviet citizen activism, the last in a long tradition of very Soviet "social organizations" *(obshchestvennye organizatsii)*. This point was driven home to me when Lydia Neekyk, who was actively involved in the establishment of the Chukotkan Association, one day described to me how she participated in writing the charter of the organization. She laughingly admitted that she and her collaborators had no idea how to write a charter, so they simply adapted the charter of the Komsomol (Communist Youth League).

In fact, social organizations had been created in Chukotka long before *glasnost'* that strongly resembled the Association and involved some of the very same indigenous intellectuals who founded the latter. In 1969, a Social Council for Work with the Population of the Peoples of the North was created in Anadyr'.[21] This Social Council was officially endorsed by the regional-level Communist Party. "The activists of the local *(mestnyi)* intelligentsia have opportunely begun to practically resolve, on a social basis, the problems of culture and daily life of the local population," stated the chair of this new council, thus seeming to imply that the council was formed as a result of a movement already initiated by these activists (Krushanov 1986:108). The council was described as having an "advisory character"; its members would be elected from among the "more active and authoritative workers of the local intelligentsia." A few of these were named: "the engineer Iurii Nikulin, the journalist Tatiana Achirgina, the artist Ekaterina Rultyneut, and others" (ibid. 109).

Some of these figures were later found at the forefront of post-Soviet social activism in Chukotka in the 1990s. Achirgina would go on in the 1990s to be one of the founders of the Society of Eskimos in Chukotka, and would serve on the board of the Inuit Circumpolar Council when the Yup'ik Eskimos of Chukotka were accepted for membership in that transnational nongovernmental organization.[22] Rultyneut, founder of the state Chukchi-Eskimo dance ensemble *Ergyron*, went on to occupy a high-level managerial position in the Chukotka Department of Culture, and in the late 1990s she became a vocal advocate of indigenous cultural revitalization. After the collapse of the Soviet Union, these individuals felt they were doing nothing so qualitatively different from what they had done in the Soviet period. Western observers might put a negative spin on this and characterize them as "Communist holdovers"; but they put a positive spin on it – they see their own careers as a more or less seamless whole, and in their own minds, they were in the past, and continue to be, social activists, working as they always had to correct imperfections in society.

When the Association was formed in 1990, it certainly followed the Soviet-era precedents for such social organizations, and it had the approval of the still-existing Communist Party. However, this is not meant to dismiss its potential effectiveness. In seeing the Association of the 1990s as just one more in a long tradition of initiatives by a Soviet indigenous intelligentsia who were following the wink and the nod of the local Communist Party, I am *not* arguing that it was therefore doomed to failure, mired in the archaic logic of the Communist system. On the contrary, given local political circumstances different from those that arose *after* the collapse of the Soviet Union and the rise of open opposition to the Party, such a supposedly "activist" organization, regardless of being state-sanctioned in the Soviet period, might have gone on to fulfill a radical agenda outside of state-scripted limitations.

However, the Association faced two obstacles. First, because it had been created during the Soviet period with the support and blessing of the local Soviet of Peoples Deputies and the Party, regional administrative authorities assumed the Association would function within certain parameters acceptable to the state – that is, according to the script – and they related to it only in that prescribed way. There was simply no precedent upon which to imagine a truly independent and defiant social organization, and no space was allowed for this to occur. Second, when a fully redesigned and incomer-dominated post-Soviet administration later ascended to power in the region after 1993, its nonindigenous leaders began to recognize the potential challenge that an independent indigenous organization might present. They quickly sought to actively coopt the Association and make it subject to their own agenda, and that agenda was decidedly hostile to Chukotka's indigenous peoples and repressive of efforts to act autonomously.

By contrast, the Society of Eskimos was far more independently activist in the 1990s than the Association. This may be accounted for in part by the Society's association with an international organization (the Inuit Circumpolar Conference). The Society was also central to a program, sponsored by Alaska's North Slope Borough, to reintroduce indigenous bowhead whale hunting as well as to monitor bowhead whale populations in Chukotka, and this was instrumental in procuring bowhead whale hunting quotas for Chukotkan indigenous peoples from the International Whaling Commission (Krupnik and Vakhtin 2002). Another factor in the Society's activism is the simple fact that its headquarters were *not* located in Chukotka's capital city, thus enabling it to escape some of the coopting pressure of the Chukotkan administration. The chair of the Society of Eskimos, Liudmila Ainana, lived on the Chukotka Peninsula in the town of Provideniya, and was thus not within such easy "striking distance" of the administration and its repressive tactics. She traveled often to Alaska, where she boldly criticized the Chukotkan administration's treatment of indigenous peoples. Alaskan Eskimos to some extent "adopted" their Chukotkan Eskimo relatives and encouraged them in their struggle for their rights, and also helped to support them materially. Ainana and others on the peninsula did eventually suffer some consequences for their bold actions and criticisms,[23] but they did not pay those consequences on a daily basis in the way that Anadyr' indigenous peoples did.[24]

Disauthenticating Discourses

The constant, repressive chauvinism of the Chukotkan administration in the 1990s, under the leadership of Nazarov, played a decisive role in defusing the energy of the original indigenous movement in Chukotka. Whereas in the Soviet period Chukotka had been created as a "national region" as a gesture to its indigenous inhabitants, in the post-Soviet period incomers increasingly claimed the region as a Russian space, "discovered" by Russian Cossacks in the seventeenth century. More than once, indigenous peoples pointed out to me the irony in the fact that Chukotka had been an indigenous space to begin with, and it was indigenous peoples who had *allowed* Russians to settle there. Sofia Rybachenko, the indigenous journalist, one day commented to me, "Russians say they 'discovered' Chukotka, but excuse me – we were here!" She then repeated a story she had heard about a Native American who had recently demonstrated the audacity of this incomer attitude by traveling to Poland, stepping off the plane, and declaring, "I have discovered Poland!" "I thought that was pretty clever," Sofia opined.

Incomers often raised the technicality that certain parts of Chukotka were only recently settled by indigenous peoples, and therefore claims to indigenousness should be considered spurious. In an article on the changing demography of post-Soviet Chukotka, one journalist at *Krainii Sever*, the regional newspaper, wrote:

> Some people are of the opinion that the Chukchi are the indigenous inhabitants of ALL Chukotka. This is not so. It will soon be 350 years since Semen Dezhnev[25] and his followers began to familiarize themselves with the coast of the Gulf of Anadyr' and the continental part of the peninsula[26] along the Anadyr' and Belaya Rivers. Indeed, at that time there practically WERE NO Chukchis there. . . . Chukchis and Eskimos (who at first waged war against one another) had a place of habitation primarily along the Arctic coast and further to the northeast and south – the later Providenskii and Iultinskii districts.[27]

These assertions elicited a letter of response from Natalia Otke, a descendant of the local Chukchi politician Otke and director of the Chukotka Regional Museum. Otke addressed what she considered several factual errors in the article, but her main concern was that the author was "negatively playing on national feelings" and "tossing oil on the fire of national relations."[28] She was answered with another long article by the same journalist in which he merely re-asserted his claims all the more adamantly.[29] The tone of these articles differed sharply from that of the Soviet era, when a discourse of international friendship and brotherhood among peoples had prevailed. However, that discourse had always carried paternalistic overtones, and was a subtle means of domination of indigenous peoples by Russians. This exchange of articles in the mid-1990s was indicative of the response indigenous peoples got when they attempted to break with the Soviet-era precedent of quietly accepting their place as "younger brothers."

A particularly indicative example of the subtle defusing of the indigenous movement occurred in April 1994, when the administration orchestrated what it called the First Congress of Indigenous Peoples of Chukotka. At first glance, it seems a mistake to call this the *first* congress, since indigenous peoples in Chukotka had gathered twice before, in 1990 and 1992. However, those gatherings had been called *conferences (konferentsiya)* of the indigenous *Association*, while this was called a *Congress (s"ezd)* of indigenous *peoples*. The person placed on the front line to organize this 1994 congress on behalf of the Chukotka administration was Aramais Dallakian,[30] an incomer and the newly appointed head of the newly created Department of Nationalities Affairs and Migration *(Upravlenie po delam natsional'nostei i migratsii)*. Millions of (old) rubles were spent on the event out of the administration's budget; participants were flown in from Moscow and Yakutiya, as well as from Alaska and Canada. In two interviews published in *Krainii Sever,* Dallakian spoke optimistically of the effect the congress would have on solving problems of "self-government of the indigenous population" and other "purely economic and social problems." He said that his congress had created a different atmosphere than the previous indigenous gatherings, which had been, "so to speak, accusatory-pleading." He praised the administration's attention to indigenous problems, asserting that 70 percent of proceeds from taxes on gold mining were spent on the indigenous peoples, who comprised only 12 percent of the total population.[31]

However, Dallakian also made one important statement that foreshadowed the direction in which the new regional politics was heading. He said that the governor himself had appeared twice at the congress, and he continued:

> By the way, [the governor] was forced to take note of the not terribly correct statements of our guests from abroad. They called for conducting similar measures exclusively on narrow national terms, thereby programming international tension. That's not something we need: In Russia, including in Chukotka, there are more than a hundred peoples and ethnic groups, and there should be no exclusions. We all have the same problems in common, we must decide them together!... In the course of the congress, this was understood even by those who started out with a confrontational attitude toward the administration and the so-called "incomers."

Dallakian was attempting to claim that indigenous – incomer tension was irrelevant to the problems that the indigenous peoples were experiencing, going so far as to attempt to delegitimate the distinction between indigenous peoples and incomers by putting the latter word in quotes.[32]

Dallakian's statement was made all the more important by the fact that it was repeated two days later in an article by a reporter who had attended the conference. She writes (at times almost word for word repeating Dallakian):

> Obviously mistaken was the statement of Caleb Panaugve,[33] our guest from across the ocean, about the necessity of carrying out such a congress exclusively "without white people." ... Supposedly the "aliens," as a majority, steam-roller and harass the locals, and they need to attain their own political freedom. Personally, I think that we are all one nation – Northerners *(severiane)*. Suppose tomorrow the Ukrainians gather their own congress, then the Belorussians, then the Russians, then the Caucasians. But truly we all have the same problems. Do we really need to solve them separately? Absurd?[34]

The writer goes on to blame such attitudes on Boris Yeltsin's statement that the regions should "take as much sovereignty as they can swallow," which she says led to the problems the country was experiencing with renegade regions such as Chechnya and Tatarstan.

The implications of the social and political realities represented by attitudes such as the preceding – that indigenous peoples had suffered no more than any other nationality, and in fact that their problems were nothing unique – began to dawn on Chukotkan indigenous peoples, and by 1995, when I arrived, it was as if I had come upon a population experiencing shell shock. The post-Soviet transformation of Russian society was a difficult time for all, bringing sweeping changes to everyone's life. Although everyone in Chukotka was experiencing radical change that was difficult to adjust to, indigenous peoples carried a dual burden. As with Russians, there was the angst of social, political, and economic insecurity in the midst of the transition. But for indigenous peoples, it also meant a change in their status, an adjustment downward to greater exclusion from the mainstream, to basic disenfranchisement – and this was on top of their Soviet-era experience of pervasive Russian chauvinism. To add insult to injury, those in power publicly denied that indigenous peoples suffered any greater problems than anyone else in Chukotka.

Conclusion

When I did not find the active indigenous movement I had been led to expect in Chukotka, my project increasingly became one concerned with solving what I saw as the riddle of the indigenous (non)movement in Chukotka. Evidence such as the newspaper reports on the Congress presented in this chapter showed that the real story to be investigated was how power relations were changing between increasingly marginalized indigenous peoples and an increasingly chauvinistic incomer population as a result of the transformation in the regional political atmosphere since the collapse of the Soviet Union. Many sources published during *glasnost'* (written by indigenous peoples as well as by sympathetic nonindigenous peoples both within and beyond Russia) place blame on the policies of the Soviet period for destroying indigenous social systems, damaging indigenous cultural traditions, and causing the loss of the indigenous languages.[35] Such accusations are more than justified. However, because the Soviet system was strongly centralized, there was at least some consistency to how policies were applied across the Soviet Union, and some recourse for appeal to the central authorities if abuses did occur locally – when there is a script, at least one can rely on most participants to perform according to their roles.

The post-Soviet system very quickly became decentralized, and the indigenous movement as it was originally conceived could not move ahead because it had become derailed by a new logic that appeared only after the collapse of the Soviet Union. Fostered in the twilight years of the Soviet era, the Chukotka indigenous movement was prepared to battle the Soviet logic that was inherent in the ideology-driven system that had colonized indigenous peoples and systematically sought to dismantle their social orders and replace them with a Soviet social order. At least in that system, indigenous peoples had a role in the script; they occupied a position that fit into the logic of the system based on Lenin's nationalities policies. The agenda of the *glasnost'*-era indigenous movement, as articulated in the documents of the late 1980s and early 1990s, was in essence to enhance the role of indigenous peoples within that logic, giving them greater autonomy culturally, economically, and politically. But the collapse of the Soviet Union also meant the collapse of such a unitary system of policy. In Chukotka, as well as in many other regions of the North, a new post-Soviet logic quickly developed that was utterly postcolonial as well. The challenge for indigenous peoples was no longer simply to enhance their part in the logic of the system, but to create from scratch a part for themselves within the new logic of a new system that was attempting to erase them from the script altogether.

By the late 1980s, Russia's indigenous peoples were free in principle to join together with indigenous peoples throughout the world in cultivating and promoting a Fourth World consciousness, and many national leaders actively sought out and interacted with their indigenous counterparts in other countries. However, in spite of the appearance in Moscow of an indigenous association that clearly intended to represent the interests of indigenous peoples of the Russian North as a whole, and a florescence of regional associations that popped up nearly simultaneously across the country, one cannot say that these phenomena were truly connected in a unified movement across Russia, even if only for logistical reasons. In fact (not surprisingly), the more far-flung the region, the less connected it tended to be to activity in the center, and Chukotka, as the most far-flung region of all, remained quite peripheral.

Yet it was not merely Chukotka's peripheralness that excluded it from greater integration with a national indigenous movement in Russia. Even locally, no coherent indigenous movement materialized, and the reasons had to be sought in the nature of local politics in Chukotka after the collapse of the Soviet Union. The incomer-dominated regional administration displayed evidence of an emerging policy that was increasingly resistant to the idea of indigenous peoples having special needs or rights. This administration proclaimed that all Chukotkans, indigenous and nonindigenous, suffered equally under the hardships of the post-Soviet transformation, and the supposedly fraternal cry of, "we're all in this together!" seemed to preclude the need for an indigenous movement. Yet indigenous peoples felt more than ever before that they were the most disadvantaged and marginalized in society.

1967

Malina Ivanovna Kevyngevyt looked around the clubhouse at the gay deco-
rations, at the bright lights strung across the ceiling, at the freshly scrubbed
teenagers and young adults all dressed in their most fashionable outfits. The
room was crowded and noisy with laughter and conversation. She thought
everyone was particularly enjoying the music – a fact which gave her a special
feeling of satisfaction, since the music being played was from the record albums
she had brought back from her trip to the big cities down south. How exciting
it was to be finished with school, to be starting her new teaching job, to have
just seen so much of the Soviet Union beyond Chukotka for the first time! She
thought of how many times her teachers had told her how great Soviet society
was; as she looked around at the bright young faces enjoying her records, even
though few of them were Chukchi faces, she tried hard to believe that she,
too, was part of this great society.

Suddenly the lights went out and the room was plunged into darkness.
The music stopped. There was a general gasp, and a few of the girls screamed.
Malina heard the shuffling of many feet on the wooden floor, a few shouts, and
some giggling, and then just as suddenly the lights came on again. Malina realized
she had been holding her breath; she gasped, and felt her heart pounding in her
throat. People in the room began to laugh and talk again, and Malina exhaled
and turned to go put the music back on. She took one step and stopped in her
tracks: Her little stack of brand new record albums was gone.

Later in the week, one of her neighbors in the teachers' dormitory took
her aside and said, "Girl, I heard your records being played in the room at the
end of the hall." Malina felt a hollowness in her stomach as she turned and
looked down the hall at the door on the end. Trembling, she walked up to the
door and knocked. The door opened, and two Russian girls stood before her.
"Yes, girl?" they asked coldly. Malina scowled and said, "I think those are my

records you have." The girls stared blankly at her. One of them said, "I don't know what you're talking about." Malina looked over the girl's shoulder and saw one of her records sitting on a table; her name was written clearly across the front of it, and she pointed this fact out to them. "Anybody could have written that on there," the other girl replied.

Malina did not get her records back.

3

THE LIMITS OF RESISTANCE

MANY CASUAL OBSERVERS, mostly outside of Russia but sometimes within Russia as well, assume that since the Chukotka Autonomous Region is so named, the Chukchi must be the majority population there. The Chukchi are by far the largest *indigenous* group in Chukotka, but they are by no means the majority in the region, and in fact, even taken together, the indigenous population is vastly outnumbered by the incomer population today. The ratio of indigenous peoples to incomers was in flux throughout the 1990s due to some very active post-Soviet migration (discussed in Chapter 7), but by the 2002 Russian census, it stood at over 30 percent indigenous peoples and less than 70 percent nonindigenous. Besides Chukchis, other indigenous groups included Eskimos,[1] Evens/Lamuts, Chuvans,[2] Yukagirs, Koriaks, and Kereks (see Table 3.1).[3] Indigenous peoples native to other regions of Russia, such as Itel'mens and Evenks, have also settled in small numbers in Chukotka.

Being such a tiny minority – in relative terms as well as in real numbers – certainly placed limits on indigenous peoples' ability to

TABLE 3.1. Population of Indigenous Peoples in Chukotka, 1997

Group Name	Population
Total regional population	87,533
Chukchis	11,895
Eskimos	1,468
Evens/Lamuts	1,327
Chuvans	937
Yukagirs	152
Koriaks	81
Evenks	53
Nentsy	19
Itel'mens	12
"Others"	1,556
Total indigenous population	17,488

Note: Reliable census data for Chukotka was notoriously hard to come by in the 1990s. Official statistics were mere extrapolations from the 1989 census, and local officials were extremely reluctant to provide more recent data. Detailed regional data from the 2002 Russian census were not made avialable until after this book went to press. This table represents the most reliable and up-to-date figures I was able to obtain.

Source: Photocopied list distributed at the 1997 Conference of the Association of Indigenous Less-Numerous Peoples of Chukotka, titled *Obshchaya chislennost' naseleniya i ego natsional'nyi sostav po okrugu na 1.01.1997 goda* (Overall population count and its national composition for the region on 1 January 1997).

launch a movement that could carry weight in Chukotkan society, even under the best of political circumstances. In Soviet times, indigenous peoples' minority status was deemphasized in favor of viewing them as a special unit in the international brotherhood of Soviet peoples. In post-Soviet Chukotka, with that family metaphor eroded, indigenous peoples were left to seek new ways to make their voices heard against an increasingly cacophonous background. In this chapter, I consider some of the options open to indigenous peoples for pursuing a movement, and I situate those options within existing anthropological approaches to studying social movements. I begin by reviewing the ways the position of indigenous peoples in Soviet society was defined ethnically.

The Less-Numerous Peoples and Soviet Approaches to Ethnicity and Nationality

The Chukchi have received a good deal of attention in scholarly literature,[4] probably in part because of the legacy of the ethnographer-exile Vladimir Bogoraz and the amount of material he published on them, and also in part simply because they are the largest indigenous group in Chukotka. Siberian Eskimos have also been well covered in ethnographic literature.[5] Material on Chukotka's remaining indigenous groups is somewhat harder to find.[6] While I generally interacted with people who identified as Chukchis more often than with those who identified as representatives of other indigenous groups, my research focused less on any particular indigenous group (along with the particularities of their ethnic identity) than on the group broadly defined (both internally and externally) as "indigenous peoples of Chukotka." Virtually every indigenous inhabitant I interviewed in Chukotka clearly identified as a member of that group in addition to his or her own specific group. This was also reflected in the frequency with which indigenous inhabitants referred to themselves as *my, korennye zhiteli* ("we, the indigenous inhabitants") in opposition to *oni, priezzhye* ("they, the incomers"). This tendency is perhaps accentuated by the fact that many indigenous peoples in Chukotka are of mixed heritage, not only from indigenous–incomer marriages, but also from mixed indigenous–indigenous marriages.

However, many of my consultees were also quick to volunteer information about the particular indigenous group with which they identified, including personal theories about their ethnic origins. Some of the urban, intellectual Chukchis I consulted told me that the word "Chukchi" was a name the incomers attached to them, while their own self-designation had been *Lyg"oravetl'an*,[7] or "the genuine people." I did not hear this ethnonym used in everyday conversation by anyone, however, and when I did ask Chukchi consultees if they felt themselves to be *Lyg"oravetl'an* rather than Chukchi, they said no. Although "Even" and "Lamut" were reported by Soviet ethnographers to be simply two alternate names for one and the same group (Levin and Potapov 1964:670), I met some people who self-identified as Lamuts and others who self-identified as Evens. I asked one Lamut woman who exactly the Lamut were, and she told me her mother always said they resulted from intermarriage between Jews and Chukchis – a theory that certainly has no precedence in existing ethnographic literature. Regarding the Chuvans, when I asked one Chuvan in the village of Snezhnoe about the origin of his people, he answered that he always understood that it was the intermarriage of Chukchis and Cossack settlers. Chukotka's indigenous people clearly did give thought to who they were.

Not only were there distinctions between different groups among Chukotka's indigenous peoples, but distinctions were made within groups as well. Coastal Yup'iks recognized a distinct difference between those native to the village of Chaplino and those native to the village of Sireniki, and distinct variations of Yup'ik were spoken in each village.[8] Chukchis strongly differentiated between coastal Chukchis and tundra Chukchis, in terms of language, cultural practices, and even imputed character traits, in a manner that reminded me of the way northerners and southerners in the United States sensed difference in one another. Even among tundra Chukchis, certain groupings of villages felt an affinity for one another and a unity of identity in contrast to clusters of villages in other parts of the tundra. In Anadyr', the circle of indigenous peoples in which I became embedded, while predominantly Chukchi, included representatives from both coastal and tundra villages.

Although in the 1990s I sometimes heard a distinctly indigenous discourse about indigenous identity in Chukotka, throughout the Soviet period, indigenous self-knowledge was assumed to be shaped by outside definitions. Soviet ethnography was pervasive in its efforts to study, define, and categorize all ethnic groups within the Soviet Union, much as other colonial powers have done all over the world, and volume after volume was published on the peoples of the North.[9] In Russian schools, indigenous children would have been taught who they were according to the authoritative definitions produced by Soviet ethnographers in these volumes, because this information was ultimately a matter of Soviet policy toward the indigenous peoples, and it trickled into the textbooks produced especially for the North (and some of the textbooks were written by the ethnographers themselves, for example, Leontev and Alekseeva 1980; see Chapter 4). The conclusions of ethnographers were made all the more authoritative because token indigenous peoples were trained in ethnography and sent back to study their own peoples.[10]

In practical terms, it did not matter who the indigenous people *felt* they were – they *were* who the Soviet government said they were. This was reinforced by the Soviet practice, introduced by Stalin in 1932, of requiring all Soviet citizens to carry internal passports (Zaslavsky 1993:33–4). Included on the passport was the infamous "Line 5," which identified the nationality of the bearer (and indigenous groups, if recognized by the Soviet government, were considered nationalities). If a child had parents of two different nationalities, only one could be chosen for entry on the passport, which the child received at age sixteen. The system was loosened during the *glasnost'* period, and a person ideally might be registered under any nationality he or she wished; thus, for example, if a Chukchi did think of herself as *Lyg"oravetl'an*, the Chukchi-language ethnonym, technically she could register as such.[11] However, national identity was so rigidly state-controlled that it was extremely difficult for "bottom-up" conceptualizations of identity to prevail. Incomers tended to be intolerant of assertions of alternative indigenous self-identity. To them there was no question about who the indigenous peoples of Chukotka were – they were who the ethnographers had already said they were, and the markers of their identity were easy to see. The Chukchi were Chukchi because they lived in *iarangi* (reindeer-skin tents), wore fur clothing, danced in a particular style, and spoke the Chukchi language. Collectively with the other indigenous peoples, they were the less-numerous peoples of the North.

This belief in the ascribed nature of ethnic or national identity is in large part a legacy of Stalin's particular twist on nationality issues. Stalin wrote, "every nation, whether large or small, has its own specific qualities and its own peculiarities, which are unique to it and which other nations do not have" (Stalin 1967, quoted in Slezkine 1994:310). Nationality was objective and consisted in specific shared traits such as language and material culture; the loss of one of these key traits, in the Stalinist view, meant the loss of a group's ethnic or national self-consciousness (Kaiser 1994:103). This helps account for the near panic I sensed from indigenous peoples who talked about how important it was to preserve the native language – in their minds, Chukchis or Eskimos who do not speak their native languages might no longer be Chukchis or Eskimos at all.

The phrase "less-numerous peoples of the North" *(malochislennye narody Severa)*, which is so pervasive in the literature on the Russian North, originated as a Soviet administrative designation for twenty-six different indigenous groups scattered all across the Russian North, from Russia's border with Finland (where Russian Saami reside) to the tip of the Chukotka Peninsula. The designation was created in the 1920s by the Committee for Assistance to the Northern Borderlands, or simply, the Committee of the North.[12] In the post-Soviet period, debate has grown concerning this official designation, particularly among ethnographers in the Russian Academy of Sciences. Some have argued to allow more small indigenous groups to be officially recognized as "less-numerous peoples" (such as the Kereks previously mentioned), while others challenged altogether the necessity of having a special category for these groups.

The term *malochislennye* is notoriously difficult to translate, and "less-numerous" is unequivocally an awkward solution. English simply has no single-word equivalent to the Russian word *malochislennye*, which combines the words *malo* (meaning "few" or "not very many") and *chislennye* (an adjective related to the verb *chislit'*, "to count," and the noun *chislo*, "number, quantity"). The word is often translated as "small," a gloss that evokes the curious impression that the people in question must be petite in stature.[13] Some writers have chosen the translation "Sparse," while others have tried such unbecoming mouthfuls as "small-in-number" and "numerically small." "Less-numerous" seems the most grammatically accurate choice, if not the most graceful.

Malochislennye has also been glossed as "minority," which comes closer to capturing its meaning than "small," but this is still a misleading translation. For one thing, Russian has a word for "minority," *menshchinstvo*, and this is not the word being used to refer to the indigenous peoples of the North. Moreover, while the concept of minority is appropriate in immigrant contexts such as that found in the United States, it is less relevant in the Soviet context. In the United States, it is recognized that people from many different ethnic backgrounds have come together to form American society (and where "melting pot" was once the metaphor, it tends now to be replaced by "mixed salad"). Hypothetically, with so many "minority" segments, a person could simultaneously belong to several different minorities or even the majority, depending on which way the segments are being drawn. For example, a person could be in the majority as "white," but in a minority as "Jewish," while someone else could be in a minority as "black," but in the majority as "Christian."

There is moreover a basis for making a distinction between "minorities" and "peoples" for the purpose of delineating rights. Erica-Irene A. Daes, as chair-rapporteur of the United Nations Working Group on Indigenous Populations, writes:

> It should be stressed that "indigenous rights" and "minority rights" are to be strictly distinguished. Indigenous "people" are the descendants of a people that has lived in the region prior to the invasion of colonizers or foreign settlers who, in many cases, have since become the dominant population. In this respect, the number of indigenous peoples does not constitute a substantive criterion. Indigenous peoples are indeed peoples, and not minorities or ethnic groups (Daes 1989:44; see also Venne 1998:90–2).

The Soviet Union did have its own ideology of bringing together many groups into one society, with the goal of creating Soviet citizens. Yet at the same time, it was always clearly kept in mind that the Soviet citizenry was made up of many distinct nationalities, not merely minority segments, and this national (rather than ethnic) diversity was

an official source of pride. It was the goal of official Soviet policy to encourage the flowering of each individual nationality's potential. This
was just as true in Chukotka as it was anywhere else in the Soviet
Union, as the Soviet historian N. N. Dikov (1989:311–12) indicates:

> The achievement of the little peoples [*malykh narodnostei*] of
> Chukotka in the building of culture is a convincing testimony of
> the concern of the Party and the government for the development
> of the spiritual culture of the peoples of our multinational Mother-
> land. These achievements speak of the advantage of socialism (even
> in its administrative-state form), having opened up a space for the
> development of the culture of all peoples – big and little.

And in the words of Innokentii Vdovin (1965:391–2), the well-known
historian and ethnographer of the Chukchi:

> In the Soviet Union, all nations and peoples have equal rights. Their
> economic and spiritual life is developed on a single socialist founda-
> tion. Economic and spiritual community is conducive to the quick
> drawing together of all nations and peoples of the Soviet Union. The
> development of the national culture of the Chukchi proceeds by these
> general laws, which are inherent to all peoples of the Soviet Union.

Thus, the concept of less-numerous peoples fits with a society that
views itself not as a multi-ethnic "mixed salad" of many minorities, but
as a family of many intact "peoples" joining together. Some of those
peoples are numerous, such as the Russians or the Ukrainians; other
peoples simply have fewer members. The Chukchi are not a minority
interspersed within a Russian society, but rather a unit alongside other
units within one overarching whole.

At the same time, Soviet nationalities policy was fraught with con-
tradiction and ambiguity.[14] Two words were consistently used to express the goals of this broad policy: "drawing together" *(sblizhenie)*
of many nationalities, and "blending" *(sliyanie)* of them (Rakowska-
Harmstone 1975:29; Slezkine 1994:344). The second word in particular betrays the assimilationist outlook of Soviet policy at the same
time that it hides the implicit assumption that Russian culture would
dominate. The previous quote by Vdovin is finished with this thought:
"Drawing together with *first of all the culture of the Russian peoples*
is a matter of conformity to those natural laws being observed in

the development of the national culture of the Chukchi" (emphasis added)(Vdovin 1965:392). Rather than imagining a melting pot in which many different nationalities and cultures each added their flavor, the concept here, at least from the Russian point of view, was rather of a smokehouse in which Russianness would infuse and improve each of the Soviet Union's many nationalities.

This idea of indigenous culture being encapsulated within and infused by Russian culture was precisely one of the key ideological obstacles that hindered the development of a distinctly indigenous social movement in Chukotka. This partly accounts for why, in spite of representations both inside and outside Chukotka that the early 1990s was a time when indigenous activism was flowering, my initial impression on the ground was that there was very little evidence of an actual indigenous movement. This led me to begin rethinking the very nature of social movements and our understanding of them.

Theorizing Social Movements

I encountered some challenges in trying to build an anthropological approach to the indigenous movement in Chukotka, and to social movements in general. In my search for theoretical precedents, I was disappointed to find that at least the recent literature included so little *anthropological* theory from which to draw. Theorizing has clearly been dominated by sociologists and political scientists,[15] and reading that literature has always been discouraging for its clear lack of ethnographic richness. Moreover, whether they espouse resource mobilization theory or "new social movements," the producers of this literature tend to favor large-scale, mass forms of protest that are seen to arise from a grassroots upswell, usually involving hundreds or thousands of people and often resulting in violent conflict. Such models generally presume an urban industrial (often specifically European) context, making them of limited utility in trying to understand the indigenous movement in the Russian North.

Oddly, anthropological literature on social movements per se is sparse; what is a virtual cacophony in the other disciplines appears as almost a silence in anthropology. A few anthropologists have bravely engaged with these theorists nevertheless, such as Arturo Escobar (1992), who manages to find what usefully remains after peeling away the Eurocentrism of Ernesto Laclau, Chantal Mouffe, and Alain T. Touraine. It was Escobar (1992:395) who stated what I considered a clarion call to anthropologists of social movements when he wrote of anthropology's "regrettable" absence from the lively debate on "the nature and role of social movements in relation to the crisis of modernity and the possibility of new social orders." Later, John Burdick also lamented anthropology's poor showing in the study of social movements, and observed, "the study of social movements remains in anthropology generally derivative from sociology" (Burdick 1995:361–2). In fact, this assertion is borne out even in the most recent review article of the study of social movements in an anthropological journal (Edelman 2001), which is devoted primarily to a review of sociological and political science theories (cf. Hodgson 2002:1046 n9).

Yet, if we look back a bit in the history of anthropology, there was a time when anthropologists *were* talking about social movements, albeit under a different heading. For example, A. F. C. Wallace examined revitalization movements, subsuming within this broad category nativistic movements and millenarian movements (Wallace 1956). Paying particular attention to the psychological processes involved in such movements, he placed within the same comparative context such seemingly divergent examples as Handsome Lake's Longhouse Religion and the Russian Revolution (cf. Clemmer 1999). Several studies address protest movements and political organizing specifically among northern indigenous peoples, such as Philip Drucker's study of the indigenous brotherhoods of the northwest coast of North America, Harald Eidheim's study of Saami political activism, and Margaret Lantis's study of a nativistic movement in Alaska (Drucker 1958; Eidheim 1968; Lantis 1973). However, such studies have become obscured from our attention because, unfortunately, anthropology textbooks have typically placed this type of material in a chapter on religion. Even if these texts acknowledge that such movements may take other, nonreligious forms, the examples given are nonetheless typically limited to cargo cults and the Ghost Dance. This pattern remains unchanged in recent anthropology texts.[16]

What has been handed down as the standard treatment in anthropology textbooks is unfortunately a distortion of the history of anthropology. Alternative anthropological treatments of movements seem to have disappeared from disciplinary memory. For example, Ralph Linton wrote a definitive review article titled simply "Nativistic Movements," published in *American Anthropologist* in 1943, that treated religious movements as only one aspect of a much wider phenomenon. Thirty years later, Lantis (1973:116) noted that Linton had outlined both magical and rational movements, both revivalistic and perpetuative, and she asserted, "anthropologists tend to remember and to write about the revivalistic and especially the magical types."[17] But she says Linton was most interested in rational and perpetuative forms, and she urges us to give them our attention as well.

As I sought in vain for recent anthropological studies of social movements, I came to see this apparent gap in anthropology to be less an absence than simply a relabeling. Where political scientists and sociologists have focused on macrophenomena and called it "social movements," anthropologists of the current generation have paid closer attention to microphenomena and called it "resistance." Particularly in the 1980s and 1990s, anthropologists took up the resistance rubric with gusto and for the most part chose not to deal with larger-scale movements.[18] Some excellent ethnographies have been produced in this vein – for example, Aihwa Ong's (1987) study of Malaysian factory women, and Jean Comaroff's (1985) study of the South African Tshidi Churches of Zion. Although anthropologists tend to invoke such studies of "resistance" as a single category, this broad rubric actually contains two very distinct approaches. Comaroff's study is an example of an approach that focuses on the creative reinterpretation of historical relationships (for example, between colonizer and colonized) through narrative and performance, a reinterpretation that "serves as a symbolic strategy for coping with historical and political-economic realities" that offer no other alternatives (Hill 1988; cf. Nash 1993).

However, as John Comaroff and Jean Comaroff (1992) have deftly pointed out elsewhere, the colonized peoples of the world do not share a unitary field of experience. The Comaroffs make a useful distinction between the "recently colonized" (and, I would add, those who have for a long time been *marginally* colonized, such as some Amazonian peoples) and those who have been drawn more fully into the consciousness of the world of the colonizer (such as Native Americans). Those in the latter group are more likely to resort to the resistance strategies of that world, what the Comaroffs call the "orthodox styles of political discourse and protest" (1992:260). I would place the indigenous peoples of Chukotka into this latter category, by virtue of the thoroughness of their colonization by Soviet ideology. In selecting modes of protest against the Russian-dominated regional administration, they almost universally gravitated to the "images, ideologies and aesthetics" (to quote Comaroff and Comaroff 1992:260) of the Soviet socialist world in which they grew up.

The second approach to resistance, into which Ong's study falls, takes its inspiration from a political scientist who, like many anthropologists, turned his attention to microphenomena: James Scott. Scott found the traditional definitions of social movements to be inadequate for describing the kind of activity he had observed among Malaysian peasants, and he sought an alternative concept. According to the conventional wisdom on social movements, writes Scott, "the degree of violence, the scope of the goals sought, and the sheer size and durability of the activity are typically invoked, singly or in combination, to develop topologies of protest or resistance" (Scott 1986:420). However, such a definition of social protest overlooks "the multitude of rather passive, reformist, episodic, and small-scale actions that fills the pages of local and provincial histories" (ibid. 421). Scott convincingly argues for the recognition of the powerful cumulative effect of seemingly trivial acts, whose eventual impact he likens to a coral reef upon which a large ship may run aground and be destroyed (ibid. 422). Scott labels this kind of incremental protest "everyday forms of peasant resistance," by which he specifically means "foot-dragging, dissimulation, false compliance, pilfering, feigned ignorance, slander, arson, sabotage, and so forth" (ibid. 419).

In seeking to understand indigenous activism in Chukotka, I found, as Scott did, that the "standard" models of social movements failed to describe what I was observing. But I also found Scott's concept of "everyday resistance" to be not entirely adequate. Everyday forms of resistance, as defined by Scott, presume a population that is of some use to the dominating power – either as a peasant agricultural class or as a laboring class that can be exploited. In such cases, the kinds of subversive activity that Scott describes – such as work slowdowns and withholding of agricultural produce – can be used as a virtual monkey wrench tossed into the works of the dominant power's goals. Scott's approach might be more appropriate for a historical examination of the predicament of indigenous peoples during the Soviet era. In the early phases of collectivization, when indigenous reindeer herds were wanted to bolster the assets of collective farms, one could point to cases in which Chukchi reindeer herders resisted by slaughtering their herds rather than giving them over to the collectives, or even by launching armed attacks against Soviet agents (Dikov 1989:211). Such resistance was far from unique in the Soviet Union, as Lynne Viola's 1996 study of peasant resistance under Stalin shows (cf. Balzer 1999). However, Scott's resistance rubric is less useful in trying to characterize the predicament in which Chukotkan indigenous peoples found themselves during the 1990s.

First of all, in the late Soviet period, Chukotkan indigenous peoples did not constitute a laboring or peasant class that could be exploited by a dominating power – to put it crudely, they were not workers or peasants, however much the Bolsheviks would have liked to imagine them to be. Reindeer herding, the occupation of the majority of Chukotkan indigenous peoples in the Soviet period (either directly or in support services within the state farm system), was considered an important economic activity in Chukotka, but from the Soviet perspective, it was important primarily in an ideological sense: It was unique to the indigenous population, and it was part of their "national character" (in the Stalinist sense discussed previously). However, in material terms, the reindeer herding economy paled in comparison to the industrial economy in Chukotka, and was in fact never a profit-making enterprise for the state. The best way for the indigenous population to be usefully exploited, again from the Soviet perspective, was to demonstrate Soviet success in constructing socialism everywhere in the

country – even in the remotest tundra. They could also serve as evidence that the Soviet Union dealt more fairly with its indigenous peoples than Western capitalist nations – the indigenous intelligentsia
were meant to be proof that indigenous peoples were better educated
and had better opportunities than indigenous peoples in the West. It
is hard to imagine where indigenous peoples could have gained much
leverage through a foot-dragging approach here.

This was all the more so in the Russia of the 1990s, when the indigenous peoples of Chukotka were deemed to be of no practical use whatsoever by the incomers who dominated the Chukotkan administration.
Nonintellectual indigenous peoples were a surplus labor force in a region where reindeer herding had all but collapsed and even industries
were proving to be unprofitable. The few jobs available, such as in
mining or oil exploitation (the potential growth industries), were routinely given to nonindigenous laborers, many of whom were imported
from outside of Chukotka. Many indigenous peoples found themselves
unemployed in the 1990s, and thus presented no value to the administration as either a productive force or a source of taxation. Indigenous
agricultural products – primarily reindeer and sea mammal meat and
byproducts – were in little demand, and the enterprises that managed
these activities (the former state farms and collective farms) were literally falling apart in the wake of privatization. From the point of view
of the Chukotkan administration, indigenous peoples were nothing
but a dependent population, and a word commonly used to describe
the role of the indigenous population was *izhdivenchestvo* – "parasitic
dependency."[19] Indigenous peoples were acutely aware of this, and
more than once, I heard indigenous consultees refer to themselves as
broshennye liudi – "discarded people."

A second reason why Scott's "everyday resistance" model did not
seem useful to me was because the indigenous protest I did observe
in Chukotka was for the most part not subtle and hidden – it was
in fact public and open. Sometimes indigenous peoples engaged directly with administrators, usually in gatherings officially called by the
administrations; sometimes indigenous peoples engaged indirectly
through material published in newspapers or broadcast on radio or

television. It happened rarely, it was practiced by only a few, and these few suffered severe consequences as a result, from being politically blackballed to being summarily dismissed from work. I did run across occasional cases of more subtle subversion, but these exceptional cases only proved the rule that Chukotkan indigenous peoples could find little room for such resistance.

For example, Sofia Rybachenko told me that the Chukchi-language staff at the state-controlled television station (which provided the only local television broadcasts in Chukotka) sometimes tried to slip critical commentary of the administration or the governor into their broadcasts. However, she went on to describe the surveillance system that had developed to deal with this. Sofia explained that the full text of each Chukchi-language broadcast had to be typed out, and a Russian-language summary also had to be typed (on typewriters with carbons – the television office had no computers at that time). The director of the television company read the Russian summaries, and if there were deemed to be any sensitive topics, the director would send for Elena Ostapenko, a highly placed Chukchi-speaking indigenous intellectual in the administration, to check the Chukchi-language transcript. If she found any objectionable material, Ostapenko would "suggest" that Sofia change it. Sometimes Ostapenko would call up Sofia at home after watching an evening broadcast, and gently complain about what Ostapenko perceived to be questionable content.

Sofia imitated for me, repressing derisive laughter, Ostapenko's wheedling tone in these conversations. "I've known her since my college days," she smirked, "because we lived in the same dormitory." Yet Sofia was also more than aware of the dangers of displaying opposition to the administration, even in the face of an old college chum. She feared losing her job, so she always made the changes Ostapenko suggested. Sofia said that sometimes she did manage to get critical material through in her broadcasts. But even when she did succeed, the impact would be minimal: Few indigenous peoples in Chukotka were fluent enough in their indigenous language to understand the broadcasts, since they had been educated in Russian-language schools and rarely had opportunities to use their indigenous language on an everyday basis.

Thus, in trying to understand the phenomena I was observing in Chukotka, I found that neither of the two predominant models – at the one extreme, large-scale mass protest, at the other extreme, subtle, subversive resistance – was entirely satisfying to me, since neither seemed to fit the situation. Alexia Bloch offers one alternative when she explores Evenki women's differing forms of resistance and accommodation to the Soviet system in which they were raised. She argues that the attention to accommodation is a means of adding complexity to the typical duality of domination and resistance, and of acknowledging that even seemingly subordinated subjects have some agency (Bloch 1996:132). Sofia's actions might certainly be characterized as a form of accommodation, and Ostapenko's all the more so. Yet I still felt there was more here – I could detect an indigenous discourse, however obscured, of indigenous rights and the need for activism as a means of bringing about change, a discourse that went beyond mere accommodation.

I found some solace in a recent book edited by anthropologists that attempts to resolve this dialectic between subtle resistance and mass protest: Richard G. Fox and Orin Starn's (1997) *Between Resistance and Revolution*. The papers published in this book focus on what Fox and Starn call "in-between social protest." Although this kind of protest might be the work of only one person or a handful of people, what distinguishes it from "resistance" is that it is *public* – it is overt and deliberate, rather than being covert and incremental. Most importantly, Fox and Starn prefer to view social protest as "a process of becoming rather than an already achieved state, the typical premise in too much of the literature on social movements" (ibid. 6). Movements do not necessarily move along a straight-line process, as Wallace's (1956) formulation implies, but rather follow meandering paths, often with false starts and seeming dead ends. This is helpful for understanding the phenomena I observed in Chukotka, which included public expressions of discontent by a few indigenous intellectuals, but did not appear as a full-blown movement, although I constantly had the impression I was observing something in the process of becoming more.

It is perhaps precisely these in-between phenomena that are most important for understanding the nature of domination and dissent.

Public and Hidden Transcripts

Not only did the administration of Chukotka deem indigenous peoples to be "unneeded" in the 1990s, it also perceived them to be a potential threat. Prominent in the rhetoric of the Moscow indigenous activists are claims to lands traditionally used by indigenous peoples, and throughout the Russian North these are almost without exception the very lands that local administrations – as well as the federal government – have their eyes on for the development of natural resources, from the harvesting of forests to gold mining to oil and gas drilling. Governor Aleksandr Nazarov made several trips to Alaska in the early 1990s, and was well aware of Alaska's experience with the Alaska Native Claims Settlement Act (ANCSA). The last thing he wanted was to establish a precedent in Chukotka of granting land rights to indigenous peoples and/or limiting the exploitation of mining resources for environmental and land-use reasons.[20] Chukotkan indigenous peoples were also aware of the situation in Alaska, and they recognized the obstacle they potentially presented to the administration. This recognition accounts for the many times I heard indigenous peoples say they believed the administration deliberately neglected their needs in the hope that they would simply go away or die off, thus eliminating any potential threat.

Although it can be said that the Russian population had dominated indigenous peoples from the beginning of the Soviet period (not to mention prior to it) and continued to dominate them in the post-Soviet period, the nature of that domination changed after the collapse of the Soviet Union and placed hardships of a somewhat different nature on the indigenous population. As discussed in the last chapter, the Soviet period was characterized by a kind of colonial domination in which the indigenous "other" had a scripted role, while in the post-Soviet period, the greatest challenge to indigenous peoples was the manner in which incomers were working to redefine social space in Chukotka such that indigenous peoples were nearly erased.[21] Following Scott, in his 1990 work *Domination and the Arts of Resistance: Hidden Transcripts*, this process can also be thought of as the rewriting of the "hidden transcript" of the dominant power in Chukotka.

Scott presents two concepts for theorizing contestation over collective perceptions of reality: public transcripts and hidden transcripts. The "hidden transcript" is any group's unofficial account of what it thinks is "really going on" between those in power and those being manipulated by it. For a subordinate group, this is "a critique of power spoken behind the back of the dominant" (Scott 1990:xii). However, Scott writes that a dominant group can just as easily have its own hidden transcript of what is actually transpiring in relations between groups, "representing the practices and claims of their rule that cannot be openly avowed" (ibid.). In contrast to both of these hidden transcripts stands the "public transcript," which is:

> ... the *self*-portrait of the dominant elites as they would have themselves seen. Given the usual power of dominant elites to compel performances from others, the discourse of the public transcript is a decidedly lopsided discussion. ... It is designed to be impressive, to affirm and naturalize the power of dominant elites, and to conceal or euphemize the dirty linen of their rule (Scott 1990:18).

In Chukotka, both the hidden and public transcripts of the dominant incomers were changing in the 1990s. The hidden transcript of the Soviet era emphasized the need to create a façade for the world to see, both within and beyond the Soviet bloc, which gave the impression that all nationalities were fairly represented in a Communist ideology. This resulted in a public transcript of socialist affirmative action that attempted to mask the dominance of Russians in virtually all spheres of life. The post-Soviet hidden transcript in Chukotka had begun to emphasize the need to capitalize on limited resources and monopolize them within incomer-dominated patronage networks. To hide the "robber baron" persona that the new administrators were taking on, the public transcript began to emphasize democratic equality and capitalist opportunity, concepts conveniently provided by Western reformers. Embodied in claims of democratic equality was the claim that everyone was "in the same boat" in Chukotka, and no particular nationality was more deserving of special assistance than any other, as was seen in the example of the Congress of Indigenous Peoples discussed in Chapter 2. Phrases such as "we're all in this together" or "we'll solve it together" sounded liberal and inclusive, but in practice this rhetoric signaled the silencing of interpretations of social relations that were inconvenient for the incomer mainstream.

The unfolding of the three "epitomizing events" in Chapter 1 revealed the gradual rewriting of the public transcript for the post-Soviet era in Chukotka, specifically concerning the administration's responsibilities to the indigenous peoples within its jurisdiction. These public actions and declarations – abandoning renovation of the *Iaranga*, closing the independent native-language newspaper, and obtaining the apparent indigenous endorsement of the Russian incumbent for governor – all said that indigenous Chukotkans no longer had any need of special treatment and they did not require their own specially prescribed space in society, but should make their own way in the context of the new market relations and democracy. The Soviet-era public transcript had been patronizing, but at least it was accommodating to indigenous participation in public life; this new public transcript was more overtly racist and exclusionary. Overall, the phenomena that were occurring in Chukotka signaled the belabored death of Soviet nationalities policy once and for all. In large part, this book is a partial documentation of its death throes in Chukotka, the process by which nationalities policy was dismanted in that region.

However, this process was not being accomplished entirely without opposition. Indigenous peoples' complicity with the public transcript in Chukotka belied the existence of an indigenous hidden transcript that was bitterly critical of the administration's treatment of indigenous peoples. The indigenous peoples' responses in the three events – demanding nothing less than their own separate meeting house, picketing the administration building in protest of the loss of an independent native-language newspaper, and rallying to support an indigenous candidate for governor, even calling in to the television station to comment on the video *Gwich'in Niintsyaa* – signaled the development of a new hidden transcript among the indigenous peoples. This hidden transcript retained elements from the Soviet era – indigenous Chukotkans had even then recognized ways in which they were discriminated against by incomers, as many people's stories revealed to me. What was added to it was, first, a new recognition that they were not alone in their plight – indigenous peoples elsewhere in Russia and in other parts of the world had the same kinds of problems, and the solutions they had come up with should in principle work in Chukotka as well – and second, that public protest as a collective activity by indigenous Chukotkans was a strategy they could consider. In the mid-1990s, this new hidden transcript was only just beginning to challenge the dominant public transcript. The three events described in Chapter 1 perhaps amounted to what Scott describes as "those rare moments of political electricity when . . . the hidden transcript is spoken directly and publicly in the teeth of power" (1990:xiii) – that is, when indigenous peoples openly defied the public transcript.

This had been done at the national level in Russia with the publication of venomous critiques by nationally known indigenous writers in the late 1980s, as discussed in Chapter 2. The subsequent creation of a national-level Association of Less-Numerous Peoples of the North, along with the appearance of regional indigenous associations, seemed to herald a change in the public transcript successfully wrought by indigenous leaders. However, as I have already argued, this action was in fact still largely in line with the Soviet-era public transcript.

More to the point, public declarations of the indigenous hidden transcript at the national level, as important as they were for opening up the possibility of a new kind of indigenous discourse, did not carry their effectiveness equally into all regions of Russia where indigenous northerners live. In the early 1990s, Boris Yeltsin offered Russia's far-flung regions a rare opportunity to grab a degree of sovereignty for themselves (a process that will be discussed more fully in Chapter 6), and this in a sense cut each region loose to develop its own character. Each subsequently became an arena of power relations with its own public and hidden transcripts, in addition to (and sometimes in conflict with) the Russian national-level transcripts. Chukotka represents a case in which those who came to power locally created an environment that was not only less than liberal in terms of its reform-mindedness, but in which the local administration seemed threatened by, and bound and determined to actively repress, all efforts at indigenous social and political autonomy and self-determination. What is most notable about Nazarov's tenure is the way he gradually brought the Russian hidden transcript of contempt for indigenous Chukotkans brazenly to the level of public discourse. Change in the public transcript could come only as equally bold declarations of the indigenous hidden transcript were made, but such declarations came with great risk.

Some Avenues of Protest

Chukotka in the 1990s was radically and almost universally changing – politically, economically, and socially. These changes had differential effects on indigenous peoples and incomers. The predicament in which indigenous peoples found themselves was frustrating: In a period of seemingly greater opportunity for all, they were more shut out than ever before; in a period of supposedly greater democracy for all, they were being newly disenfranchised. Something had to be done, and yet the avenues for action seemed to be narrowing. Non-indigenous administration officials frequently claimed that indigenous peoples had plenty of avenues for solving their problems and representing their interests. They pointed to the token indigenous peoples who held high-level positions in the administration, such as Ostapenko, or to Aleksandr Omrypkir, president of the regional Association, who was often depicted in the administration-controlled newspaper as a quintessential indigenous "leader." However, the phrase I often heard from indigenous peoples in Anadyr' to describe these high-ranking and administration-favored indigenous peoples was that they were far too "fond of their own armchair" *(on / ona liubit svoe kreslo)*, and therefore would never really challenge the administration or be effective in bringing about change. Thus, indigenous peoples in

Chukotka were left to seek ways to act on an individual, professional, or communal basis.

What options did they have to express their dissent and pursue change in what they saw as an unsatisfactory social order? One approach often used by indigenous peoples internationally is a strategy that has been termed the "boomerang effect" (Sikkink and Keck 1998:12–13). This refers to the pressure that foreign interests can bring on a government that is allegedly violating human rights within its borders. Victims of such violations are often powerless to elicit any response from their own government to their grievances, but by contacting sympathetic foreign governmental agents (such as legislators) or international nongovernmental organizations, they can indirectly bring pressure on the government of the offending country from the outside. International pressure on behalf of Chukotkan indigenous peoples could in principle be brought to bear on both the Russian federal government as well as the administration of Chukotka. Chukotkan indigenous peoples were indeed in contact with indigenous advocacy organizations in the United States, Canada, and Europe, and were beginning to make their case at the United Nations Working Group on Indigenous Populations sessions in Geneva. The Inuit Circumpolar Conference showed interest in helping indigenous organizations within Russia. Besides this, sympathetic academics (including Russians, Europeans, and Americans) began in the 1990s to conduct "expeditions" to Chukotka, most having a fairly open agenda of pro-indigenous advocacy.[22] However, the boomerang effect was having minimal impact on the Russian federal government in the early 1990s. In Chukotka, it was even having a negative effect, inspiring the administration to take preventive measures against interference from outsiders – such as complicating the federal border zone law with more restrictive local regulations that created obstacles for foreign visitors, and cultivating an attack on the activities of outsiders in Chukotka through items placed in the local media (these matters are discussed more fully in Chapter 6).

A second possible approach for Chukotkan indigenous peoples was to seek greater legitimacy within the existing system, and to build a coalition with sympathetic nonindigenous peoples to help them achieve the numbers needed to gain election to public office and bring about change through the newly established "democratic" means. This was a more or less "natural" course for indigenous peoples raised in the Soviet system to pursue, since they were accustomed to being involved in both regional and national politics throughout the Soviet period. Several indigenous leaders in Chukotka, such as Vladimir Etylin, Maia Ettyryntyna, and Larisa Abriutina, had experience working in public office, and they had the precedent of indigenous peoples being elected to the Regional Soviet to bolster their legitimacy among nonindigenous peoples. This made the prospect of forging an electoral coalition with nonindigenous peoples quite possible, all the more so since the proportion of indigenous peoples in Chukotka was creeping up as nonindigenous immigrants to Chukotka moved back to their homelands by the thousands after the collapse of the Soviet Union. This kind of coalition building was precisely the kind of approach that seemed to be working in Canada, bringing about the creation of the new territory of Nunavut.[23] Chukotkan indigenous peoples remained vastly outnumbered by incomers, but in principle, it seemed possible to build an effective coalition.

However, there was a significant obstacle to this approach, related to the nature of electoral politics in Chukotka. Although Chukotka regularly held elections that were touted by the administration as being "democratic," in fact there was widespread corruption. For each of the several elections that took place in Chukotka since the time I began my research in the mid-1990s, consultees reported countless incidents of voting irregularities, from outright fraud at the polling place (such as attendants stuffing ballot boxes, and workplace managers completing ballots for voters who did not show up) to voter intimidation (managers pressuring employees to vote for certain candidates, polling place attendants telling voters how they should vote as they handed them their ballots, election observers being arrested on orders from district bosses, and so on). Chukotka is not unique in this, nor, perhaps, in the lack of verifiable documentation of these irregularities. It must be understood that local attempts to document and report such incidents only led to more aggressive intimidation, and thus polling place corruption in the 1990s will probably never be officially documented. The net effect of this state of affairs, nonetheless, is that attempts to change the status quo through the "democratic process" were stymied by the flaws in that process.

Short of these more sweeping strategies, indigenous peoples were left to seek more incremental avenues of protest. The urban indigenous intelligentsia were more likely to consider active protest. For nonintellectual indigenous peoples in the city and for those living in villages, activism did not seem to be a viable option. In my interviews with villagers in western Chukotka, I often encountered the attitude that the problems they faced were the responsibility of some authority higher up. Rather than seeking solutions that they could implement locally, they were passively waiting for someone else to take the initiative. The attitude is even less surprising when one considers that local government in Russia continues to be designed and administered by Russian federal law, and in Chukotka, this has resulted in a structure by which decisions are passed down from district bosses to village administrators appointed by them.

For example, the outskirts of Snezhnoe, where I lived for several months, were littered with a veritable junkyard of scrap metal and broken-down vehicles. Children liked to play in the cab of a rusted-out crane and do a tightrope walk along on the edge of an old tractor's shovel, antics that never failed to make me cringe with apprehension. When I asked villagers about it, they sighed and responded that, in the past, scrap metal of this kind would have been periodically gathered up and hauled down to the beach, where barges returning empty after delivering loads of coal and supplies upriver would pick it up and take it away for recycling. They agreed it was an unsightly and dangerous mess, but they said no one ever organized them to clean it up – they were waiting for initiative to come from above. No such order came down from the district level, and so no one at the village level acted. When I asked if it would be possible to negotiate locally with a passing barge captain to take the metal, they said, "Sure, but who is going to organize it?"

Thus, individual initiative was hard to come by. One form of proactive response that all indigenous peoples did take – from villagers to urban intellectuals – was to write open letters to government leaders and send them for publication to newspapers.[24] Writing such letters to, or for the benefit of, government officials is a very long tradition in Russia, tracing back to the petitions sent to Tsars by peasant subjects and sometimes conquered indigenous peoples.[25] As Viola writes in her book on peasant resistance under Stalin against the collectivization and "dekulakization" of the 1930s:

> Peasants wrote letters to Stalin and Mikhail Kalinin, newspapers, and Party and government agencies in their efforts to gain redress. They wrote their letters individually and collectively. They protested bravely, begged humbly, and they asserted the rights of Soviet citizenship (Viola 1996:91).

Even the national movement that created the Association of Less-Numerous Peoples of the North began with a letter to Soviet President Mikhail Gorbachev, written by several prominent indigenous writers.[26] Such letters appeared in the pages of *Krainii Sever* nearly every week in the mid-1990s. The letters might be addressed simply to the editors of the paper or to particular government officials. Even Chukotka's governor sometimes used this tactic to register his protest with the federal government. For example, the front page of the 21 September 1996 issue of *Krainii Sever* carries a letter signed by the governor (acting in his capacity as a representative to the *Sovet federatsii* or upper house of legislature) and three federal ministers, addressed to Russian Minister of Finance A. Ia. Livshits. The letter complains about the delay in the disbursement of federal funds to the region for the payment of salaries.

The letters that appeared in *Krainii Sever* during the 1990s fit very well the tenor that Viola describes for the peasant letters she found. For example, in December 1996, a letter titled "We Have Forgotten the Taste of Bread!" and signed by sixteen residents of Snezhnoe appeared in the paper.[27] The following are excerpts from this letter:

> Esteemed editors of the newspaper *Krainii Sever*! The reindeer herders of the state farm "Anadyrskii" appeal to you . . . it has already been three years in the brigade since we have been supplied with the necessary provisions of food and ammunition. And if they do bring supplies, it barely lasts us a month. . . .The *tundroviki* [those who live in tundra] are not receiving their salary. Those on vacation are forced

to go back to work when they don't receive their money. For several months, mothers have not been paid their lump sum allowance for children. At the main settlement, in order to obtain provisions of food, each herder figures something out as best he can, but we've already forgotten the taste of bread. . . . The head of administration of the village absolutely does not respond to our needs, and yet it is indeed his direct responsibility to bring in to school the children who have already been in the tundra for two months too long and are not studying. And one more question: What does the *AKB*[28] exist for in the village if it has not once visited the reindeer brigade to show videos? In conclusion, esteemed editors, we would like to ask of any interested persons: How are we supposed to go on living?

The letter was written by reindeer herders, not intellectuals, and they knew that this was an acceptable form of protest. They also knew they might suffer repercussions from the village mayor or the director of the reorganized state farm; but in their desperation, they perhaps reasoned that things could not get much worse for them. One of the signers I recognized as a young man who was one of the first to come knocking on my door for a visit after I arrived in the village. Having emboldened himself with a bit of vodka beforehand, he burst through the door with a friend in tow and immediately said, "Patty! I want you to take a letter for me to Boutros Boutros-Ghali! I'm going to write and tell the United Nations what is going on here!" He would not be satisfied until I promised to deliver his letter. That letter never appeared, but the previously excerpted letter, written shortly afterward, seems to have taken its place.

For his part, the governor of Chukotka wrote letters back to the people; his open letters appeared frequently on the front page of *Krainii Sever*. In so doing, it was as if a transaction were completed – a letter for a letter – while the prevailing conditions remained unchanged and specific problems remained unaddressed. The governor often blamed authorities higher up for creating conditions that left him powerless to effect any change, and letters like the one from Snezhnoe in fact provided him with fuel for his own grievances. The letter to Livshits was a case in point; it implied that the governor bore no blame for the salary delays, even though the federal government frequently lamented that federal funds sent to the regions for salaries were used for other purposes.

Following Nazarov's first-time election to his previously appointed post of governor, a letter appeared in the 28 December 1996 issue of *Krainii Sever* addressed to "Dear fellow countrymen, respected northerners," and signed, "Sincerely yours, Governor Aleksandr Nazarov." The letter reads in part:

> Behind us is the first free election for the head of the executive power of the region in the history of Chukotka. It did not go off simply in this complex socioeconomic atmosphere that our region is experiencing, but amidst a sharp political struggle. . . .
>
> Yes, many of us today are not living at all sweetly. Our common headache is the delay in the payment of salaries. I understand that I carry personal responsibility before you, my fellow countrymen, to see that you are able to buy necessities and feed your children. . . .
>
> . . . The people did not give in to the dubious promises and provocations [of other candidates in the election]. On the contrary, they drew closer to simple, worldly truths. This is the path to unity, to consolidation: that we should decide all pressing questions together, jointly, having faith in one another, and not separately, in an atmosphere of dissidence, societywide suspiciousness, and enmity. . . .
>
> Dear fellow countrymen, I assure you that all my strength, knowledge, and experience will be directed exclusively to making Chukotka a truly enlightened region, so that you may live calmly, confidently, happily. . . .
>
> Away with drunkenness, parasitic dependency [*izhdivenchestvo*], and other vices! Beloved work, valued relaxation, the bringing up of children – these are our reference points. Physically healthy, spiritually sound, highly educated, and cultured people should live in Chukotka. . . .

The familiar slogan of the post-Soviet public transcript is evoked, that everyone in Chukotka is in the same boat and everyone should work together to solve common problems. This public transcript is further refined as the governor provides a profile of the ideal citizen of Chukotka: healthy, educated, and cultured. The problems that had long been associated with the indigenous population – drunkenness and *izhdivenchestvo* – are to be solved simply by bidding them to go away. The letter does not suggest a single concrete solution, and indeed, that is not its purpose.

These letters were cumulative and sometimes competing contributions to the public transcript about social conditions in Chukotka. Ultimately for indigenous peoples, this was a losing proposition, since the local administration tightly controlled what appeared in the state-funded media, and this was the only mass media that existed in Chukotka.

Conclusion

In terms of the indigenous movement in Chukotka, the mid-1990s were a kind of "bottleneck" period, an almost liminal phase in a process of moving from Soviet to post-Soviet logic. Confronting *either* a radical social transformation such as occurred with the collapse of the Soviet Union *or* a repressive administration like that of Nazarov's might have been surmountable; but in concert, these factors proved to be disorienting enough that even the most prominent among the indigenous intelligentsia had trouble finding their footing. Letter writing was a relatively safe means of articulating a critique of power, but it would take some time before avenues of action could be found.

1971

"Lina! Lina! You're in the paper!"

Malina Ivanovna turned to see her friend Tonia running up to her and waving the latest issue of *Soviet Chukotka*, the newspaper published down in Anadyr', the capital city. "Look, they wrote about you!" she cried excitedly.

"Oh, right, I knew that was coming out," Malina Ivanovna said nonchalantly. But she had not seen the article yet, and so she stood shoulder to shoulder with Tonia to peer at the paper. The article was written by the Russian secretary of the Provideniya Executive Committee – not a bad person to have notice you. It started with a charming little opening, describing how every morning Malina Ivanovna Kevyngevyt, the chair of the village soviet, hurried into the little administration building over which a red flag flew, and tackled the mass of work for the day. She was praised for her competence in listening to the villagers' needs, answering questions, and considering a myriad of proposals. Malina Ivanovna was described as a "pretty, swarthy woman . . . energetic, intelligent, highly erudite." The article talked about how difficult the job of chair was and how well Malina Ivanovna handled it. "Oh, Lina," cooed Tonia, "You should join the Communist Party. They would take you in a minute."

Malina Ivanovna smiled; lots of people in the village had offered to sponsor her membership in the Party. She looked again at the article, returning to the physical description of herself: "Swarthy. . . . " Why did he have to use that word? Something about it left Malina Ivanovna feeling ill at ease. Swarthy. She wouldn't have minded just being called a "pretty woman."

4

TOWARD A HISTORY OF
SOVIET CHUKOTKA

AS I SPENT more and more time among indigenous peoples in Anadyr',
it became clear that whatever indigenous activism did exist there –
both during the Soviet period as well as after the collapse of the Soviet
Union – was the province primarily of the educated, urban intellectuals of that city.[1] I consequently came to focus my ethnography more
and more exclusively on them, and to seek more historical material
that would help me contextualize their experiences. The history of
Chukotka and its indigenous peoples is in many ways quite similar to
the history of other regions and other indigenous groups in the Russian
North. In sketching out Chukotka's history, therefore, my main goal is
to pay particular attention to the historical processes that produced
Chukotka's indigenous intelligentsia. In subsequent chapters, I will
go on to explore ethnographically the experiences of this intellectual
community in the 1990s.

Accounts of the history of indigenous peoples of the Russian
North often emphasize the prerevolutionary colonial phase, high-
lighting the burdensome tribute demanded by often-maverick Tsarist
administrators.[2] This history is certainly important for Chukotka, since

it has shaped the conditions in which Chukotka's indigenous peoples live today, as well as their relations with incomers. However, since plenty of works already provide background on the prerevolutionary history of Chukotka,[3] and since my own research has focused on the Soviet period, this book's historical treatment favors the latter. By the same token, when the Soviet period is discussed in historical accounts – whether of indigenous peoples or others – a common trope is the absurd and sometimes cruel overzealousness of the postrevolutionary political and social organizers. To be sure, the process of sovietization had some horrifying aspects that everyone now admits were at best mistakes and at worst crimes. At this point in Soviet historiography, I feel there is no sense in beating a dead horse, and therefore I will not place much emphasis on recounting these abuses in Chukotka. Moreover, my research in Chukotka drove home to me the recognition that indigenous peoples and incomers alike remember Chukotka's Soviet history, and while their interpretations of that history may differ, for the most part, no one views this history in purely negative terms. This chapter considers both the positive as well as the negative consequences of indigenous encounters with the Soviet system. The goal is to provide a framework for understanding the position of indigenous peoples in the incomer-dominated post-Soviet politics of Chukotka in the 1990s.

I begin with a brief overview, and take as my arbitrary (although admittedly somewhat poetic) starting point the ethnographer-exile Vladimir Tan-Bogoraz, who arrived in Chukotka in the late nineteenth century and eventually produced what is now the most well-known ethnography of the Chukchi (Bogoras 1904–9). Well into the early twentieth century, indigenous peoples in Chukotka continued to pursue a lifestyle more or less resembling that described in Bogoraz's ethnography: the sedentary coastal peoples (Chukchis and Eskimos) engaged in sea mammal hunting supplemented by fishing and gathering, the tundra-dwelling peoples (primarily Chukchis, but also Chuvans, Koriaks, Evens/Lamuts, and Yukagirs) engaged in nomadic reindeer herding or hunting, supplemented by fishing and gathering. All peoples interacted with one another – sometimes with hostility, more often amicably, traveling great distances across Chukotka to trade with one another and with incomers. At the beginning of the twentieth century, indigenous peoples still vastly outnumbered incomers in Chukotka, and so their impact was relatively insignificant.

A qualitative change began to occur when Russia was thrown into a civil war as a result of the Bolshevik Revolution that turned St. Petersburg upside down in 1917 and spread from there across the country. The shock waves did not begin to hit Chukotka until the early 1920s. Once the civil war was brought under control and the country began to stabilize, indigenous peoples in Chukotka began to receive more visitors in the form of young propagandists for the Cultural Revolution, which was unleashed on the countryside throughout Russia from the late 1920s to the late 1930s. Suddenly the most remote tundra camps were overrun by these young zealots, whose primary goal was the "liquidation of illiteracy."

The mammoth task of turning an indigenous population that was considered entirely illiterate into professional and skilled workers capable of reproducing Soviet society was taken on in large part by young Russians who came to Chukotka with missionary zeal. Among the first were the young disciples of Bogoraz and another ethnographer of the peoples of the North, Lev Shternberg. Bogoraz and Shternberg argued that the very people who were most qualified to take on the administrative tasks in the North were the ethnographers they were currently training. Said Bogoraz:

> We must send to the North not scholars but missionaries, missionaries of the new culture and new Soviet statehood. Not the old ones but the young ones, not the experienced professors but the recent graduates, brought up in the new Soviet environment and ready to take to the North the burning fire of their enthusiasm born of the Revolution (quoted in Slezkine 1994:159).

They were able to find plenty of young people who fit this profile. As one of Bogoraz's students wrote from the field, "I am still unable to get to my place of work . . . but I will jump off anywhere in Chukotka and get there somehow. I am not the kind to go back" (Slezkine 1994:168). Tikhon Semushkin[4] immortalized this phenomenon in his novel *Alitet Goes to the Hills*, a fictionalized and idealistic account of the establishment of Soviet power in Chukotka, which won the Stalin Prize in 1948.

In it, Andrei Zhukov, a geography student from Petrograd University, is sent to Chukotka in 1922 to survey its coast, and he is able to communicate with the locals because "an old professor at the university who had spent some years in exile in this region had imparted to Andrei Zhukov his entire Chukchi vocabulary" (Semushkin 1952:142).

Jumping ahead to the 1960s, we find a generation of literate adult indigenous peoples who were more comfortable speaking and reading Russian than their own native language. They had been transformed into voracious readers of newspapers, magazines, and books,[5] and even the most remotely located tundra herders had seen films from Moscow and Leningrad by virtue of traveling cinema tents (Dikov 1989:365–7). In newspaper articles, they read about the successes of their compatriots who had become doctors and teachers, had earned higher degrees, had been elected to local and national political offices, and had even been accepted as members of the Communist Party. Some of the short stories and novels they enjoyed reading had been written by indigenous peoples who had been honored with admission to the Soviet Writers' Union (such as Iurii Rytkheu, Vladimir Sangi, and Uvan Shestalov). This chapter examines how such a transformation of the indigenous population was achieved.

What Is To Be Done?

Those knowledgeable of Russian history will immediately recognize the provenance of the title of this section and its relevance for any discussion of intellectuals in Russia. *What Is To Be Done? (Chto delat'?)* is the title of a novel written by the radical revolutionary Nikolai Chernyshevsky during his imprisonment by the Tsarist authorities for his revolutionary activities of the late 1850s (Chernyshevsky 1986). Chernyshevsky's writings had developed a set of ideas that influenced an entire generation of Russian revolutionaries (Walicki 1979:188). The novel provided a set of fictional characters who possessed all of the idealistic qualities of a politically engaged intelligentsia that he had propounded in his earlier writings. The question of the title refers to the social problems of the nineteenth century, which provided the motivation for the various strands of the revolutionary movement that formed during that time. The answer was embodied in the characters of the novel, whose self-sacrificing devotion to the peasantry and fearless, decisive action to overturn the status quo were clearly meant to be emulated.

The phrase "what is to be done?" has been used over and over since the appearance of Chernyshevsky's novel. Vladimir Lenin, as a fledgling revolutionary, was deeply moved by Chernyshevsky's writings (including the novel *What Is To Be Done?*), and used the phrase as the title of his own pamphlet outlining his vision for a revolutionary Marxist party (Walicki 1979:190). The phrase can be found frequently in Russian newspaper and journal articles that discuss current social problems. One recent use of it can be found as a subheading of an article in an issue of *Foreign Affairs* by Grigory Yavlinsky, leader of the Russian democratic reform party *Yabloko* (Yavlinsky 1998:78). I use the phrase here to highlight the fact that the indigenous intellectuals in Chukotka, like Russian intellectuals, took on as their calling the burden of focusing on what was to be done about the social condition of their people (cf. Haruchi 2002:92).

The indigenous intelligentsia was based on the ideal of the Soviet intellectual, an image that in turn had roots in the Russian intellectual movement of the late nineteenth and early twentieth century (Diakonova and Romanova 2003). Indigenous politicians' speeches of the Soviet period were rhetorically indistinguishable from the speeches of their Russian politician counterparts; indigenous writers' poems, stories, and novels reflected the themes and styles of the Russian writers they read in the course of their training, such as Alexander Pushkin, Anton Chekhov, and Leo Tolstoi (Slezkine 1994:369). This intelligentsia was created entirely from scratch out of transformed reindeer herders and sea mammal hunters, and humble beginnings came to be a kind of calling card that assured impeccable credentials. A favorite rhetorical device when presenting a biographical sketch of an indigenous intellectual was to start with the phrase "born to a family of herders (or hunters, fishermen, and so on)." The average Soviet (read: Russian) citizen was meant to marvel at what socialism could accomplish in even the remotest locations.

It became a matter of Soviet policy and ideology that every nationality, no matter how small, needed its own indigenous intelligentsia to symbolize its highest potential (Slezkine 1994:157; Uvachan 1990:45).

For the most part, the indigenous intelligentsia in Chukotka, as in other parts of the Russian North, was a deliberate creation of the Soviet state, a centrally planned product. "We cannot move ahead if we will not work intensively on the creation of the indigenous peoples' own intelligentsia," wrote Anatolii Lunacharskii, the Soviet commissar of education in the 1920s (quoted in Udalova 1989:101). Special emphasis was placed on the development of indigenous literature; as the historian N. N. Dikov (1989:285) writes:

> The conception and development of literature among the peoples of Chukotka, who formerly did not even have a writing system, was one of the most important proofs of the realization of the Leninist plan of Cultural Revolution.

As many indigenous peoples as possible were funneled into the primary educational system, and from there a certain number of them were drawn into the postsecondary institutions and tracked to fulfill all the roles that were needed in order for the Soviet government to be able to make claims to the existence of an indigenous intelligentsia. The most visible and iconic among these were writers, legislators (People's Deputies), and journalist/translators, but also important were teachers, doctors, technical specialists, artists, and other "cultural workers" (Dikov 1989:416–17). Taken together, they came to be known as *mestnaya natsional'naya intelligentsia*, "the local national intelligentsia" (with "national" glossing as something similar to what we would understand "ethnic" to mean today).

Revolutionary and Early Soviet History of Chukotka

From the Soviet perspective, the history of Chukotka as a Soviet political entity begins during the Civil War between the Bolshevik Red Army and the counterrevolutionary White Army, locally referred to as "White Bandits" (cf. Flerov 1973:54).[6] In 1919, the Kamchatka *Revkom* (revolutionary committee) sent two young Russian Bolsheviks, Mikhail Mandrikov and Avgust Berzin', to Anadyr' to form an underground movement in Chukotka to undermine the White Army forces resident there. They drew several other incomers into their revolutionary circle, such as Aleksandr Bulatov and Vasilii Titov, and even managed to re-cruit a couple of local russified Chuvans, Mikhail Kurkutskii and Nikolai Kulinovskii. This core circle of revolutionaries came to be known as the First Revolutionary Committee of Chukotka, or *Pervyi Revkom Chukotki*, an emblematic group that remains well known in Chukotka to this day. Sources tell of how the counterrevolutionary Whites in Anadyr' were on the verge of discovering this group when it made a cataclysmic decision on the night of 16 December 1919 to attack the White forces in Anadyr', overthrowing them and setting up a revolu-tionary committee the very next day. As the lore goes, they immediately set about freeing victimized indigenous Chukotkans from the debts of the greedy merchants and began to take steps toward the liquidation of capitalist dominance in Chukotka, with the goal of securing the border against incursions from the United States and establishing a Soviet state monopoly on local trade (Zhikharev 1961:43–4; see also Semushkin 1952).

However, it seems the youthful *Revkom* made a few mistakes. Al-though the *Revkom* set about to nationalize the property of merchants in Anadyr', it did not manage to seize the stores of guns and ammu-nition. The merchants remaining in Anadyr' took advantage of this and organized an effort against the *Revkomtsy*, planning to do away with the revolutionary leader Mandrikov. On the morning of 31 January 1920, the armed merchants surrounded the *Revkom* office and opened fire. Titov was killed, others were wounded, and Mandrikov decided to surrender. The survivors were imprisoned, but their captors elimi-nated them by feigning to transfer them to another location and then shooting them at a lonely place along the road. The remaining *Revkom* members had meanwhile been away in Markovo, and they were am-bushed as they returned unawares to Anadyr'. All of the survivors were eventually executed (Zhikharev 1961:60–1).

The victorious merchants immediately set about restoring every-thing as it had been before the Bolshevik overthrow, reappropriating seized property and setting up a local governing council. With time, the Kamchatka *Revkom* received news of the deaths of the Anadyr' *Revkom*, and sent a telegram demanding to know the details. The merchants pre-tended to be socialists, and answered with a declaration claiming that

they were merely part of a cooperative commune, peacefully working together for the good of the collective. Soviet sources allege that
they forced local residents to sign an affidavit in support of this new
administration. Apparently to complete the illusion, they formed an
Anadyr' branch of the Russian Communist Party of Bolsheviks, and
sent telegrams all over Russia announcing this new branch of the Party.
However, because Mandrikov, Berzin', and their cohort had managed
to take their revolutionary movement to Ust'-Belaia and Markovo (an
old Russian settlement) before they were killed, they still had followers
in these towns, and these did not fall for the ruse of the Anadyr' merchants. The headquarters for the work of establishing Soviet power in
Chukotka simply shifted to Markovo and became the Second *Revkom*
of Chukotka (Zhikharev 1961:63).

The Markovo *Revkom* appealed to the Kamchatka *Revkom* for help,
and in response the latter sent word to the Anadyr' merchants that they
were fooling no one. The Kamchatka *Revkom* warned that the deaths of
the Anadyr' *Revkom* would not go unpunished, and that it was sending
a commission on the first steamship in the spring to investigate. "Not
waiting their arrival," writes Dikov, "some of the conspirators fled to
Alaska, while others remained in Anadyr', discontinuing their political
activities" (1989:148). The struggle was not yet over, however, for the
Civil War continued to rage on in the Russian Far East. It was not until
the spring of 1923 that Red Army Commander M. P. Volskii in Kamchatka
issued an order declaring that the liquidation of the White forces in
Chukotka was finished (ibid.:156).

Although a memorial to the members of the First *Revkom* of
Chukotka (featuring a statue of Mandrikov) was erected in Anadyr' by
the summer of 1921 (Dikov 1974:158–9), the Second Chukotka *Revkom*
never found the bodies of the heroes. It was not until 1969 that a tip
from an elderly indigenous man who said he remembered seeing them
buried led to the recovery of the bodies in the cemetery of Tavaivaam.
Excavations indeed turned up the eleven bodies of the *Revkom*
members. In a solemn procession, they were paraded from Tavaivaam
up through the city of Anadyr' to the site of the memorial, where "those
who first brought to this far region the Leninist word of truth" were
buried with full honors[7] (Krushanov 1986:111). In a speech made at the

PLATE 4.1. Memorial to the *Revkomtsy* on Mandrikov Plaza in Anadyr'

graveside, the first secretary of the Chukotka Communist Party said, "The activity for which the *Revkomtsy* were killed brought to the peoples of Chukotka freedom, culture, wealth, high quality of life – that is, all the blessings that are unapproachable by little nationalities living in the capitalist world" (ibid.). A new monument consisting of life-size statues of several of the members, along with large plaques over the grave site naming each of the heroes, was later added to the expanded memorial site, which is now called Mandrikov Plaza (see Plate 4.1).

Throughout the 1920s, the Second Chukotka *Revkom* worked to expand and consolidate Soviet power in Chukotka. Several Bolsheviks were sent up to Chukotka (mostly from Kamchatka or Vladivostok) to round out the personnel needed to begin the work of politically organizing the indigenous population; building offices, housing, and schools; and bringing Soviet-style cultural enlightenment to the region. Administratively, Chukotka's fledgling Soviet communities had up to this point been subsumed within Kamchatka Province, but on 10 December 1930, Chukotka was for the first time given its own territorial definition when it was re-created by the central Soviet government as a "national region" within the Russian Soviet Federative Socialist Republic (RSFSR). According to the rhetoric of Soviet nationalities policy, "the little peoples of the peninsula received national statehood *(gosudarstvennost')* in the form of a national region" (Dikov 1989:192). This was ordained in a resolution of the Central Executive Committee of the USSR that simultaneously created fifteen other national regions throughout Russia (all but seven of these were later dissolved) (Taracouzio 1938:415–18). The region remained administratively subordinated to Kamchatka Province until 1951, when it was passed over to the jurisdiction of Khabarovsk Territory (Dikov 1989:460).

At the time of its ordination as a national region in 1930, Chukotka had six districts: Western Tundra (population 1,100); Eastern Tundra (population 1,500); Chaunskii (population 2,000); Chukotskii (population 4,000); Anadyrskii (population 4,000); and Markovskii (population 2,000) (Vdovin 1965:330). Over the years, the Soviet government redrew the boundaries around and within Chukotka several times; today there are eight districts, with the last district, Shmidtovskii, being created in 1974 (see Map 4.1). Less than 4 percent of Chukotka's total population was nonindigenous in 1930; by 1938, the figure had already risen to 16.4 percent (see Table 4.1).

TABLE 4.1. Ethnic Breakdown of Chukotka's Population, 1930–89

Ethnic Group	1930	1938	1959	1970	1989
All groups	14,500	18,390	46,689	101,191	164,783
Chukchis	11,060	12,101	9,975	11,001	11,914
Eskimos	1,261	1,280	1,064	1,149	1,452
Evens (& Evenks)	625	1,989	820	1,061	1,479
Yukagirs/Chuvans	1,000	–	214	~200	944
Russians	297	3,020	28,318	70,531	108,921
Others	257	–	6,298	17,249	40,073

Notes: "Others" includes Ukrainians, Belorussians, Armenians, Tatars, and other nationalities of the Soviet Union. Evens and Evenks were combined in 1930; thereafter the figures represent only Evens, except in 1938, when Evens were combined with Yukagirs and Chuvans. The category Yukagirs and Chuvans was expanded in 1959 and 1970 to include all other indigenous peoples. Koriaks are not listed because data are not available for them in all years.
Sources: Kotov et al. 1995:188, 191; Leontev 1977; Vdovin 1965:330.

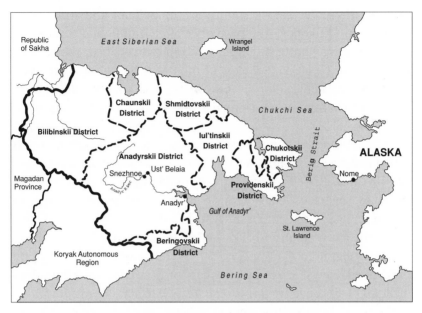

MAP 4.1. The Chukotka Autonomous Region

Collectivization: Indigenous Peoples as Moveable Parts

Among the many transformative processes happening in Chukotka in the early and middle Soviet period, probably the most disruptive was the collectivization of all indigenous occupations (that is, reindeer herding, sea mammal hunting, fishing and hunting, and fur trapping). The process of collectivization in the North is remarkably consistent throughout Russia; it was driven both by the mandate to establish conditions that would facilitate industrialization, as well as by the ideology that the application of socialist economic principles would naturally improve any kind of economic activity, even something as alien to the average Russian as reindeer herding.[8] More so perhaps than other parts of the Russian North, Chukotka became a testing ground for experimental policies in the collectivization process. The idea seemed to be that if it could be made to work in Chukotka – a place so far from the center and so unnervingly close to capitalist America – then it could surely be made to work anywhere. Therefore, Soviet planners were all the more zealous about pushing policies and strategies to the limit in Chukotka – the pace of collectivization had to be faster, the state farms had to be bigger and more diversified, the reindeer herds had to be larger. Scholars of the late Soviet period would describe the collectivization process in Chukotka as "marked experiments of social engineering aimed at destroying nomadic ways of life" (Pika 1999:96).

Considering its remoteness from the center – even from established centers in the Russian Far East – collectivization started very early in Chukotka; efforts were already under way by the early 1920s. By the 1930s, several collective farms had been established in Chukotka, and in the 1940s, the emphasis shifted to the consolidation *(ukreplenie)* of the many small and dispersed collective enterprises into larger and more centralized units. This process continued into the 1950s, and progressed alongside a complementary project, which was the reorganization of all collective farms *(kolkhozy)* into state farms *(sovkhozy)*. While the collective farms had members who theoretically set their own production quotas and paid themselves out of their own profits, the state farms had employees who executed a plan handed down by the Ministry of Agriculture. Most significantly, this meant unequivocally that reindeer herding should no longer be considered a way of life *(bytovoe kochevanie)*, but rather a form of production *(proizvodstvennoe kochevanie)*, a branch of the Soviet economy in which the herders were merely employees of the state (Slezkine 1994:341; Ustinov 1956). Increasingly, these consolidated state farms were treated as productive branches of the Soviet economy just like any other, and were made subject to the production quotas of centrally determined five-year plans.

The role of indigenous peoples in these collectivized operations shifted over the years. In the beginning, special efforts were made to appoint indigenous peoples to fill governing positions in the collective farms (cf. Flerov 1973:128). These efforts were driven by Lenin's policy of "indigenization" *(korennizatsiya)* (Liber 1991). Lenin had taken the stance of granting the right of self-determination (in theory, at least) to all of the nationalities within the Soviet Union, from Ukrainians to Tatars to Chukchis, believing that as class consciousness grew, national identity would weaken and ultimately become irrelevant. Until such a time, however, there was a need to emphasize the equal right that each nationality had to participate in economic as well as political processes, so that none would feel agitated on national grounds. To accomplish this, Lenin encouraged the recruitment of representatives of indigenous nationalities to hold key positions in economic enterprises as well as in local political structures, and especially in the Communist Party (Vakhtin 1994:54). Lenin's motives were certainly not altruistic; the intent of this policy was to create among indigenous peoples a cadre of political elites who were competent in the precepts of Marxist-Leninism and who would remain loyal to the authority of the Party (Kaiser 1994:105, 132).

In Chukotka, recruitment of indigenous peoples was also partly motivated by the fact that there were not yet enough trained Russians to cover all of the positions. Historical accounts take great pains to point out the high percentage of indigenous peoples staffing the collective farms in these early years as a great boon to the indigenous population and a credit to the Soviet system (Dikov 1989:216). However, as more Russians arrived in Chukotka with desirable professional skills, the percentage of indigenous peoples in collective farm management positions declined, and the majority of indigenous peoples came to occupy a laboring class within the state farms. This was more a byproduct of systematic racism and the Soviet version of the "glass ceiling" than a reflection of the real skill level of these indigenous managers – many Russians undoubtedly felt uncomfortable having indigenous peoples in superior positions (cf. Schindler 1997:198).

The abuses of the collectivization process are a frequent focus of the critical discourse of indigenous intellectuals, both within and beyond Chukotka, in evaluating the treatment of indigenous peoples during the Soviet period. At the same time, I found that Chukotkan indigenous peoples, both those living in the villages as well as the urban intelligentsia, almost universally spoke in nostalgic terms of their experiences in the state farms. This is understandable given the relative stability and social security that the state farm provided, and the sensation of chaos that prevailed in villages after the state farms were reorganized.[9] Most of the indigenous peoples who experienced the traumatic early years of collectivization in Chukotka are long dead, and the remaining generations all grew up in villages where state farms were already a fact of life – the state farm in effect *was* the village to them; it was the social system in which their families were embedded.

But perhaps more importantly for the indigenous intelligentsia, the state farms – located in the tundra and on the sea coast and so closely associated with the quintessential indigenous pursuits of rein-deer herding and sea mammal hunting – came to embody an important locus of indigenous identity. Virtually all of Anadyr's indigenous intel-lectuals over the age of thirty-five have roots in Chukotka's villages, and virtually all of these villages were oriented around a state farm. They share this common experience not only with one another, but with the indigenous peoples who remain in the villages and lead a ru-ral lifestyle. Moreover, virtually all Anadyr' indigenous peoples have relatives who remain in the villages. This makes the current fate of these formerly state farm-based communities a key issue on the ac-tivist agenda of Anadyr's indigenous intelligentsia, and a key point of connection between their own urban lives and the rural lives of village indigenous peoples.

The Communist Party and the Politicization of Indigenous Chukotkans

As a result of Lenin's policy of indigenization, indigenous peoples were drawn not only into the economic life of the region, but into its politi-cal life as well. They were slotted into administrative offices, recruited into the Komsomol (Communist Youth League), and nominated for membership in the Communist Party. Party organizing, which began in 1924, was begun first among the incomer population; a few repre-sentatives of the Party were sent to Chukotka from Petropavlovsk-on-Kamchatka with the explicit task of forming the first cell of the Russian Communist Party of Bolsheviks (Vdovin 1965:337). In 1926, a Party gath-ering was held in Uelen that brought together candidates for Party membership from the villages of Naukan, Chaplino, and Dezhnev.

Party membership was considered a privilege, not a foregone conclusion, and members were accepted only in stages, starting with a period of candidacy. Thus, it was not until 1928 that Uelen was deemed ready for an official Party cell, made up of three Party members and one candidate for membership – all nonindigenous.

These early Soviet agents found indigenous peoples frustratingly dispersed throughout the tundra, and thus hard to recruit for possible Party membership. They began their task by targeting the settled peoples along the coast, and in 1930, the first three indigenous Party members were initiated, and a few more indigenous inhabitants were tapped for Party candidacy (Vdovin 1965:339). Various strategies were developed to attract more indigenous candidates: organizing professional associations among indigenous inhabitants, rounding up women for enrollment in reading lessons, and opening little schools to teach political awareness *(politshkola)*. Little by little, indigenous inhabitants were drawn into the Party, and by the mid-1950s, they numbered 478 in Chukotka's Communist Party, or 17.7 percent of its total membership (Dikov 1989:289). However, most Chukotkan indigenous peoples never experienced Party membership; by 1985 only 1,223, or less than 10 percent of the indigenous population, were members of Party organizations (Dikov 1989: 372–3). Party involvement would be the province of only an elite segment of the indigenous intelligentsia.

Administration in the region took the form of regional, district, and local soviets (governing councils). Soviets were formed in a pyramidal structure: Village and town soviets formed the base of the pyramid, district soviets formed the middle section, and the Regional Soviet formed the top point. Regional Soviets across the Soviet Union in turn formed the base of another pyramid that culminated in the Supreme Soviet in Moscow (Hahn 1988:84–5). Indigenous inhabitants had been sought out to serve as chairs of local soviets from the beginning of the work of the Chukotka *Revkom*. Soviets headed by indigenous peoples were called "clan" *(rodovye)* soviets at first, but were renamed "indigenous" *(tuzemnye)* soviets in accordance with a decision of the Far Eastern Territory Party and Executive Committee that all soviets should be organized only on a national-territorial principle ("clans" by then were seen as survivals of a "primitive" society that needed to be eliminated).

Even the nomadic reindeer herders were organized into "nomadic" *(kochevye)* soviets (Dikov 1989:166).

In April 1932, the first Chukotka Regional Congress of Soviets was held (Dikov 1989:192–3; Vdovin 1965:331). According to historical accounts, the two most important steps at this first congress were to create two bodies: the first Regional Communist Party organization, and the first Regional Executive Committee, which would carry out the resolutions of the Regional Soviet. A Russian incomer, M. Tselousov, was named first secretary of the Regional Communist Party; a Chukchi, Tegrynkeu, was named chair of the Regional Executive Committee. Thus was established in Chukotka the pattern of naming a Russian to head the Party and balancing that by naming an indigenous leader to head the Executive Committee (Uvachan 1990:43). This pattern was repeated consistently throughout the Soviet period – there was a very deliberate effort to balance Russians and indigenous peoples in these two highly visible leadership positions, as well as to maintain proportional indigenous representation in the Regional Soviet. In 1954, for example, out of fifty-three deputies elected to the Regional Soviet, seventeen (32 percent) were indigenous (Dikov 1989:289), which roughly matched the ratio of indigenous peoples to incomers at that time.

The policy of indigenization was ultimately reflected in the way the Soviet government organized the political structure not only in regions like Chukotka but throughout the entire country. In 1936, the first constitution of the Soviet Union was ratified, and it called for a new national-level legislative body called the Supreme Soviet *(Verkhovnyi sovet)*. This was a bicameral legislature that met briefly each year in Moscow, divided into a Soviet of the Union and a Soviet of Nationalities. The Soviet of the Union was dominated by Russians. The Soviet of Nationalities, however, was intended to provide representation to all of the nationalities in the Soviet Union (including Russians). Each different type of territorial formation (union republics such as Ukraine or Kazakhstan, autonomous republics such as Yakutia, provinces such as Kamchatka, and national regions such as Chukotka) was allotted a set number of seats, and each of the national regions, most of them created in the 1930s, had the right to elect one representative to it, regardless of the size of the population in the region.

TABLE 4.2. Deputies Elected to the Soviet of Nationalities of the USSR from Chukotka and Also Serving as Chair of the Regional Executive Committee

Session	Year	Deputy
1st	1937	Tevlianto
2nd	1946	Otke
3rd	1950	Otke
4th	1954	Ivan Rultytegin
5th	1958	Ivan Rultytegin
6th	1962	Olga Dmitrievna Nutetegryne
7th	1966	Olga Dmitrievna Nutetegryne
8th	1970	Lina Grigorevna Tynel'
9th	1974	Lina Grigorevna Tynel'
10th	1979	Lina Grigorevna Tynel'
11th	1984	Nadezhda Pavlovna Otke
CPD*	1990	Vladimir Mikhailovich Etylin

Note: CPD = Congress of People's Deputies of the Soviet Union.
Sources: Dikov 1989; *Verkhovnyi Sovet SSSR* 1954, 1959, 1962, 1966, 1970, 1974, 1979, 1984, 1991.

In the entire course of the history of the Soviet Union, twelve sessions of the Soviet of Nationalities were elected, including the *glasnost'*-era Congress of People's Deputies of the USSR.[10] Each of the twelve sessions included a representative from Chukotka, and seven different deputies were elected over the years, all of them Chukchis (see Table 4.2). In all of the national regions across Russia, the indigenous representative to the Soviet of Nationalities was always the titular nationality of each region; thus, Chukotka always sent a Chukchi, Evenkiya always sent an Evenk, and so on, but Eskimos, Chuvans, Evens, and the other small groups in Chukotka and in other regions never made it into national politics (see the appendix). No Chukchi, or any other indigenous person from Chukotka, was ever elected to the Soviet of the Union. The first Chukchi to be sent to the Supreme Soviet was Tevlianto, who was concurrently elected chair of the Chukotka Regional Executive Committee.[11] Hereafter, this became the standard pattern: Whoever was elected chair of the Regional

Executive Committee in Chukotka went on the occupy Chukotka's seat in the Soviet of Nationalities. The one exception to this was the final deputy, Vladimir Etylin, who was chair of the Chukotka Regional Soviet of Deputies rather than of the Regional Executive Committee, and was elected in 1990 to the newly created Congress of People's Deputies of the USSR in Moscow.[12]

I. S. Vdovin (1965:333) sums up indigenous participation in Soviet government this way:

> In agreement with the new Constitution, the small peoples of the North received the right through their own representatives in the Soviet of Nationalities to direct participation in the legislative activities of the higher organs of the Soviet state.

Of course, these higher organs of the Soviet state had no significant power in Soviet government; they met only a few days per year in a ceremonial gathering in the Kremlin, at which they rubber-stamped predrafted legislation and resolutions. The real work of government was carried out by a permanent Council of Ministers, which was guided by the Politburo, the core of power within the Party. Absolutely no representatives of the Peoples of the North ever served in that body, or came close to it. Nevertheless, indigenous peoples elected to the Soviet of Nationalities did get to travel to Moscow, see the halls of power within the Kremlin, and network with other indigenous politicians, and they were able to learn much about the way power worked in the Soviet system. They were also viewed with respect by indigenous peoples in their home regions and looked to as leaders.

For those who were active in the Party and in government, however, daily life could be difficult. My frequent consultee, Lidia Neekyk, told me of a childhood spent on the road following her father, who was employed in the Party. He was first elected Party Secretary in Lidia's natal village of Uelen, and then was promoted to a regional-level position in the Party. This required him to travel frequently to villages throughout the region, and to relocate his family periodically as he was transferred from place to place, eventually coming to Anadyr'. These travels took a toll on the family, and at one point, when Lidia's father announced that he had been transferred to yet another Party organ,

Lidia's mother declared that enough was enough. The couple divorced, and the mother remained settled with her children in Anadyr' while the father moved on to yet another town.

On a separate but parallel track with the Communist Party was the development of the Komsomol. *Komsomol* is an abbreviation of *Kommunisticheskii Soyuz Molodezhi*, which is in turn a shortened form of *Vsesoyuznyi Leninskii Kommunisticheskii Soyuz Molodezhi* or *VLKSM* (All-Union Leninist Communist Union of Youth, or Communist Youth League). The Komsomol organization was essentially a training ground for future Communist Party members, although in many cases the zealous young Komsomol showed more passion for Communism than even their bureaucratic Party leaders (Kochan and Abraham 1962:357). In 1928, the Komsomol organization in Kamchatka sent a representative to Chukotka, and in that year the Komsomol established a cell in Uelen. By 1945, 72 percent of all Komsomol members in Chukotka were indigenous (Dikov 1989:258; Vdovin 1965:340), but the proportion was never that high again; by 1980, it was only 14.2 percent (Dikov 1989:291, 373), falling as the proportion of indigenous peoples in the total population also fell.

It was young Komsomol members who carried out much of the work of the Cultural Revolution in the Chukotka tundra, leading a "literacy assault in the tundra"; they also formed the nucleus of the teaching personnel in Chukotka's rural areas (Dikov 1989:228, 255). In those early years of the 1920s and 1930s, many young indigenous people were involved in this work. As one indigenous Komsomol is reported to have said before the secretary of the Chukotka Regional Party in 1933:

> I only now understand why the Russians came to us. I understand that you came to teach us how to better build our lives, so that we live just as you live in the mainland. But I have come to understand this so quickly because I myself speak Russian well, I am literate, I have read much, and I understand what I have read. But many Chukchis are still illiterate, they speak very little Russian and see Russians rarely.... We need to work more and prepare faster our own local cadres! (Vdovin 1965:341).

However, later generations of Soviet youth did not take the Komsomol nearly so seriously. In the village of Snezhnoe, I learned much from sitting in on several tea-time conversations between two Chukchis of the generation born in the late 1960s: Nikolai Rultytegin, a local reindeer herder, and Marina Peliave, a graduate student from the Anadyr' research institute who accompanied me to Snezhnoe. The two met for the first time on this trip to the village, and they took obvious pleasure in comparing their experiences of growing up in two different villages in Chukotka's western tundra. Much laughter surrounded their recollections of what seemed to them the artificial zeal of the Komsomol. They had both learned an alternative interpretation of what the Komsomol initials VLKSM stood for: *Vozmi Lopatku, Kopai Sebe Mogilu*, which means, "Grab a shovel, dig yourself a grave!"

Nevertheless, the rhetoric of enthusiasm with which indigenous peoples were bombarded could be seductive. They were regularly praised for their miraculous achievements and the wondrous swiftness of their progress from primitive communal tribes to exemplars of socialist development. As the ethnographer Vdovin writes in typical style:

> The Chukchi, Siberian Eskimo, and other peoples of the North of the USSR, as a result of the consistent realization of Leninist principles of national politics by the Party, made an enormous leap from primitive-communal relations, passing over capitalism, to socialism (Vdovin 1965:398).[13]

The indigenous peoples knew they were supposed to see themselves as special in the vast brotherhood of Soviet peoples. Those from their number who had gained national notoriety were often placed in the limelight, under which they marveled publicly at the heights to which the peoples of the North could attain. A typical example of this is the Evenk ethnographer Vasilii Uvachan, who was elected to five terms in the Soviet of Nationalities between 1950 and 1974. In a speech before the Supreme Soviet in 1963, he declared:

> In the great constellation of brotherhood and friendship of the peoples of the Soviet Union, the small peoples of the North occupy a deserving place. It is not for nothing that it is said among the people, "Even small stars beautify the heavens" (Uvachan 1963:422).

In Chukotka, also, ceremonies of ritual amazement over the achievements of the indigenous peoples were held with great pomp. Dikov describes a festival celebrating the fortieth anniversary of the Chukotka National Region, held in December 1970, to which "distinguished visitors" were brought from Yakutia, Magadan, and other surrounding territories to congratulate their fellow northerners on their achievements to date. Dikov writes:

> Those appearing at the festival gathering convincingly showed what an enormous leap the peoples of Chukotka had completed in their own development, striding out of a patriarchal-clan way of life toward the heights of socialist civilization. . . . In what branches of economy, science and culture have they not worked, these progeny of simple reindeer herding and hunting families? (1989: 324).

What other possible response on the part of the indigenous population could be intended aside from pride in themselves and gratitude toward those who had made this great leap possible? By the 1970s, Chukotkan indigenous peoples – especially the intelligentsia – knew what roles they were expected to play, and had learned their cues well.

Soviet Education of Indigenous Chukotkans: "The Preparation of Cadres"

The main engine behind the "enormous leap" of the indigenous peoples of Chukotka was education, and this is perhaps where Soviet practice in dealing with its indigenous population differs most sharply from the practice of other colonial states. Leningrad was the central headquarters both for planning the education and "civilization" of indigenous northerners as well as for training teachers and cultural professionals to go to the regions of the Russian Far North and carry out this work. In 1925, the Committee of the North[14] began the project by creating a special department for indigenous peoples within Leningrad University (Dikov 1989:185; Slezkine 1994:180). This later became known as the Institute of the North, whose mandate was "the preparation of workers of secondary and higher qualification for soviet-party construction and building culture, as well as scientific cadres for northern studies" (Dikov 1989:185). Several particularly talented young indigenous people were found and brought to Leningrad in order to be trained and then sent back among their own peoples. However, as work intensified in the North, more qualified teachers were needed to go to the villages of the North, including Chukotka, to teach in "national schools" (schools for indigenous children). In 1930, a special division devoted exclusively to training teachers for the North was created within the Herzen Pedagogical Institute in Leningrad (Vdovin 1965:385), and this ultimately became the Faculty of the Peoples of the Far North (*Fakul'tet Narodov Krainego Severa*, or *FNKS*).[15] This faculty at first trained mainly nonindigenous teachers, but later indigenous peoples also began to join the faculty. As the faculty took on a more significant role in training indigenous peoples to be teachers, the separate Institute of the North of Leningrad University that had been created by the Committee of the North was closed.

The first crop of indigenous students to be sent to Leningrad for training came from all across the Russian North in 1925. Among them was the first Chukchi to be sent, Tevlianto (Dikov 1989:185; Vdovin 1965:325). Tevlianto made it through the program with flying colors, and was later elected to the Soviet of Nationalities (as discussed previously). He was officially revered as a hero of the indigenous intelligentsia, becoming a prototypical Chukchi intellectual in whose image many were to follow: raised from humble beginnings, educated outside of Chukotka, and brought back to serve as a highly visible representative of the indigenous intelligentsia.

However, before any Chukotkan indigenous people could aspire to higher education, they had to be put through primary and secondary schooling, and for that, schools had to be built in Chukotka. The first Soviet school for indigenous children was opened at the "culture base" *(kul'tbaza)* in Uelen in 1923, and thereafter the number of schools grew steadily. Culture bases were the front-line Soviet strategy for establishing civilization in the North. The typical culture base included a residential school, library, portable film projector, health clinic, midwife station, mechanical repair shop, veterinary station, store, and cafeteria. In Chukotka, these were primarily set up in the villages of the Chukotka Peninsula, which were more accessible because of their proximity to the coast, while culture bases did not reach the villages located deep in the inland tundra until much later.

In the interim, these remoter regions were reached by the mobile component of the culture bases, the "red tents" *(krasnaya iaranga)* (Dikov 1989:219; Slezkine 1994:229). Vdovin (1965:324) describes one of the first red tents this way:

> It was the usual Chukchi *iaranga* with a large *polog* [inner room], which was heated and lit by a kerosene lamp. . . . This was the first cultural institution in Chukotka, earmarked for service to the nomads. The red tent was an organizer of Soviet cooperative work in the tundra and a bearer of Soviet culture. It was here that the first reindeer herders saw cinema, heard radio, received the first qualified medical assistance, saw doctors and teachers, and experienced the diversity of the concern of the Soviet power for them.

The red tents eventually evolved into the *AKB (Agitatsionno-Kul'turnaya Brigada,* or "propagandizing-cultural brigades"), an institution that was attached to the village House of Culture. The employees of the AKB lived in the village, but would regularly travel by helicopter to the reindeer camps to deliver reading material, hold political education seminars, and provide entertainment in the form of live concerts (cf. Kerttula 2000:12). AKBs were still functioning in Chukotka in the 1990s, although they were more likely to deliver videos that could be shown on a VCR powered by a generator (Jean-Claude Van Damme movies were a particular favorite among Snezhnoe reindeer herders).

Many of the first "schools" for indigenous children existed without a building; classes were held in earthen dug-out houses, *iarangi*, or imported canvas tents (Dikov 1989:253). Schools for Russian students were generally separate from schools for indigenous students (Dikov 1989:219; Vdovin 1965:386). In the 1930s there were some experiments with "nomadic schools" *(kochevye shkoly)*, which involved a Russian teacher who traveled with a nomadic reindeer herding group in order to school the children without taking them away from their parents, but these schools were soon abandoned (Taracouzio 1938:487–8). Instead, emphasis was shifted to establishing residential schools *(shkoly-internaty)*, located so as to be accessible by an encircling network of nomadic reindeer herding settlements, where children of herding families could be kept in one place and educated while their parents continued their mobile work in the tundra.

All of the textbooks used in primary schools throughout the North were published in Moscow or Leningrad, and virtually all textbooks for studying the native languages of the North were published by the company *Prosveshchenie* (literally "Enlightenment," figuratively "Education"), which is still located above the well-known book store *Dom Knigi* ("House of Books") on Nevsky Prospect in St. Petersburg. The northern division of the publishing house was in the 1990s under the direction of Vladimir Grigorevich Rakhtilin, a Chukchi from the Chukotka Peninsula area. The authors of these school primers were either Russian linguist-ethnographers of the North or indigenous linguist-ethnographers brought up through the Leningrad higher education system (and in many cases, individuals from both categories collaborated). Many of the Chukchi language primers were produced wholly or in part by the late Petr Ivanovich Inenlikei, a prominent Chukchi linguist who also wrote Chukchi–Russian dictionaries (Inenlikei 1982). Inenlikei was an example of an indigenous intellectual who not only successfully navigated the educational system through the postsecondary level by graduating from the Herzen Pedagogical Institute in Leningrad, but went on to do graduate work in the Institute of Linguistics of the USSR Academy of Sciences (Dikov 1989:309) and taught at the Faculty of the Peoples of the North. Within the logic underpinning Soviet nationalities policy, there was a certain poetic symmetry to a life like Inenlikei's, raised through the system of indigenous education in the North and dedicated in turn to perpetuating that system. Dikov singles him out as a "model" of a young Chukchi intellectual.

The textbooks produced by indigenous scholars such as Inenlikei, or by ethnographers of Chukotka (such as that by Leontev and Alekseeva 1980), were tailored specifically for life in Chukotka, but they nevertheless served as vehicles for exposing indigenous children to Soviet values and ideology, not to mention indoctrinating them into the cult of Lenin (see Plate 4.2). The colorfully illustrated primers contained abundant representations of reindeer and sea mammals, as well as indigenous peoples dressed in traditional clothing, but there were just as many representations of indigenous interaction with industrial technology (trucks and planes, radios and telephones, military

PLATE 4.2. Chukchi school primer depicting Chukchi children in red Young Pioneer scarves on Red Square in Moscow

hardware). Narrations of the life of Lenin were standard for inclusion, and were accompanied by drawings of Lenin both as a curly-headed lad and as an adult father figure. Indigenous children were shown wearing the red neckkerchief that signaled membership in the Young Pioneers, one of the first rungs on the ladder toward membership in the Communist Party.

At first, the preferred language of instruction in the schools for indigenous children was the native language of the children attending. One problem was in deciding which dialect of the many regional variants to choose as the literary dialect for the school primers and dictionaries that would be published (cf. Bloch 1996:77). Eventually, educated indigenous intellectuals would produce native-language literature – poems, stories, novels – and also native-language radio and television programming, not to mention the textbooks and dictionaries previously discussed. To accomplish this, the intelligentsia had to develop standard literary languages. The presence of literary versions of the indigenous languages masked the diversity of each language, but did not affect the presence of regional dialects in everyday speech. Literary

Chukchi, for example, was based primarily on a coastal dialect of Chukchi concentrated around Uelen. In Snezhnoe, Nikolai Rultytegin spent an afternoon with me curiously browsing through a Chukchi phrase book I had been given as a gift. As he read, he pointed out which words were "correct" and which ones were "incorrect" – meaning they were inconsistent with the dialect he learned growing up in the western tundra.

In the case of Chukchi, not only were there regional dialects, but there was also variation in men's and women's pronunciations (cf. Dunn 2000). Where men pronounced the phoneme *r* in a word, women replaced it with the phoneme *ts*. Special verbs have been invented to describe this phenomenon: men *rekat'* (they "pronounce *r*"), while women *tsokat'* (they "pronounce *ts*"). Sofia Rybachenko talked about how initially horrifying it was for girls to start school and find they were expected to speak the men's dialect of Chukchi, and moreover, to pronounce all of those rolling *r*s of the Russian language. "I was ashamed to *rekat'* at first," she said, smiling at the recollection of her childish embarrassment, "but I eventually got used to it." She adopted this literary standard for her classroom speech, but she had to code switch between the school setting and settings dominated by older women in the community, who continued to *tsokat'*. In her own television broadcasts, she had long since adopted the men's dialectical pronunciation.

Soviet agents in Chukotka encountered several problems with using the indigenous languages in schools; the first was the fact that teachers, who were not indigenous, had first to learn the languages in order to teach in them. Later on, indigenous teachers would be trained, but even then, a tension remained between two ideals: one of teaching indigenous children in their own languages, and one of training indigenous students who could go on to higher education in technical schools and universities where only Russian would be spoken. Eventually the difficulties of organizing instruction of more advanced subjects in indigenous languages meant that Russian won out, a trend that could be observed throughout the USSR. Indigenous children were first given full immersion in the Russian language until they could understand it well enough to learn in it, and then they were taught subject material in Russian (Dikov 1989:279–80). It would take some years before indigenous students could actually join Russian students in the classroom, but when they did, it marked a complete abandonment of the idea of providing education to indigenous children in their own languages.

This grew to be a matter of concern to linguists, and in 1967, a study was undertaken by the linguist G. A. Menovshchikov and the ethnographer V. V. Leontev to determine how the use of Russian in schools was affecting children's knowledge of their native languages. When it came to be understood that a whole generation of indigenous peoples had grown up more fluent in Russian than in their own native languages, the researchers recommended that Chukotkan schools again take up indigenous-language instruction (Dikov 1989:362–3). Eventually, indigenous languages were added back into the school curriculum as elective subjects, meaning anyone could take them, including Russian students (cf. Krupnik and Vakhtin 2002:20). Indigenous teachers who taught native languages in school more often than not had learned these languages themselves as essentially a second language during their university studies at the Faculty of the Peoples of the Far North, since they had grown up with at best only a passive knowledge of their own native languages (cf. Pika 1999:148–52).

However, the events of the 1970s for the time being swept aside all aspirations to provide instruction in indigenous languages. As the pace of industrial development picked up, Russian immigration to Chukotka, exploded and attention shifted to providing schools for this new, growing segment of the population. The number of "national" schools dropped dramatically. Educators disagreed on whether special schools for indigenous children were needed at all, and in the end, many of the schools were closed or converted into Russian schools, which indigenous children were allowed to attend. A later invention introduced kindergartens for preschool children aged one to five years[16] (Vdovin 1965:387), which grew at the same time as "national" schools declined and exacerbated native-language loss among indigenous children (Dikov 1989:362). One type of school for indigenous children that did not decline, however, but remained even into the 1990s was residential schools.

Residential Schools

From time to time, I ran across people in Chukotka who claimed that residential schools *(shkola-internat)* virtually no longer existed in the 1990s, which I believed until I began to stumble upon them myself, and came to realize they could still be found throughout Chukotka. Even Anadyr' supported a residential school, located in the village of Tavaivaam. It was used primarily as a daytime kindergarten for many city children, but had several beds for children of village reindeer herders whose parents were away in the tundra. Residential schools are one of the most controversial elements of Russian colonization in the North. Most works on the Russian North at least mention residential schools,[17] but only recently have they begun to be investigated ethnographically. Alexia Bloch's dissertation work focused primarily on a residential school in one of the district centers in the Evenki Autonomous Region; a substantial component of her analysis is personal narratives of Evenki women's experiences of resistance or accommodation to residential schools (Bloch 1996:107–33). Elena Liarskaya, in her dissertation work on residential schools in the Yamalo-Nenets Autonomous Region, argues for viewing residential schools not only in negative terms as an agent causing indigenous children to lose their indigenous culture, but in positive terms as an agent enabling them to learn the norms of village life, allowing them the option to switch back and forth between both settings with relative fluidity (Liarskaya 2001). Most other accounts of residential schools unfortunately render them rather as if they were monolithic entities, both in terms of their negative effects on indigenous populations as well as in terms of their practical structure and function.

Chukotka's residential schools in the 1990s were variable. In a small, predominantly indigenous village, the one and only school might have been both a school and a dormitory, attended on a residential basis by the children of tundra reindeer herders, and on a daytime basis by the children of parents living full-time in the village (such was the case in Tavaivaam). Larger villages, were more likely to have a simple dormitory *(internat)* for indigenous children whose parents resided in the tundra, and these children would walk over to the regular town school to attend classes. In Snezhnoe, for example, the village school offered instruction to all village children in a residential school, but this went only up to the third grade; thereafter, all of the village's children had to travel to Ust'-Belaia, a town 18 kilometers downriver, to live in the *internat* and attend the town's school. Snezhnoe had tried to establish a school for upper grades in the early 1990s, but the effort failed. The mayor of Snezhnoe lamented that he had been unable to get a single teacher to come to Snezhnoe to teach the added grades, not even with the incentive of a free deluxe apartment (deluxe in this case meant the presence of cold running water as opposed to no plumbing at all). The existing four teachers tried to handle teaching the new classes in addition to their own, but the effort failed, and the upper grades were closed.

Soviet historical accounts do not hide the fact that most indigenous parents in Chukotka objected to having their children taken from them and placed in residential schools, although they deemphasize the compulsory nature of attendance. Tikhon Semushkin's first novel, *Children of the Soviet Arctic*, is a fictionalized account, based on his own experience, of the creation of Chukotka's first residential school in 1928 at the culture base of the coastal village of Lavrentiya (cf. Vdovin 1965:324). Semushkin's account takes great pains to demonstrate that indigenous parents were gently persuaded to enroll their children, and won over by what even they could see as the benefits their children would receive at the residential school. "We don't intend to do anything by force," says the Soviet recruiting agent to indigenous parents, "We do not wish harm to your people. You know that. We want to come to a voluntary understanding on both sides" (Semushkin 1934:29). Those indigenous peoples who publicly acknowledged the necessity of their children's education were highly praised for their perceptiveness. Dikov ecstatically quotes "the Chukchi Tunatugi" as saying, "The Chukchi were illiterate, they didn't think about cleanliness. Today it's different, my daughter studies in school. Many of us have understood that you have to live cleanly, culturally, and not as we lived before" (Dikov 1989:220).

Yet it is well known that such peaceful acceptance of residential schools was rare if it ever occurred at all, and many stories are told of children being taken away forcibly, sometimes violently, from their parents and placed into the residential school (cf. Kerttula 2000:14). Vakhtin writes:

> As a result of the boarding-school system, children became fully state-dependent in many places and deprived of a family upbringing. They also lost their native mother tongues. At the age of fifteen or seventeen, they returned to their families as complete strangers, with no knowledge of traditional native culture or of home life. Parents also suffered since, in many cases, they lost all their feeling of responsibility toward their children and delegated it all to the state (1994: 61).

Enough criticism of residential schools surfaced in the Soviet period that by the 1980s many of them were being converted into regular day schools (Vakhtin 1994:61). In the 1990s, indigenous activists and ethnographers alike began calling for greater investment once again in nomadic schools that would provide education to the children of reindeer herding families without separating children from their parents and their family cultural traditions (Pika and Prokhorov 1994:161).

While criticism of residential schools is generally justified, both Bloch and Liarskaya urge us to recognize that not all indigenous accounts of life in residential schools are negative. I was also surprised to hear many positive comments about indigenous peoples' personal experiences in Chukotkan residential schools. The late Maia Ettyryntyna, a Chukchi doctor who went on to become a deputy in the RSFSR Congress of People's Deputies, expressed gratitude that she had been given the opportunity to attain an education that had brought her so far. As we sat sipping tea in a café in Moscow, she said that she had been able to experience the best of both worlds, Russian and indigenous, since she spent her summers at home with her family in the tundra. From her perspective, the residential school system was responsible for the creation of an indigenous intelligentsia in Chukotka, and that intelligentsia played an important leadership role in Chukotka today.

Nikolai Rultytegin, the reindeer herder in Snezhnoe, told me a residential school story that confused me at first, because I took it for one of the horror stories about mistreatment. He told of how the school's *vospitatel'* ("upbringer" – cf. Bloch 1996) would make the boys sit on the ends of their beds every morning with their legs extended, so that he could see the bottoms of their feet. Any boy who had a hole in his socks would have his feet whacked with a yardstick. When I expressed shock at such cruel treatment, Nikolai laughed and said this man had actually been one of the best influences in his life, because he forced the boys to be self-reliant. "We learned that nobody else was going to look after us – you had to look out for yourself," he said. Nikolai's account is ironic, since most of the criticism of residential schools claims just the opposite – that the experience taught children to be dependent. Even Ettyryntyna commented that the residential school experience rendered most indigenous peoples psychologically unprepared for life as it was changing in post-Soviet Russia, since it conditioned them to relate to the government as children to a parent.

Others echoed this idea. Lidia Neekyk's husband, Vladik, shared with me a particularly interesting residential school experience that he also tied to the problems that the indigenous movement was experiencing in Chukotka. Vladik compared his own experience in a residential school to his experience serving in the Soviet army:

> Look, you have a men's collective [just like in the army], because boys and girls are separated from each other. And everything happens by the bell. There's a bell in the morning – ring! – and you get up and do your calisthenics. Then – ring! – and you make your bed; ring! – and you go brush your teeth; ring! – you go have breakfast, and so forth.[18]

Vladik said his residential school experience was sometimes a source of conflict between him and Lidia, who never attended residential school and therefore found it difficult to understand the effect it had on him. But Vladik insisted that the effect of residential school is significant for anyone – that it takes away one's ability to take initiative on anything.[19] For this very reason, according to Vladik, it was hard to find leaders among indigenous peoples. Those with residential school backgrounds were more likely to say, "if you want to be mayor, go ahead and do it – I'll be glad to help you in any way. But for *me* to become mayor – I just can't do it." Moreover, Vladik said that indigenous people who were raised in a residential school tended to look with suspicion on those indigenous people who did become leaders: "It's like they think, what are you doing? Now you're one of them. Come down here on our level and be equal to us."[20]

However, even from indigenous consultees who said they valued their Russian residential school education, I collected many narratives of the traumas involved. Sofia Rybachenko spoke often about her experiences in Russian schools, and the common theme running through all her stories was her youthful shock and incomprehension as she was confronted with Russian ways:

> You just can't imagine what it was like when they suddenly came and said, "No, you can't live like that anymore, you must move into a house like we live in and do everything as we do." Imagine – it would be as if someone suddenly came to you and said, "You have to move out of your apartment and live like the Indians do."

In her first couple of years of school (in the 1950s), Sofia spoke little Russian, and barely understood what was happening in the classroom. She talked about how difficult it was to imagine things that that the teacher described, such as ancient Egypt with its pharaohs and pyramids – she simply had no point of comparison within her own experience to reference this new information. She recounted one class in which the lesson plan called for the students to draw a picture of a cucumber – a staple food in European Russia. But Sofia had never seen a cucumber and had no idea what the teacher wanted them to draw. The teacher finally gave them an empty jar of pickles with a drawing of a cucumber on the front. Sofia drew this image, still having no idea what a cucumber was.

Attending school in a later generation, Marina Peliave appreciated her Russian education for allowing her to attend the Faculty of the Peoples of the Far North in St. Petersburg and go on to graduate study at the research institute in Anadyr'. However, she also recalled many painful moments from her residential school experience. Most distressing, she said, was to be on the helicopter taking children back to school after spending holidays with their families in the tundra. "By the time the helicopter was full, every child would be crying, even the older boys," she said. "And back in the *iarangi*, the parents would be crying, too." Marina's mother worked with the reindeer brigade, but sometimes she would visit town and stay in the family's apartment; yet even when their mother was home, the children were not allowed to stay with her, nor even to take their meals with her. "We used to sneak out of the school at lunchtime when she was home," said Marina, "just so we could taste her cooking."

Conclusion

Indigenous peoples and incomers alike were caught up in a storm of political and economic change throughout the Soviet-era history of Chukotka, and the main difference was in who was controlling the momentum of that change. From Civil War to Cultural Revolution to industrialization, all the struggles of the wider Soviet Union were played out on Chukotkan soil. The indigenous peoples of Chukotka experienced a deliberate transformative assault on their lifestyle and values that resembled, in an almost Fordist fashion, similar assaults on other northern peoples. Their intended place in the array of Soviet national success stories was predicted, achieved, and then celebrated. Through an increasingly Russian-dominated educational system, they were made into literate, socially aware Soviet citizens, even at the village level, and some among them were prepared to take up positions within an indigenous intelligentsia. They were given a role in both regional and national politics, and groomed for membership in the Communist Party. All of this activity was part of the image that the Chukotka Autonomous Region was expected to have, as a territory with a significant indigenous population. By the 1980s, indigenous peoples had already seen several generations of radical change, but it would all begin to seem mild compared to what would come when Soviet power was finally toppled.

1980

"May I speak to Malina Ivanovna?"

"Speaking." Malina Ivanovna did not recognize the male voice at the other end of the line. The man introduced himself as an ethnographer from Moscow. He was in Chukotka for a summer research expedition to study Chukchi traditional spiritual culture. He was particularly interested in folktales with a spiritual theme, and he knew she performed in a folkloric theater troupe. He would be in Anadyr' for a few days before moving on to the peninsular villages; would she be so kind as to meet with him for an interview?

Malina Ivanovna twisted the phone cord around her forefinger. "How long will it take?" she asked. She had met with an ethnographer once before when she lived in Sireniki, a woman from Leningrad. The woman came one day and asked her questions about the Chukchi language. She came again the next day, and the next. Malina Ivanovna had spent hours and hours with her. The woman went back to Leningrad and got her doctoral degree, then made her career on the material she collected in Chukotka, but Malina Ivanovna never got a thing in return – not so much as a postcard from Leningrad.

The man said it might take a few hours, but that they didn't have to do it all in one sitting.

Malina Ivanovna thought about the tape recordings she had been making of the folktales she remembered from her childhood. She had in mind to give them to her daughters someday, a kind of legacy. She tapped her fingernails on the table.

"I have been feeling rather ill this week," she said finally. "I think it is my blood pressure. I need to rest. I'm sorry."

She hung up the phone.

5

INDIGENOUS CULTURE IN
A RUSSIAN SPACE

THIS CHAPTER FOCUSES on analyzing Chukotka as a physical and social space shared by indigenous residents and incomers. I discuss how
they did that during the "dark decade" of the 1990s, and how incomers
managed to inscribe their dominance on a space that was originally
thought to belong to indigenous residents. I begin with an overview of
the region, considering how the vast space of Chukotka was negotiated
in logistical terms. Then I turn to a description of the central place of
my ethnography, the city of Anadyr', giving attention to the competing ideas I encountered about whose space this was – indigenous or
incomer – and who "naturally" belongs where. Finally, I turn to consider the importance of culture as a means by which incomers spatially
defined and dominated indigenous residents.

Space and Movement in Chukotka

Chukotka is a predominantly wilderness territory nearly the size of
Alaska. It has no railroads whatsoever, and only a few intercity roads,

all unpaved, connecting towns in Chukotka's industrial mining areas.[1] When I first arrived, I noticed a paved road leading out of Anadyr', and for a long time I imagined, without giving it much thought, that this road continued west and eventually led one to Yakutsk. This perception was shattered one summer day when I decided to take a walk down this road and found that it merely circled around and led right back into the city – a surreal experience that drove home the realization of just how isolated Anadyr' is.

However, by the late Soviet period, even Chukotka's most rural residents were hardly aware of this isolation, since such colossal effort (and government subsidy) was put into maintaining its communication and transportation infrastructure. Movement through this vast territory was necessary, given the way the Soviet central planning system was designed. Economic and political centralization meant that goods, cash, and people had to move continually from the center to the periphery. People were moved from European Russia to Chukotka in order to carry out the Soviet plan for socialist development in the North. Incomers were moved from the cities to the villages to provide the social services needed to maintain the collective farms, as well as to bring "enlightenment" to the indigenous residents. Remote reindeer camps were dependent on the delivery of staple foods and supplies from the center. Indigenous children whose parents lived in the reindeer camps were flown back and forth from residential schools. Villagers had to travel to the city hospital to treat major injuries and diseases and to give birth. Individuals, especially if they were affiliated with the party, tended to be shuffled from location to location to take up new posts. And finally, the Soviet government, in its perpetual quest for greater "efficiency," maintained a continual flow of bodies around Chukotka by frequently closing whole villages and moving their residents to other villages. Any point in the region could be reached by air because of the ubiquitous Soviet MI-8 military helicopter, which picked up where the region's myriad small propeller jets left off. It hardly seems possible that anyone could ever feel settled or rooted under these circumstances.

Granted, the reliance on air travel had its pitfalls, and could at times be excruciatingly difficult. Flights could be grounded by bad weather in any season, and it was not uncommon for travelers to be unexpectedly stranded in airports for days or weeks. Given the great distances, and the inherent difficulties of transportation, one might expect that people would simply stay put unless they absolutely had to move. Thus, it was rather surprising to find that Chukotkans engaged in *so much* travel, even voluntarily. Gold miners and reindeer herders were flown back and forth from work at the mine or reindeer camp to leisure time in village or city; AKB brigades were flown to remote reindeer camps to bring reading material and to perform for the herders. And everyone flew back to the *materik* ("the mainland," as western Russia is referred to in the Russian Far East) for summer vacation, a social benefit for northerners subsidized by the state. Even some indigenous residents managed to activate this privilege, and I was often shown family photos depicting Chukchis frolicking in the surf of the Black Sea at Sochi.

For most indigenous Chukotkans, movement was nothing new. Chukchi reindeer herders had long been systematically nomadic (Krupnik 1993), and I heard several accounts of how during the Soviet period, herding families would periodically pack up a veritable wagon train of reindeer sleds with trade goods and head off several hundred kilometers to a trade fair, often traveling from the inland tundra to the coastal areas of the Chukotka Peninsula. Herding camps had to be moved every few days in order to bring the reindeer to fresh pastures. This had long been a topic of vigorous debate among Soviet ethnographers, policy makers, and administrators, who considered such perpetual motion unnatural, or at least unprogressive; one should live a settled life in a square house, not a portable life in round tents (Slezkine 1992), and thus one of the central goals of Soviet development in the North as it pertained to the indigenous peoples was the "settling of the nomads" (e.g. Gurvich 1962:27). The Soviet era brought a kind of lockdown among the nomadic herders by establishing administrative boundaries around the state farm beyond which reindeer herders were forbidden to pass.[2] Thus, it is rather ironic that once the Soviets had managed to settle these nomads in villages, they immediately introduced frenetic mobility.

It is important in Chukotka to take note of differential access to different kinds of mobility. Everyone moved in Chukotka, but each person moved according to different motivations and opportunities. In the Soviet period, indigenous residents were generally forced to move (as in the examples of children being taken to residential schools and villagers being relocated after their villages were closed), while nonindigenous residents tended to have more control over their movement (for example, they took their post in Chukotka in response to the incentive of higher pay and lucrative benefits, and they planned their vacation to visit relatives back in European Russia). In post-Soviet Chukotka, there was a widening "mobility gap" (quite literally) between indigenous residents and nonindigenous residents. As will be discussed more fully in Chapter 7, the 1990s saw a massive outmigration from Chukotka, as residents sought better conditions in the temperate zones of Russia. It was primarily nonindigenous residents who had access to the resources (money and family connections elsewhere in Russia) to make this migration possible. It is true that many indigenous residents preferred to remain in their Chukotkan homeland anyway, but I did have conversations with several indigenous residents (both in the city and in the village) who dreamed of a more prosperous life in western Russia and were working to save the money to get there, and I knew some who had already relocated there.

Despite the mobility gap, several Chukotkan indigenous residents – primarily from among the intelligentsia, but not exclusively – gained remarkable access to sites around the world after *glasnost'*. Inhabitants of tiny coastal villages on the Chukotka Peninsula began traveling to Alaska and Canada as early as 1989 on sponsored exchange programs,[3] while a few urban intellectual Chukotkan indigenous residents traveled to such destinations as England, Norway, Switzerland, the United States, and Canada. And while the former traveled primarily as tourists in cultural exchanges, the latter traveled with a consciousness of the international movement to promote their rights and interests as indigenous peoples, in partnership with other indigenous peoples around the world. In 1990, while as a first-year graduate student I was just beginning to learn about the Chukchi from Bogoraz's ethnography and was trying, starry-eyed, to imagine them living in their reindeer skin tents in the tundra, Chukchi activists were already becoming global jet setters.

The Socialist City

Since I had originally envisioned my research taking place in Chukotkan villages, I thought that Chukotka's urban spaces would be something I would simply pass through on my way to its rural expanses. I did not suspect that I would find in the city such a fertile field for my study. However, the more time I spent in Chukotka's capital city of Anadyr' and the more I was drawn into the social networks of indigenous residents living there, the more I realized that the city was the most appropriate place to be. Anadyr' was not the only place in Chukotka where indigenous intellectuals could be found – there were seven other district centers in Chukotka, small cities where educated indigenous residents resided. I also encountered intellectuals living in villages, such as the late writer Liubov' Petrovna Uvarovskaya in Snezhnoe (Uvarovskaya 1992). However, as the regional capital, Anadyr' was the key center for Chukotka's indigenous intelligentsia. All of Anadyr's major educational institutions were there, such as the Teacher's College *(Peduchilishche)*, the Teacher's Finishing Institute *(Institut Usovershenstvovanye Uchitelei)*, and the Medical College *(Meduchilishche)*. These not only provided training for indigenous residents, but also provided employment to already-educated indigenous residents, regardless of where they had been schooled.

Studying indigenous residents in arctic cities is perhaps developing into something of a precedent; Alexia Bloch's study of Siberian Evenks was focused primarily in Tura, the small capital city of the Evenk Autonomous Region (Bloch 1996); Nancy Fogel-Chance (1993) has studied Iñupiaq women in Anchorage; and Ann Fienup-Riordan, who has long studied Yup'iks in Alaskan villages, now writes as well about the Yup'ik community in Anchorage (Fienup-Riordan 2000:151–68). The word "city" evokes for most readers images of a certain kind of place, perhaps one that is clean and graced with monumental architecture. Anadyr' would defy almost anyone's stereotypical image of a capital city, primarily because the difficulties of constructing buildings on permafrost make maintenance of a concrete city in the tundra a challenge. In fact, the city looked to me so dilapidated that my first impression upon arriving was that I had entered a war zone.

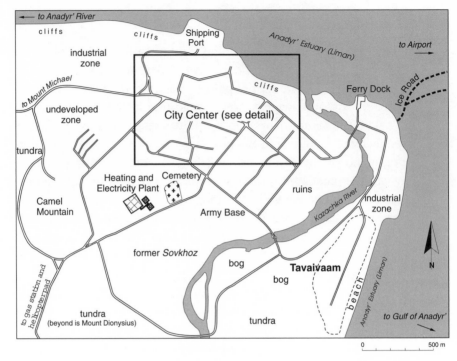

MAP 5.1. Anadyr'/Tavaivaam

Anadyr' is a small (population 11,280[4]) and very Soviet city improbably plopped down in the middle of the Chukotkan tundra (see Map 5.1). It is built on a broad slope rising upon an enormous cape that is bordered on one side by the broad mouth of the Anadyr' River and on the other by the Anadyr' Estuary *(liman)* that leads to the Gulf of Anadyr', which in turn opens up to the Bering Sea. Indigenous residents enjoyed telling me, with a smirk, that their ancestors had called the site upon which the city was built "place of death." Nevertheless, it is a site not without beauty. When one climbs high enough in the town and looks back down, the sea suddenly appears all around. Craggy mountains lie beyond the water, capped with snow even in the peak of summer. The landward side of the cape opens up suddenly to endless tundra, flat and broad, rolling away until it dissolves into mist. Beyond this, most of Chukotka's landscape is folded into low, rugged mountains, but around the city all is flat save for a single, broad-backed mountain called Mount Dionysus, rising abruptly out of the tundra about 30 kilometers outside of town. In the course of my stay in Anadyr', I watched as the mountain's appearance changed with the shifting of the weak arctic light and the shadowy veils of mist that gathered about it. In winter, it was shrouded in snowy whiteness, which transformed to glowing, pale pink in the afternoon when the sun was fading, and a terrible, icy blue in the twilight.

The natural beauty of the tundra and mountains that surround Anadyr' stand in stark contrast to the city itself. The historical roots of Anadyr' date back to 1889, but the contemporary city very much reflects the Soviet ideal of the Siberian socialist utopia – a modern, concrete city with all the requisite amenities. From a distance, Anadyr' appears as a chalky white expanse spreading up the slope of the cape, inspiring the poet Andrei Gazha to describe it as "white city, with its stories reaching up to the blue!"[5] In winter, this pristine image is transformed to a black stain against the surrounding white of frozen tundra and sea. Most of the buildings in Anadyr' are five-story prefabricated apartment blocks, built during and since the time of Nikita Khrushchev. Most of these are virtually identical; they were pieced together from standard cement slabs with a hole cut out for the window, each building twelve slabs long by five slabs high. A stockpile of these ready-made pieces cluttered one side of town, where a factory once produced building materials. Faded paint on many of the buildings bore traces of Soviet-era design sense, which tended toward colorful geometric patterns outlining the otherwise monotonously similar windows. Huge tile mosaics still adorned the windowless ends of a few of these buildings – a racing dog sled, an indigenous woman reaching toward a bright sun, a map of Chukotka graced with a red flag that declares "All power to the soviets!"

Pedestrians walking among these buildings are able to peer at their undersides, since all the buildings are propped up on steel and concrete stilts to keep their warmth from melting the permafrost below them and slowly sucking the buildings down. Even so, some buildings did befall this fate, and stood empty and boarded up as a result of subsidence. On the outskirts of town there were two districts of ruins where

PLATE 5.1. Panoramic view of Anadyr'

older wooden buildings and smaller concrete buildings stood at wild angles, fallen off their foundations, collapsing from within. Although they looked as if perhaps an earthquake shook them up like so many houses of cards, they in fact reached their current state in slow motion, sinking and shifting year after year with the thawing and refreezing of the ground. In 1998, even the capital's central administration building, nicknamed the "White House," began to crack apart noticeably and had to be abandoned. In 2002, it was demolished.

While Anadyr's municipal center was oriented around a complex of several public and commercial buildings, shops and government offices could be found tucked away on the first floors of apartment buildings throughout most of the city. The city had no concept of zoning, which made it a hodge-podge of mixed use. Children's playgrounds were likely to turn up anywhere. The city cemetery, with grave markers a mixture of nameless wooden posts and constructivist style metal "tombstones" bearing ceramicized photographs of the deceased, spans a slope directly below the twin smokestacks of the roaring, smoke-belching heating and electricity plant (see Plate 5.2). The cemetery is shadowed by a black mountain of coal, which is uncontained and runs off with rainwater and melted snow into the cemetery and down the street. And scattered in multitudinous clusters virtually wherever

PLATE 5.2. Anadyr's heating plant and cemetery

a bit of extra space in the city landscape exists are makeshift storage huts *(sarai)* and steel shipping containers *(konteinery)*, also used for storage. Since living space is very limited in the apartments, and there is no on-site storage space for residents, nearly every family kept a *sarai* or *konteiner* somewhere under lock and key for extra belongings, small motor vehicles, and food stored for winter. These clusters of storage units resembled little villages of their own, and tended to become gathering places for the city's men.

Anadyr' has its own airport, but it was built on the opposite side of the estuary from the city. Travelers must therefore be transported across the water to catch their flights. In summer, one could take a small ferry, the *Kamchatka,* which putted noisily across the estuary in a fair rendition of the *African Queen.* In spring and fall, when the estuary filled up with crushing, grinding ice floes, the only option was a brief and quite expensive flight across by helicopter. In January, the estuary freezes solid, and a road is carved across the ice to connect the city and the airport. The entrance point to this road on the city side of the estuary for years was marked with an iron archway emblazoned with the words "Happy Trails!" *(Schastlivogo Puti!)*, which was an incongruous sight in the summer when it led to nothing but an expanse of water. All winter long, vehicles crawled in and out of this access point like ants at the entrance to an anthill.

In spite of its monstrous structures, which gives it the feel of a largish city, the space that Anadyr' occupies is actually quite small. The length of it can be walked in less than half an hour, and would just about fit between two Moscow metro stops. On all my visits, the streets were always teeming with people, busy, well dressed, and friendly, bustling in and out of shops and offices. Since most shopping was done on foot, people typically did a little shopping every day. The demographic profile of the town was clearly a diverse mix of age groups: – Children dashed through the market square; elderly folks stepped gingerly along the rough sidewalks; adult men and women strode back and forth looking most businesslike; and young parents (usually mothers, but sometimes lone fathers) wheeled infants in old-fashioned prams with hoods. These prams were the best evidence I saw of what an intimate, small-town setting I was in; when mothers made their rounds,

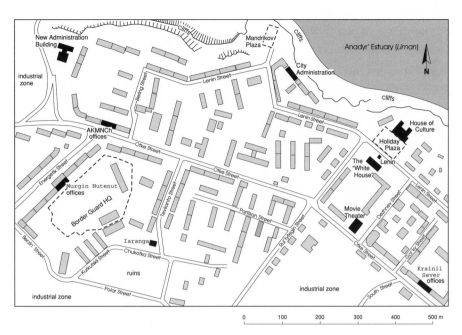

MAP 5.2. Anadyr' Detail

they simply rolled up to a shop, parked baby and carriage outside, and walked away from it, having no fear of anything untoward occurring in their absence.

As an American accustomed to cities that are laid out on a grid with well-marked streets, I found the organization of Anadyr' haphazard at best (see Map 5.2). There were no street signs directly on the streets, and often the buildings that were labeled with a particular street address were located far from the street itself, standing next to buildings belonging to a different street address. The entire city was a complex web of avenues of movement around and among the clutter of buildings. The main streets were paved (though crumbling), but there were several unpaved minor streets, and these seemed to me identical in appearance to the maze of back alleyways lacing the city, making it a challenge to determine which meandering gravel track was actually a named street. All of this complexity would be daunting enough to the newcomer even with a street map in hand, but in fact no municipal street map has ever been published.

Overlaid upon this convoluted web of streets, sidewalks, and alleys was another category of walking surface altogether that, for lack of a better designation, I dubbed "pipeways."[6] A tangle of pipes emerged from the power plant and proceeded to snake its way throughout the city, delivering its steamy heat. The pipes were not buried, but rather ran along the surface of the ground, wrapped a foot thick in insulation covered with a metal shell. In most cases, these fat tubes were covered with a square housing of concrete, and it was the tops of these housings that became a walking surface. Pipeways laced the city, sometimes running alongside streets and alleys, sometimes projecting at odd angles, and residents used them heavily as pedestrian shortcuts. A peculiar advantage of pipeways in winter was that their warmth kept them relatively free of ice, making them the least treacherous walking surface. The only disadvantage was getting up and down the usually ice-slicked wooden planks thrown up against them here and there for pedestrian access.

The pedestrian tour in Anadyr' in the 1990s was further complicated by the condition of the paved surfaces, which resembled an obstacle course. One had to step carefully over broken patches of concrete and watch out for steel rebar sticking out at threatening angles. In many places, the pavement had dissolved altogether, and people picked their way across rough gravel surfaces littered with large pebbles. This was especially a challenge for the city's women, since the current fashion in Anadyr' favored high-heeled shoes in the summer months. Anadyrites seemed rather stoic about the physical appearance of their surroundings, as I watched them picking their way through the streets with calm patience. But they occasionally expressed frustration. A brief article appeared in the 17 August 1996 edition of *Krainii Sever* with the headline "Ruins." Next to it were two photographs of crumbling wooden buildings in the city, some of which were no more than a pile of sticks. The article begins sarcastically:

> In the first place, the "landscape" you see in the picture has nothing whatsoever to do with Africa or Latin America. It isn't even one of the countries of the "Third World" – this is Russia. In the second place, these picturesque ruins were not shot in Chechnya or Abkhazia or Karabakh. Because this is not the result of battles in one

of the "hot spots" of the CIS [Commonwealth of Independent States] –
this is Chukotka. And in the third place, these wrecked houses are
not located in Iultin or Mandrikovo or Poliarnyi. This is not one of
the "closed towns"[7] – this is Anadyr'. The capitol of Chukotka? The
very same!

Inscribed on all this apparent pandemonium was nevertheless a
detectable attempt to reproduce the Soviet social order as it existed in
Moscow and other cosmopolitan centers of the Soviet Union. A pen-
sive, granite Lenin stood before the (former) central administration
building, overlooking a large plaza on which all Russian State holidays
were held. On the other side of the plaza stood Anadyr's impressive
House of Culture (the building was demolished in 2002). The three-
story building was painted white with pink facing, and over the door
was a faded, twenty-foot socialist realist mural of a parading man and
woman. Above the mural, just below the peaked roof, was a gigantic
white bas-relief seal of the Soviet Union. Anadyr' was also given its
movie theater, its museum, its library – all the trappings of a "cultured"
Soviet city. There were reminders of the Cold War era, such as the
large compound inside the city that still served as the headquarters
for the ever-present Russian border guard. This location was at one
time outside of the city proper, but the residential space grew to engulf
it, until a rifle-toting sentry at the entrance to the compound stood
alongside a kindergarten playground. These scenes reminiscent of
the Cold War were sometimes ironically juxtaposed to reminders of
recent social and political changes, such as the sound of American
pop music (anything from the Beatles to rap) floating down from
open windows.

Although Anadyr' may seem to outsiders to be a remote location
in the middle of the tundra, its inhabitants cling to their identity as
city dwellers. Anadyr' had existed in some form since 1889 (when it
was established as the post Novo-Mariinsk), but the most progressive moment of its history is considered to be the year 1965, when it
was officially designated as a full-fledged city. This city identity was
especially important to incomers – indigenous residents were more
likely to call Anadyr' jokingly a "big village," usually in reference to the
speed with which gossip circulated around it. One can view Anadyr'

as an example of the Russian way of constructing and using space in Chukotka, which radically differs from the way indigenous residents originally interacted with the physical spaces of Chukotka. Chukchi reindeer herders lived in lightweight, round, portable dwellings made of reindeer skin *(iarangi)*, and they moved with relative fluidity across the tundra. Even settled coastal dwellers, whose homes were similar but permanent, maintained a more fluid continuity between the space of the village and the space of the nearby tundra, as well as the sea (Kerttula 1997:216–18). Incomers, by contrast, longed to be anchored to one site and to walk among monstrous and immovable structures, even if it meant a colossal investment of financial and material resources and scientific expertise to mitigate the enmity of the permafrost toward heavy concrete buildings.

However, indigenous residents and incomers alike participated in ascribing meaning to the contrasting spaces of city and tundra. Although at times one could hear the tundra described as an "indigenous" space and the city as a "Russian" space, such a dichotomy is too simplistic to capture the sometimes competing interpretations of these two social spaces. Many incomers saw the tundra as a source of mineral wealth (gold or oil), or as a vast "backyard" for weekend hunting (moose, caribou, and geese) or fishing, and for this purpose any quality of "indigenousness" that might otherwise adhere to the tundra seemed irrelevant. Conversely, there were some indigenous residents who had been born and raised in either the city or the village and felt most comfortable in an apartment with all the amenities. In the village of Snezhnoe, I encountered several indigenous residents who had never traveled out to the tundra reindeer brigades because their jobs kept them in the village, and some were beside themselves with the amusing irony that I, an outsider and a neophyte, had been there before they had. Still, to some extent, the presence of incomers in city spaces and indigenous residents in tundra spaces seemed somehow natural to Chukotkans. Most adult indigenous residents were familiar with the tundra because they had lived at least part of their life either in the tundra or close to it in a village, while the average incomer had never set foot in the tundra (beyond perhaps a berry-picking escapade on the outskirts of Anadyr') and in fact had no desire to be plunged into that wild and unforgiving environment. Incomers routinely marveled at my own willingness to travel to the tundra.

Indeed, the city remained a place if not literally for Russians, then at least for Russianlike people. Indigenous residents who had lived permanently in the city for some time frequently commented to me that they lived *po-russkii* ("in the Russian way"), that is, residing in apartments, eating Russian foods like potatoes, cabbage, and cucumbers, and comporting themselves reservedly on the streets. If they did *not* comport themselves thus, they drew negative attention to themselves. Marina Peliave remarked that she had always been aware of one noticeable difference between incomers and Chukchis in Anadyr: When Chukchis encountered one another on the street or in shops, they greeted each other with laughter and lively chatter, while surrounding incomers looked on sternly and silently. She said she always felt that incomers disapproved of their noisy and uninhibited behavior, and that this was disconcerting to her. Whether or not Russians were in fact looking with disapproval upon Marina is less important than Marina's perception of incomer–indigenous relations. She learned how to act differently when she was in Russian social spaces in order to avoid attracting what she felt was negative attention.

The "National Village"

Down the hill from central Anadyr', seeming to lie at its feet along the coast of the estuary, is the "national village" of Tavaivaam. When I first arrived in Anadyr', a Russian colleague at the research institute, knowing my research concerned indigenous peoples, suggested I would be interested in visiting Tavaivaam; he described it as a "part of town" that was mostly inhabited by indigenous residents. Indeed, only about 8.5 percent of the inhabitants of Anadyr' were indigenous, while in Tavaivaam the proportion was about 78 percent indigenous. In spite of Tavaivaam's proximity to Anadyr', in all of my discussions with city residents, I clearly sensed that the village was assigned social meaning as an *indigenous* space, not a Russian space. There was an objective reason for this. Administratively, thirty-seven villages in

Chukotka were set apart and given a special status as "national villages" *(natsional'noe selo)*, meaning they were "places of compact residence of Less-Numerous Peoples of the North."[8] These villages were the beneficiaries of special programs, and in Chukotka, indigenous inhabitants of these villages had rights to "privileges" *(lgoty)*, such as free breakfast at school for children.

Anadyr' and Tavaivaam have long been linked by a single road, with pavement on the city end, and gravel on the village end. Tavaivaam's tiny cemetery lies along this road, wedged between a warehouse and a city shipyard (which is apparently where the bodies of the *Revkomtsy* were found). The village was provided its own modest House of Culture, or "the Club," as everyone referred to it, and the village administration was housed in the same building. The other main buildings in Tavaivaam included a small shop across from the Club, a kindergarten (which had also served as a residential school for children of reindeer herders living in the tundra), a health clinic, a warehouse, and a fish-processing barn. Residential housing came in various forms: a block of three-story apartment buildings in the center of town (where most residents lived); a three-story dormitory (so dilapidated that it was finally torn down in 1999); a few one-story wooden duplexes (rat-infested and without plumbing); and a set of clean-looking, relatively new two-story apartment buildings. Another "modern" three-story cement apartment block stood prominently empty on the main road. It was constructed in the early 1990s up to the point of installing the window glass, but was then abandoned due to financing problems. Given the severe shortage of decent housing in the village, the frustrated villagers regarded the gaping windows lined with broken glass as a continual taunt.

Although the village was supplied with running water and with heat from the central power plant, not a single building in Tavaivaam was equipped with hot water. Apparently, Tavaivaam once did have hot water, when the main power plant was located along the estuary not far from Tavaivaam. But that plant was destroyed in a severe winter storm in the 1980s, and the new power plant was built high up the hill on the far side of the city. The village was promised hot water; in fact, a set of heating pipes ran downhill from the power plant toward Tavaivaam, all the way up to the edge of the village, but there the pipes abruptly stopped. As with the abandoned apartment buildings, construction on the pipes was halted, although only a few meters remained to be built. Nikita Suslov, who worked in the village's House of Culture, said that city officials had appeared at a village gathering and said, in effect, that village inhabitants were accustomed to harsh conditions (being mostly indigenous with presumably tundra roots), and therefore they could manage without hot water until the city could find the resources to complete the construction. Those who wanted a hot shower managed it only by jerry-rigging a connection from the steam heating pipes and siphoning off hot water.

The central focus of life in Tavaivaam throughout the Soviet period was its state farm, which was originally named "Stalin" and changed to "Twenty-Second Party Congress" after Stalin's death.[9] I often heard stories of what a successful and exemplary state farm it was. Maia Ettyryntyna, Chukotka's representative to the federal Council of the Federation from 1993 to 1995, became very animated when I mentioned the Tavaivaam state farm during our 1996 interview. She told me it had been a "Millionaire state farm," one of the most productive and profitable in the region. The main enterprise of the state farm was reindeer herding, and at its height in the late 1970s it managed as many as ten separate reindeer herds totaling over twenty-seven thousand head of deer, which grazed in the broad, flat tundra south of Anadyr' and Tavaivaam. Each herd was the responsibility of an individual brigade, and the position of *brigadir* was prestigious among the indigenous inhabitants. The state farm at one time employed most of the village inhabitants, with indigenous residents working directly with the herds or in the fur sewing shop or the fish processing base, and incomers filling the professional positions or driving tractors and *vezdekhody* (a kind of passenger tank used in the North).[10]

After the Soviet Union collapsed, when Boris Yeltsin decreed that all agricultural enterprises must reorganize into new, privatized forms,[11] Tavaivaam's state farm technically dissolved, and in its place, four private "farms" *(fermerskoe khoziaistvo)* were created with the names Chirynai, Kenkeren, Eupolian, and Topolovoe. These were headed by former state farm reindeer herders, and their Chukchi-language names reflect the nativistic outlook of their new directors. However, the state farm had been so central to the identity of the villagers that everyone still referred to these reindeer herding enterprises collectively as the *sovkhoz*, as is generally the case in villages all over Chukotka, and indeed all over Russia. Yet unlike most villages in Chukotka, where a "rump" state farm remained after smaller enterprises hived off, Tavaivaam's reorganization was more radical – all of the assets of the state farm were divided among the four enterprises, leaving nothing behind. This proved fateful for the survival of reindeer herding in Tavaivaam, for the directors of these new enterprises simply did not have the knowledge and experience needed to turn reindeer herding into a capitalist enterprise. When I arrived in Chukotka in 1995, only two or three viable herds were said to be left in the tundra, and it soon became clear that even these were doomed. Department of Agriculture figures show the combined head counts for the four enterprises dropped from over twenty thousand in 1985 to less than eight thousand in 1995. By the time I returned in 1998, all four of the new enterprises were defunct, and no reindeer herds whatsoever were left.

Even more central to the identity of Tavaivaam villagers than the state farm was the tundra itself, where the reindeer herds had grazed. A large proportion of villagers, both men and women, had been employed directly in the brigades and commuted back and forth between tundra and village in helicopters or in the state farm–owned *vezdekhody*. During the summer and on school holidays, children were sent to live with their families in the tundra, returning to the village residential school in the fall. The tundra was also an important supplier of sustenance to the villagers; besides consuming the meat of the reindeer that grazed on the tundra, villagers gathered mushrooms, berries, and a variety of plants, as well as hunted birds and other animals (and in this they often had to compete with Russian weekenders from Anadyr' who seasonally flocked to the surrounding tundra).

Up to the mid-1990s, Tavaivaam still functioned much as it did in its state farm days. Many former state farm workers had been left unemployed, however, since in the process of reorganizing and creating the four new enterprises, some elements of the collective operation (such as the fur sewing shop) were dropped by the wayside. Ultimately, especially as the reindeer herding enterprises failed, the shock of all the changes plunged many into depression, pushing alcoholism and suicide rates in the village to high levels. At the same time, some villagers were determined to provide a sense of purpose to residents, particularly to the village's many children. There were programs in the Club and in the village kindergarten to involve children in art, dance, and athletics, and nature walks to the tundra were occasionally organized (cf. Van Deusen 1999:61).

I later learned that Tavaivaam had actually been annexed by the city of Anadyr' in May 1994, a move that was very controversial and had both its defenders and its critics, even among the indigenous population. Accounts of the annexation were somewhat conflicting. Maia Ettyryntyna told me that the annexation was the result of a city resolution. Anastasia Zinkevich, who claimed to get her information from a pro-indigenous deputy in the Chukotka regional legislature, told me the annexation was the result of machinations by Aleksandr Nazarov himself. Nazarov had apparently wanted to merge some of Chukotka's eight districts, presumably in the interest of trimming regional budget expenditures, but was thwarted by the fact that such restructuring was within the exclusive competence of the federal government. So he instead took action that was within his own competence and administratively merged several "national villages" into larger towns nearby. Both Ettyryntyna and Zinkevich asserted that Tavaivaam lost its status as a "national village" when it was annexed; Ettyryntyna opined that the city accomplished the annexation as a matter of convenience – it wanted to save the money that would otherwise have gone to support privileges for the indigenous population.

Many villagers were unabashedly vocal in their criticism of the merger, saying it was unfair to the villagers to be ruled by an outside administration that only ignored them. Some cited the lack of hot water as the ultimate hypocrisy on the part of the city: By annexing the village, the city wanted to claim it as belonging to the city, but it refused to deliver all of the city's services. Viktor Serekov, then president of the Anadyr' Association of Indigenous Peoples, stated in a public meeting in 1996 (discussed in Chapter 1) that he believed the annexation was patently illegal. In stark contrast, some in the city administration spoke almost evangelically about all of the benefits Tavaivaam had accrued with the annexation. The mayor of Anadyr', Viktor Alekseevich Khvan, twice appeared at meetings of the City Association of Indigenous Peoples in 1996 and tried to persuade a disgruntled crowd how lucky they were to be patronized by the city. Tavaivaam's mayor at the time, Galina Ivanovna Notatynagyrgyna, spoke in one accord with him, and published an article in *Krainii Sever*[12] that persuasively defended the annexation. In any case, for all practical purposes, Tavaivaam became simply one district of the Russian-dominated city of Anadyr', and since it remained a poorer district populated predominantly by indigenous residents, it began to take on the quality of an ethnic ghetto.

The Relentless Significance of Culture

What the city did seem to gain from Tavaivaam was a living museum of Chukotka's indigenous cultures, a conveniently close location where incomers could safely observe indigenous culture and still be home in time for dinner and the evening news. Public holidays were periodically held in Tavaivaam, to which city residents were always invited. Anadyr' celebrated an impressive annual array of holidays and festivals, from the wild spring carnival Smelt Festival held on the frozen estuary in April, to the more somber Revolution Day[13] in November. Most of these were Russian state holidays, but a very few were considered "national holidays" of Chukotkan indigenous residents. All of these holidays were codified in a resolution of the governor that included an official calendar of thirty-five holidays, nine of which were indigenous "traditional" holidays.[14]

The Russian State holidays were without exception held in the plaza in front of the Anadyr' House of Culture, under the watchful eye of the granite Lenin (see Plates 5.3 and 5.4), often with performances by the professional State Chukchi-Eskimo Ensemble *Ergyron*"[15] and sometimes by any one of several "amateur"[16] indigenous ensembles, performing dance and song in colorful costumes. These holidays were attended by vendors selling grilled *shashlik* (shish kabob) and hot dogs, while fresh beer from Anadyr's own brewery was dispensed from

PLATE 5.3. Lenin overlooks a holiday on the main plaza before the House of Culture in Anadyr'

PLATE 5.4. A holiday on the dirt main street next to Tavaivaam's House of Culture

a gigantic yellow keg mounted on a truck, and bottles of champagne were passed among small groups of (mostly incomer) celebrants. The "indigenous holidays" were held in Tavaivaam, without the vendors, but with the indigenous amateur ensembles. The one exception to this pattern was the International Day of the World's Indigenous People, a new holiday invented in the context of the United Nations International Decade of the World's Indigenous People (1995–2004), which was commemorated on 9 August with a parade of Chukotkan indigenous residents through the streets of Anadyr' ending on the city's central plaza, where additional festivities were staged.[17]

I did not have to wait long to have my first taste of an indigenous holiday in Tavaivaam. In October 1995, two weeks after I first arrived in Anadyr', I was told there was going to be an indigenous festival down in Tavaivaam to commemorate the tenth anniversary of the village's resident folk ensemble, *Emnung* (Chukchi for "tundra"). It was open to all, and I was urged to attend. I looked forward not only to seeing an indigenous performance for the first time, but also to my first visit to an indigenous village. When I arrived in the village, all was quiet on the main street save for a few children hanging about next to a ramshackle two-story wooden building. I asked them if there was a festival going on somewhere, and they pointed to a door leading in. This unassuming building turned out to be Tavaivaam's House of Culture.

I found my way down a dim, creaky hallway to a room that was utterly jammed with people, half of whom were standing against the walls. Bright lights blazed from the back of the room to illuminate the scene for the Chukchi TV cameraman who was busily at work recording the event. At the front of the room, a small group of people, mostly children, were dancing and singing in Chukchi. The ensemble was not limited to indigenous participants; two blonde girls, a Russian woman (who turned out to be the director of the Tavaivaam House of Culture), and a nonindigenous man (an Australian linguist who had come to write a grammar of the Chukchi language) were also dancing with them. The obvious leader of the ensemble was a fortyish Chukchi man with an impish grin and darting eyes. Dressed in a reindeer-fur suit with an elaborately trimmed fur hat, Boris Vasilevich Etuve energetically leapt about the room orchestrating the performance. He introduced each piece first in Chukchi and then in Russian, and provided commentary on the historical origins of the dances. At one point, he performed in a two-man Chukchi-language skit, playing a staid and dignified reindeer to the Australian linguist's cackling trickster-fish character, a comic performance that caused the audience to roar with laughter.

Emnung's program lasted about an hour, and was followed by a ceremony to congratulate Etuve for his ten years of exemplary service to the village as director of the ensemble. One by one, people stood up to praise "Boris Vasilevich" for his work to "promote and preserve indigenous cultural traditions," and he was presented with gifts such as books, music cassettes, and videos. There was a virtual frenzy of laudatory speeches, and every gift presentation was accompanied by hearty applause from the audience. The longest and clearly the most authoritative speech was made by Raisa Shakina, a Russian woman whom I later came to know as the ebullient director of the Chukotka Regional Center for Folk Culture, located in Anadyr's House of Culture. Shakina gushed with enthusiasm as she praised Boris Vasilevich's talent and dedication. Brimming with emotion, she said, "Our two cultures, Chukchi and Russian, have always honored and respected one another." She dramatically concluded speech by presenting Boris Vasilevich with a brand new television.

I expected the evening to end with this energetic climax, but in fact, I had only seen the first half, the indigenous half; now would come the Russian half. The program was turned over to a buoyant Russian master of ceremonies who wore an ill-fitting satin suit with glittering sequin trim. At this point it became clear that a large portion of the assembled audience were themselves performers, many of them children accompanied by their parents, who were waiting for their turn to appear. This Russian half of the program included three boys with expressions of stern concentration performing a Cossack dance, complete with spoon playing; a three-girl ensemble of accordions and bayan; and a man playing balalaika while singing a sad Russian ballad in a deep bass voice. Each act was energetically introduced by the M.C., who himself eventually performed, singing along to a pop music recording.

The evening was structured as though an even exchange were being made: indigenous cultural traditions for Russian cultural traditions. This exchange had been charged with energy and enthusiasm
throughout the evening, and the participants evidently meant to show
their sincere appreciation for each other's culture. Yet there remained
an awkwardness about it, highlighted by the sense that the underlying control was in the hands of only one of the groups – the Russians.
The subtext seemed clear: It was by virtue of the authority of Russians
and their culture that the indigenous cultural traditions were being
recognized as having merit (further validated by the presence of the
news media – although the cameraman was Chukchi, he nevertheless
worked for the Russian state television company). The inverse situation – a delegation of indigenous residents from Tavaivaam visiting the
House of Culture in Anadyr' with gifts and praise for the director of
Russian cultural programs there – was unthinkable. It was clearly the
incomers who were allowing and controlling a space where indigenous
culture could be exhibited and appreciated.

About a year after I had witnessed this first of many indigenous
cultural events I would see in the course of my research, an interview
with an employee of the Tavaivaam House of Culture, Nikita Suslov,
provided belated validation of the awkwardness I had felt at that first
performance. I asked Nikita for an interview after I heard him stand
up at the meeting of the Anadyr' City Association of Indigenous Less-
Numerous Peoples of Chukotka and openly criticize the administration
of Chukotka. During our interview a few days later, he was still full of
agitation and I had only to mention my interest in relations between
the administration and indigenous residents for him to spill out a flood
of invective. "All they do is give us holidays and pretend that everything
is fine," he hissed. "They show us off to international audiences and
say 'see how well our traditional cultures are doing!' Dance, sing, they
tell us, but they won't help us where we really need help!" These words
provided evidence of local awareness that indigenous residents were
not only being ghettoized in a "cultural space" provided and controlled
by incomers, but that this was a kind of diversionary tactic, a way to
shift attention away from more pressing indigenous concerns (poverty,
lack of housing, and health care, for example). It also indicated the

presence of a latent indigenous political critique. Nikita paid a price for his open criticism; when I returned to Chukotka in 1998, he had lost his job at the House of Culture, and he made it plain to me that he believed he had been fired for political reasons.

In the course of my research in Russia, I saw many examples of this pattern of incomers giving indigenous residents a special and limited place in cultural space, usually with a magnanimous flair that tread a fine line between sincerity and patronization, while at the same time turning a deaf ear to their complaints about their economic or political position in Chukotkan society. It was at the event in Tavaivaam where I first began to see how incomers were paternalistically asserting dominance over indigenous residents in a subtle, spatially inscribed way by encouraging them to stay within that cultural space and take on a role as cultural tokens of Chukotka. It would be difficult to overstate the centrality of culture in Chukotkan society during this period. In fact, as Nikita Suslov emphasized, it did seem odd that so much attention would be given to culture, and so much public money spent on it, when so many other pressing social ills were in such obvious need of attention.

But in Chukotka, the "problem of culture" qualified as one of these social ills. When I talked with indigenous consultees about their most pressing problems, they invariably pointed to indigenous language and culture, and their perception that they were deteriorating. In the newspaper, on the radio, at public meetings, and in my conversations with both indigenous residents and incomers, the need to preserve and promote indigenous language and culture was continually raised. A plethora of cultural organizations and institutions had been developed, both formal and informal, devoted to promoting indigenous language and culture in one way or another. Some were in the form of educational institutions, from courses in indigenous language and traditional culture at the Teacher's College, to art and music programs at the *Natsional'nyi kolledzh iskusstv* (National College of Arts). There was the regional museum, as well as the Center for Folk Culture. Others were in the form of the many performing ensembles in Anadyr' – besides *Ergyron*, there was one in the National College, the city had one called *Atasikun*, Tavaivaam had *Emnung*, and there was a children's ensemble at the *Dvorets Pionerov* ("Pioneers' Palace," a children's recreational facility).[18] There were also social clubs, most notably the Chukchi-language club called *Chychetkin Vetgav* ("Our Indigenous Speech"), which met periodically to converse in Chukchi over tea.

All of these manifestations of culture were very much Soviet in style and legacy, and similar manifestations could be found all over the country for other "national cultures" (including Russian culture). However, there was a difference between the ways that incomers and indigenous residents approached the issue of *indigenous* culture in Chukotka. Incomers could agree that indigenous culture had intrinsic value and was worth preserving for its own sake, and they felt the best ways to do that were to collect and display artifacts, teach indigenous languages as subjects in schools, support traditional indigenous per-formative and applied arts, and so on. For indigenous residents, the issue had more urgency. They did not see indigenous culture as worth preserving because of its intrinsic value; rather, it was the very essence of who they were, and in talking about the preservation of culture, they were talking about the very survival of their own consciousness as peoples. Nevertheless, many indigenous residents accommodated the incomers' agenda for cultural preservation, perhaps because it seemed to be the only option available to them for having at least some space to assert their cultural identity as indigenous residents (cf. Bloch 1996).

Incomers' views about culture (and to a large extent indigenous residents' views as well) were strongly influence by the Stalinist concept of culture and ethnicity, as discussed in the previous chapter. Moreover, a basic Arnoldian framework can be detected in the Stalinist concep-tualization that two general types of culture could be distinguished: There was culture in the general sense, which meant things like the arts and media, literacy, good hygiene – anything that facilitated in-doctrination into Marxist-Leninist principles and the assimilation of all within the territory of the Soviet Union into a single Soviet people (cf. Anderson 1996:104). This was ostensibly de-ethnicized, but was essen-tially Russian. Then there was "traditional culture," which in simplistic terms meant everything that was written in books by ethnographers who had studied non-Russian peoples. At the start of the Soviet era, these were marked as the very characteristics that had to be rooted out in order for socialism to progress, but they were ultimately considered charming, interesting, or utilitarian enough to merit preservation in books and museums and certain performing venues, and as evidence of the Soviet Union's international character and friendship with all peoples.

Early in Stalin's regime, the academic discipline of ethnography was attacked for being too protective of "fragile" indigenous cultures, and not sufficiently devoted to the supreme goal of socialist development. After being threatened with complete liquidation, the discipline of ethnography was finally reduced to being merely a sub-discipline of history (Slezkine 1991). Thus, under Stalin's influence a generation of not only ethnographers but all "cultural workers" was raised with an understanding that the essence of their work with indigenous cultures was historical, that their task was description and preservation of things of the past, while pushing indigenous peoples themselves toward greater harmony with progressive socialist ideals and practices. Wherever living humans were found to be engaging in practices of the past, it was assumed that their culture was on the brink of imminent death (cf. Slezkine 1994:392). Its passing would be mourned, but this was considered an inevitable result of the progress of socialism, and the struggle to prevent its passing was considered futile and indeed regressive.

What purveyors of this discourse forgot was that such pronouncements of imminent death have been made about indigenous peoples of Chukotka for generations. For example, the final words of Valdimir Bogoraz's monolithic ethnography of the Chukchi (well-known to all northern specialists) are:

> From all that has been said, the general conclusion may be drawn that the Chukchee tribe, Reindeer or Maritime, being very primitive, may continue to exist in its barren desert only if left alone by civilization. As soon as the latter comes too near, the Chukchee must follow in the way of so many other primitive tribes, and die (Bogoras 1904–9:733).

Bogoraz made this prediction at the very beginning of the twentieth century. Yet at the beginning of the twenty-first century, the Chukchi, as well as the Eskimos, Evens, Lamuts, Chuvans, and others, were not dead yet, although I often heard them spoken of as if they were.

Nevertheless, these views still held sway in Chukotka in the 1990s. In conversations with Chukotkans of every ilk, I found no perception that indigenous culture may change and, in spite of its superficial lack of resemblance to the indigenous culture of one hundred years ago, remain just as indigenous as ever. Yet change is the very nature of culture. The metaphor of cultural death is persistent and deeply rooted in popular imagination, not only in Chukotka; Ann Fienup-Riordan also struggles with it as she writes about the growing Yup'ik population in Anchorage, Alaska. Writes Fienup-Riordan:

> Yup'ik communities are not disintegrating, their lifeblood gradually seeping away. Many can be seen as actually expanding and recreating themselves in unprecedented ways until today, when they are as strong and vital as at any time in their 2,500-year history (2000:152).

Fienup-Riordan focuses on kinship and exchange relations as the core of this extended Alaskan Yup'ik community. Yet in Soviet ideology, kin relations were actively sublimated to the importance of unity among all as one Soviet family.

The "cultural workers" who were commissioned to manage indigenous culture in Chukotka were the *metodisty* ("methodologists") of the Center for Folk Culture in Anadyr'. Virtually all of them incomers, these were people who expressed genuine admiration for indigenous cultures. Nonindigenous residents who relocated to remote regions like Chukotka to staff such centers tended to be "true believers," aficionados of the traditional cultures who sincerely lamented their passing. The *metodisty* were quite popular among indigenous residents in Anadyr', who recognized their sincerity and appreciated the attention they paid to their traditional culture. Indigenous residents viewed the Center and its staff as a resource. The *metodisty* indeed celebrated traditional culture; yet, at the same time, they failed to see that their very efforts to preserve it also tended to freeze it and to encourage everyone to think of it as something dead and embalmed for posterity. The analogy to Lenin's body preserved and displayed on Red Square hardly needs to be invoked.

Technically, the Center for Folk Culture was the government agency responsible for dealing with all traditional culture. This could include the traditional folk culture of any nationality; but the Center's direc-tor, Shakina, admitted that the Center was primarily concerned with "the indigenous nationalities." The Center was administratively sub-ordinated under the regional Department of Culture, which in turn answered to the federal Ministry of Culture in Moscow. The Center had an incomer director, an indigenous deputy director, a staff of in-comer *metodisty*, and an indigenous clerical staff. One of the *metodisty* described the mission of the Center as being essentially salvage ethnography: Realizing that civilization was moving in on indigenous peoples (as though this process was as yet incomplete), they endeav-ored to travel to villages and collect as much indigenous culture as pos-sible before it disappeared altogether. They published booklets filled with sheet music and lyrics of indigenous songs, stories passed down through generations, recipes for "national dishes," and drawings of ob-jects of material culture. Items such as fur boots, bags, and toys were put on display in glass cases. The *metodisty* did not merely collect ma-terial in a passive way; they actively organized "indigenous" festivals in all eight districts of Chukotka in turn, and then stood by to record the proceedings. Once this act was complete, it was felt that at least these bits of folklore had been "preserved" for posterity, even if the culture died out. They also held out some hope that through their work they might pump life back into indigenous culture and begin to revive it, so that it could remain as a kind of living museum, if nothing else (cf. Bloch 1996:187).

John Sharp (1996:91) uses the phrase "polite domination" to char-acterize this kind of paternalistic appreciation of culture. He writes, "Those who are in a dominant position can afford to objectify 'oth-erness,' and to insist that those who want to be different play out their differences according to a script of which they are not the sole authors." Indeed, the *metodisty* were quite active in scripting per-formances of indigenous culture. The work and the attitudes of the *metodisty* exemplified also the spatial and temporal distancing de-vices outlined by Johannes Fabian (1983). The most "real" indige-nous culture today was thought to be "out there" in the tundra, and it was most real of all "back then," before indigenous residents got acclimated to living in comfortable apartments with amenities like

electricity and running water. For example, at the Anadyr' Smelt Festival in 1996 (which centered around a smelt-fishing contest on the
frozen estuary), I was talking with a *metodist* of the Center for Folk
Culture who, like I, was snapping photographs of the festivities. We
both caught sight of a Chukchi woman who was dressed in a reindeer fur coat and hat (see Plate 5.5). The *metodist* nudged me with his
elbow and said, "Take a picture of that, because it won't be around
much longer." Ironically, the woman in question was a television reporter, and she was dancing to rock music blaring from a boom box
alongside fellow members of an aerobics club who were clad in running suits. To me, this woman embodied a quintessential picture of
"Chukchi culture" in the 1990s; but the *metodist* had edited out the
contemporary music and the nontraditional dance form, and focused
only on the recognizably indigenous face and traditional fur clothing.
He was looking for the best fit with his image of "real" Chukchi culture.
Ironically, I heard some indigenous residents say that they would just
as soon wear reindeer fur coats all winter, even in the city (they are
warmer and more comfortable), but if they did, incomers would stare
at them and sometimes even make fun of them. This made them uncomfortable, so they wore "Western" clothes. The festival was a kind of
liminal setting to which wearing "ethnic" clothing seemed acceptable.

The concept of culture in Chukotka was also suffused with a kind
of ecological ethic. Indigenous culture had its own "habitat" where
it could exist *au naturel*, and that was the tundra; but in the city, it
was best captured in controlled museum displays. As Arjun Appadurai
(1990:13) notes:

> [States] are everywhere seeking to monopolize the moral resources
> of the community, either by flatly claiming coevality between nation
> and state, or by systematically museumizing and representing all the
> groups within them in a variety of heritage politics that seems re-
> markably uniform throughout the world.

Sergei Sheptsov, an incomer acquaintance in the Chukotkan administration, beautifully articulated this concept of "museumizing" culture
as he told me about a winter festival that used to be held in Anadyr'
at the conclusion of the annual long-distance dog-sled race *Nadezhda*
("Hope"), which terminated in Anadyr'. During this festival, Chukchis

PLATE 5.5. Chukchi woman dancing in "traditional" clothing at the annual Smelt Festival in Anadyr'

set up their *iarangi* in the plaza by the administration building, and staged various events showcasing traditional culture, such as a competition to see who could most quickly light a cooking fire, and exhibitions of women's sewing skill. Sergei, who had only recently moved to Chukotka, was romantically swept away by the color and pageantry of the scene around the *iarangi*; he told me he could not take his eyes off the indigenous people as they worked, because he was so impressed by their skill. I was genuinely moved by Sergei's vivid descriptions and obviously sincere appreciation of indigenous culture; yet, at the same time I recognized that what he appreciated was the exhibition quality of the culture. He told me he spent hours in the cold strolling among the *iarangi* and taking everything in – in this sense, it seems as though to him the experience was both like visiting a museum and watching a cultural performance. It was a living museum diorama, an expression of indigenous culture carried out in a safely circumscribed space. As long as the indigenous people devoted their energies to *these* kinds of demonstrations, they would not be demonstrating in front of the administration building.

There is also an element of what Renato Rosaldo (1989:69) calls "imperialist nostalgia" in these attitudes toward indigenous culture. Addressing primarily nineteenth-century European colonialism, Rosaldo proposes that colonial officials "often display nostalgia for the colonized culture as it was 'traditionally' (that is, when they first encountered it)." Incomers viewing these living dioramas might have imagined what it was like to be on one of the first Russian expeditions to the wilds of the Far North. Rosaldo proposes that, under imperialism, "people mourn the passing of what they themselves have transformed.... Nostalgia is a particularly appropriate emotion to invoke in attempting to establish one's innocence and at the same time talk about what one has destroyed" (ibid. 69–70). Rosaldo sternly concludes that "nostalgia at play with domination ... uses compelling tenderness to draw attention away from the relation's fundamental inequality.... Ideological discourses work more through selective attention than outright suppression" (ibid. 87). Attention in Chukotka was selectively focused on the traditional side of indigenous culture, editing out the realities of contemporary daily life for indigenous residents.

In the view of some incomers, the presence of actual indigenous residents was not even required in order for indigenous culture to be enjoyed and even preserved. For example, being Chukchi or Eskimo was not a prerequisite for a position with the state Chukchi-Eskimo ensemble *Ergyron*. In fact, not a single Eskimo was in the ensemble in the 1990s. The remaining performers were not even all Chukchis, and the artistic director of the ensemble at the time was a Buryat woman. The same was true of the many amateur performing ensembles found in the towns and villages – one did not necessarily need to be indigenous to dance with them. Indigenous residents explained this by saying they were simply nonconfrontational by nature, and would not presume to turn away an incomer who had the desire to dance with them. Moreover, the National College of Folk Arts – greatly touted as supporting the development of traditional indigenous culture – had only 50 percent indigenous enrollment, and a few nonindigenous children danced in the school's indigenous folk ensemble. Although the administration's representatives often touted the National College as an example of the generous support of the administration for the indigenous population, much of the curriculum of the college was devoted to nonindigenous art, music, and dance. All students, indigenous and nonindigenous, were required to study classical ballet and piano.

For its part, the regional administration found a way to use indigenous residents and their culture as a kind of capital.[19] As representatives of the "traditional culture" of Chukotka, indigenous residents could be used as a marketing tool to draw attention to Chukotka and help attract investors to develop mining and fishing enterprises and other forms of business. The governor himself, Aleksandr Nazarov, cited the need to show the face of Chukotka to the investing world as the justification for staging the "Days of Chukotka Culture" in November 1996, an ostentatious and expensive exhibition of "Chukotkaniana" in Moscow. For this publicity extravaganza, Nazarov flew Chukotkans of every ilk to Moscow, from indigenous dancers and singers, to museum personnel with their exhibits, to businesspeople. He even planned to fly mushers with their dogs and sleds, but bad weather grounded the flight that was to carry them from coastal Chukotka. Displays and performances were arranged in a Moscow park, and the public was invited to come and experience a taste of Chukotka.

Similarly, *Ergyron* was often used as the iconic face of Chukotka. A photo in one of Russia's national newspapers, meant to publicize a deal between the Chukotka administration and a Moscow processing plant regarding Chukotkan salmon caviar, shows the governor of Chukotka, the president of the cannery, and three smiling members of *Ergyron* dressed in traditional costume, posing with generous platters of salmon.[20] *Ergyron* was even employed as a campaigning tool during the 1996 presidential election. Governor Nazarov, as a member of former Russian prime minister Viktor Chernomyrdin's political party (*Nash Dom Rossiya*, or "Our Home is Russia," also referred to at that time as the "party of power") was expected to do his part to bring in the local vote for Yeltsin. *Ergyron* was sent on a tour of all the districts of Chukotka to "drum up enthusiasm for the election" (according to one dancer in the group), although taken in the context of the flood of pro-Yeltsin rhetoric in the administration-owned media at that time, it was clear that *Ergyron's* effort was meant to rally the vote for Yeltsin specifically.

On an everyday basis, indigenous residents were most visible in Chukotka when they dressed in their traditional costumes and performed their traditional dance and song. The many amateur ensembles in Chukotka performed on numerous occasions throughout the year at public holidays, both Russian and indigenous. Incomers usually flocked to these performances, armed with cameras and video recorders; for their own part, they claimed these manifestations of indigenous culture as part of the heritage of the region they called home (cf. Krupnik and Vakhtin 2002:20). Only in the context of indigenous residents performing or producing handicrafts did I hear praise for indigenous residents from incomers, many of whom otherwise tended to express racist attitudes toward them. This kind of public performance of indigenous culture was supported financially by the administration[21] – one of the few sources of unbegrudging government support that the indigenous population enjoyed. In fact, an entire branch of the region's educational system was designed to channel students into eventual work in performing ensembles and other culturally oriented endeavors. The regional Department of Culture established a network of village music schools in the 1990s, and the best students were selected to come to Anadyr' and enroll in the National College.

Indigenous residents clearly loved their performing traditions, and engaged in them with relish. Discussions among indigenous residents about the need to preserve and promote indigenous culture included these performance arts, but extended as well to the indigenous languages and to the traditional economies of reindeer herding and sea mammal hunting. There was ample evidence that it was precisely in the practice of traditional economies by whole indigenous families that the languages and cultural traditions were best preserved. But from the perspective of the administration, the traditional economies were nothing but a drain on resources, while the more colorful manifestations of indigenous culture at least had some usefulness to make the administration's investment in them pay off. Funding them was cheap, but could still be publicly touted as assistance to the indigenous population.

However, in order to use this "cultural capital" more efficiently, the administration needed maximum control over cultural space and indigenous representation in it, and in many ways, the administration worked to usurp the control of indigenous cultural manifestations from indigenous hands. Some of this had its roots in the Soviet period, such as the professionalization of the ensemble *Ergyron*. *Ergyron* was founded in 1968 when particularly talented performers were rounded up from Chukotka's villages and brought to Anadyr', "summoned to preserve the better examples of the national art of the minor peoples" (Dikov 1989:368). This was a common practice all across the Soviet North, and each "national area" had its own performing ensemble. But the post-Soviet period brought fresh cases of incomer cooptation of indigenous cultural productions. One such case is the administration's takeover of the native-language newspaper *Murgin Nutenut* in 1995, discussed in Chapter 1.

This created an uncomfortable paradox for indigenous residents: The loss of language and culture was one of the key concerns of the indigenous population, a concern I heard articulated over and over by many of the indigenous residents with whom I interacted; yet their own culture was a source of their exploitation by the dominant power.

Very few indigenous residents explicitly told me that they saw this as a form of exploitation; however, occasionally I would hear outbursts that signaled to me the indigenous residents' lack of satisfaction with the status quo, such as the previously mentioned comments of Nikita Suslov. Moreover, although *Ergyron* performances remained popular among indigenous residents, nearly every indigenous person I spoke to about *Ergyron* commented that the kind of dancing and singing the ensemble performed was almost laughable in terms of how little it resembled Chukchi and Eskimo dancing as they knew it, and was developed primarily to entertain those outside Chukotka (*Ergyron* has toured frequently outside of Russia, even in Europe and the United States). Moreover, many asked me rhetorically how it was possible for an ensemble to be both "Chukchi" and "Eskimo" at the same time. To outsiders, the two performing traditions looked pretty much the same, and it made sense to be inclusive and represent both indigenous traditions with one effort. But to Chukchis and Eskimos, they were distinct traditions, and it seemed a little bit absurd to lump them together.

Conclusion

The uneasy juxtaposition of Anadyr', the capital city, and Tavaivaam, the indigenous village annexed by the city, seemed to embody the awkwardness of the position of indigenous residents in Chukotkan society – forced to exist in a Russian space, and yet ghettoized into a cultural sphere within that space. The indigenous peoples of Chukotka were a small minority of Chukotka's population, and the attention their cultural performances received seemed disproportionate. Chukotka's administration continually tried to convince indigenous residents that this was a good thing, for which they should be grateful. Yet it was not indigenous culture *in vivo* that garnered this attention, but a particular, prescribed manifestation of that culture, packaged and performed for an incomer audience. The special cultural institutions that were charged with managing indigenous culture in Chukotka were guided by a Stalinist concept of culture that recognized authenticity only in particular manifestations that fit a preconceived idea of what "traditional"

indigenous culture should look like. This "traditional" indigenous culture was continually proclaimed to be dying even as new samples of it
were gathered, preserved, and displayed. Indigenous residents at times
resisted, at times accommodated this packaging of their own culture,
but either way, they could not help but notice that they got the most
attention and support when they fit the "traditional" stereotype.

1989

Malina reached for another cookie, keeping her eyes on the French folklorist as he talked to the little group assembled for tea. Could he be serious about wanting to learn to speak Chukchi? What use could they have for the Chukchi language in France! She glanced over at her friend Tonia, who returned the glance with eyebrows raised in mock incredulity, and Malina struggled to suppress a smile. So now foreigners were interested in the Chukchi, and came all this way just to have a look. May wonders never cease.

The French folklorist had started talking about his admiration for Chukchi culture. Yes, he had read Bogoraz, and he knew that the Chukchi had a deep, spiritual respect for nature, and he was very interested in shamanic practices . . .

Foo! Again with this Bogoraz! Sure, Malina had been eager to get a hold of the translation of his ethnography of the Chukchi when it had appeared not long ago, and she had enjoyed reading in such detail about her ancestors. But she was already getting sick and tired of everyone quoting him as the absolute authority on Chukchi culture. Good grief, he traveled around Chukotka for, what, a few years? And damned if she believed he was fluent enough in Chukchi to work without a translator. So how could his book embody the absolute truth about the Chukchi?

Besides, she knew that Bogoraz could not have possibly found out everything about Chukchi culture, even if he had been fluent in the language. The richest, most precious parts of her culture were private family matters, secrets that no one would have talked about with a Russian outsider. There were some things she had never even told her husband.

Well, fine, let them quote their Bogoraz, she thought. It seems to be good publicity for the Chukchi, and the devil knows, we can use it.

6

TRANSFORMATION OF LOCAL POLITICS IN CHUKOTKA

THIS BOOK ARGUES in part that a major factor disrupting the momentum of the indigenous movement in Chukotka in the 1990s was the change in local political dynamics that occurred after the collapse of the Soviet Union. The shift of power from the center to the periphery was a common experience across the Russian North, but the subsequent local political dramas took shape differently in each region. This chapter examines the particularities of local politics in Chukotka. The rise of a new figure, the "governor," and the particular character of the governor who took power in Chukotka were significant factors in the development of public and hidden transcripts in Chukotka that were so hostile to indigenous self-determination.

The Creation of Magadan Province and the Escalation of Development

To understand the political changes that took place in the 1990s, we must back up a bit and examine the changes in Chukotka's territorial-administrative status that occurred in the late Soviet period. In December 1953, Magadan Province was formed and Chukotka was subsumed within it, being transferred from its brief association with Khabarovsk Territory (Dikov 1989:288). Chukotka made up 62 percent of the territory of the new province, but nevertheless, all administrative functions were shifted to the city of Magadan, while agencies in Chukotka were reduced to the status of branch offices. Chukotka had always been technically subordinated to other administrative centers (first Kamchatka, then Khabarovsk), but the relationship had always been looser, with Chukotka maintaining a great deal of autonomy. The caveat to this, of course, is that *all* territories of the Soviet Union were fully ensconced in the central planning system, in which lines of authority ran from the local administrative organs all the way to the Presidium of the Supreme Soviet and the Politburo of the Communist Party. However, in this case, Chukotka did experience a drastic shift in its administrative functions.

The death of Joseph Stalin and the rise to power of Nikita Khrushchev in 1953 ushered in the "Thaw" period in the Soviet Union: the relaxing of the authoritarian nature of the Soviet state. Within a few years, the population of Magadan Province dropped dramatically as prisoners were released from labor camps (Stephan 1994:256). However, these reforms did not ease the pressure on Chukotkan indigenous residents by incomers; in fact, the real pressure had not even begun yet. The Soviet government was now ready to extract the fullest development potential out of the Northeast, and a fresh, productive volunteer workforce was needed. As stated in a resolution of the Magadan Province Party conference in May 1954:

> The formation of Magadan Province was a clear manifestation of the concern of the Party and the government for the further and more rapid development of the productive strength of the Northeast of our country, and for the raising of the material well-being and cultural level of the toilers in the province (Dikov 1989:288).

From here on, particular attention would be paid to organizing mining operations, consolidating state farms, preparing cadres, and searching for new forms of organization in the work of reindeer herders

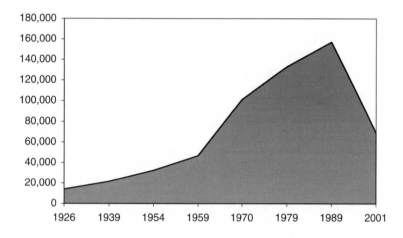

Sources: Goskomstat RSFSR 1991; Krushanov 1982:115; Leontev 1977; Petrenko 1998; Vdovin 1965; 2002 figures provided by the *Komitet Gosudarstvennoi Statistiki* online at http://www.gks-ru/PEREPIS/tabl_1.htm.

FIGURE 6.1. Population Rise and Decline in Chukotka, 1926–2002

(ibid. 289). Thus, the departing prisoners were soon replaced by young and ambitious industrial workers, attracted to the North in part by their own romantic ideals and thirst for adventure, but even more by the state's promise of high salaries, extended paid vacations, tax breaks, and other advantages (Slezkine 1994:338).

This new surge of incomers to Chukotka was the beginning of a dramatic demographic shift. Up to 1954, the incomer population of Chukotka had grown very slowly, increasing on average by only 730 people per year[1] (Leontev 1973:21). After 1954, the rate of immigration increased drastically (see Figure 6.1). Between 1959 and 1970, Chukotka had far and away the highest net gain of Russians in comparison with the rest of the Soviet Union (Kaiser 1994:176–7). Not only the rate, but also the nature of the immigration changed. In the 1930s and 1940s, the immigrants had been primarily intellectuals – doctors, teachers, agricultural specialists, and administrators (labor was handled by the prison population). A large proportion of them settled in Chukotka's villages, and for the most part they harbored optimistic ideals about helping the indigenous population, however misguided their efforts may seem to contemporary observers (Leontev 1977:11). In the

1960s and 1970s, much to the contrary, the immigrants were of a more materialistic bent – loggers, hunters, miners, and construction workers who had come *za dlinnym rublem* (meaning, essentially, "for the big bucks"). These new immigrants settled mostly in cities and industrial settlements (such as gold mining encampments). The indigenous population meant nothing to them except perhaps as a bit of exotica to be viewed on the way to the worksite.

Moreover, this new wave of immigration shifted the balance in Chukotka from a primarily rural population to an overwhelmingly urban population (see Table 6.1). These towns and cities were unequivocally nonindigenous spaces; by 1970, only 17.7 percent of all Chukchis, for example, were settled in urban areas (Savoskul 1989:114). In 1965, the year Anadyr' was officially christened a city (and thus become the easternmost city in the Soviet Union), the first apartment complexes with hot and cold running water were built, along with the House of Culture. Plans were made for a movie theater, printing house, bathhouse, and beer brewery. Anadyr' had become the dreamed-of "cultural center of Chukotka" (Krushanov 1986:71–2).

By the end of the 1980s, industrial occupations, along with the suppliers and transport services that supported them, vastly outnumbered

TABLE 6.1. Urban and Rural Population of Chukotka, 1939–2002

Year	Total Population	Urban – %	Rural – %
1939	21,500	15.3	84.7
1959	46,689	62.1	37.9
1970	101,184	69.2	30.8
1979	133,000	69.9	30.1
1989	157,000	72.6	27.4
1997	87,533	69.8	30.2
2002	53,600	66.0	34.0

Sources: Goskomstat Rossii 1994; Ivanov 1996; Kotov et al. 1995; Leontev 1977; Vdovin 1965. Figures for 2002 provided by the *Komitet Gosudarstvennoi Statistiki* online at http://www.gks-ru/PEREPIS/tabl_1.htm.

TABLE 6.2. The Structure of Employment in Chukotka in 1990

Type of Occupation	Percent of Working Population
Culture	24.8
Mineral mining	16.6
Commerce and suppliers	12.4
Transport	11.5
Other industry	9.8
Construction	7.7
Rural economy	7.2
Housing and communal services	5.9
Communications	2.0
Organs of government	1.3
Credit and finance, insurance institutions	.8

Note: "Culture" includes education, public health services, physical culture and sport, and culture and science. "Mineral Mining" includes mining for gold, tin, tungsten, and oil. "Other industry" includes nonferrous metallurgy, coal, electricity, food processing, light industry, and construction materials. "Rural economy" includes reindeer herding, hunting, fishing, and sea mammal hunting.
Source: Kotov et al. 1995:224.

other kinds of occupations in Chukotka (see Table 6.2). This period of intense industrial development in the Chukotka National Region culminated in another change in the region's status in 1980. In the wake of the new Soviet constitution of 1977, the Supreme Soviet passed a law in 1980 that changed all of the "national" regions to "autonomous" regions (Dikov 1989:375), and the Chukotka National Region became the Chukotka Autonomous Region.[2] The only reference made to the indigenous peoples in the law was in Article Twenty-Nine, which stated that measures would be taken to develop indigenous culture, art, and literature (Vakhtin 1994:9). What was formerly seen as a form of territorial self-determination for small nationalities was now seen as merely another kind of unit amid all of the other territorial units in the Soviet Union. The fact that the proportion of indigenous residents in Chukotka had fallen below 20 percent perhaps made this conceptual shift easier to accomplish (see Figure 6.2).

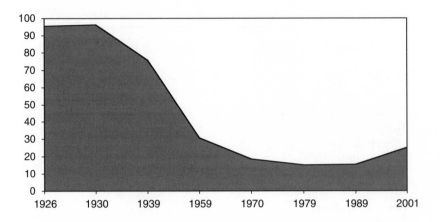

Sources: Kotov et al. 1995; Krushanov 1982:115; Petrenko 1998; 2002 figures provided by the *Komitet Gosudarstvennoi Statistiki* online at http://www.gks-ru/PEREPIS/tabl_1.htm.

FIGURE 6.2. Indigenous Population as a Percent of Total Population, 1926–2002

Given that indigenous residents were all but invisible in the law accomplishing this change, one would think they might have begun to feel threatened. However, in his role as enthusiastic apologist for the Soviet power, Vasilii Uvachan, the prolific Evenk ethnographer and Soviet people's deputy, for his part found a silver lining:

> Changing the name "national region" to "autonomous region" is a timely move and has principally theoretical and practical significance. First of all, the name "autonomous region" more fully reflects the deep socioeconomic, ethnic, and demographic changes occurring in the life of the regions, and more precisely reflects their multinational composition. Secondly, it unifies the terminology that conforms to the Soviet science and practice of governing under a determined form of autonomy (autonomous republic, autonomous province, autonomous region). Thirdly, the autonomous region is a category that reflects the contemporary level of political, economic, social, and cultural development of the peoples of the North (Uvachan 1982:26–7).

Then again, another interpretation remains evident: The change served the whims of bureaucracy and Soviet logic at the time.

Perestroika and the Declaration of the Chukotka Republic

The period of *glasnost'* and *perestroika* not only resulted in radical restructuring – that is, dissolution – of the former Soviet Union, but also affected the internal federal structure of Russia itself. In 1990, as pressure to dismantle the Soviet Union began to increase in response to a rash of national sovereignty movements all over the country, Russian Republic President Boris Yeltsin took on the role of provocateur by declaring in a speech in Tatarstan in August that all of the various territorial formations within Russia should "take as much sovereignty as they can swallow."[3] Earlier in the year, Yeltsin had stated, "I believe that, within the borders of the Russian Federation, independence *(samostoiatel'nost')* must be given to all autonomies" (Dunlop 1993:62). In response to this invitation, republics, territories, and provinces all over Russia began to declare their essential sovereignty and equal status with all other Russian territorial divisions in relation to the central federal power in Moscow.[4] Among the first was the Republic of Karelia, which declared itself sovereign within Russia in August 1990. One of the most contentious cases was Tatarstan, which went a step further and declared itself a union republic independent of Russia in September 1990, thereby seeking to elevate its status unilaterally to be equivalent to other Soviet republics such as the Ukrainian Autonomous Soviet Socialist Republic(ASSR) or the Kazakh ASSR (Graney 2001). So many declarations followed that the phenomenon was dubbed the "parade of sovereignties."[5]

This trend inspired activists among of the Nivkhi and Nanai, who were never granted their own territorial unit during the Soviet period, to attempt to create autonomous units for their people for the first time. They were greeted with derision – what had been called a "parade" when it involved republics within Russia was now called a "farce of sovereignties" when it involved the "small nationalities" of the Russian North.[6] Although in theory even these small nationalities had been granted "statehood" *(gosudarstvennost')* within the Soviet Union when national regions were created for them (Dikov 1989:192), this kind of discourse betrayed the fact that, in practice, no one really took them seriously as ethnic homelands.

Tired of living in the shadow of Magadan Province, Chukotka joined this first wave of declarations of independence. In October 1990, the Chukotka Soviet of People's Deputies (led by the Chukchi chair, Vladimir Etylin) made a unilateral decision to separate from Magadan Province. The Chukotka Soviet issued a resolution, signed by Etylin, to the Magadan Province Soviet declaring itself the Chukotka Soviet Autonomous Republic.[7] This new title was used prominently and frequently in the newspaper, and even appeared on postcards and stationery, and collected resolutions of the region's legislature in 1991 were published under this title as well. The declaration of republic status in itself is significant; by making the declaration, Chukotka showed that it not only wanted independence from Magadan Province, but it also aspired to a higher status within Russia's federal structure.

The Magadan Province Soviet vigorously objected to the move; a flurry of missives flew back and forth between Anadyr' and Magadan, culminating in a personal visit to the Chukotka Soviet of People's Deputies by the chair of the Magadan Province Soviet of People's Deputies, V. I. Kobets. According to Etylin, Kobets wagered that he could persuade the Chukotka deputies in person to veer from the path they had taken; instead, his visit hastened a vote on the matter by the Chukotka Soviet, which stood its ground.[8] The Soviet Union had in the meantime dissolved, and far-reaching changes were only just beginning to take shape at the Russian federal level. Russian law confirmed Chukotka's separation from Magadan in June 1992,[9] but Magadan appealed to the federal level, and the Russian Federation's fledgling Constitutional Court ultimately took up the matter. The Constitutional Court uphold Chukotka's separation from Magadan Province in a decision issued in May 1993.[10] Although it did not manage to retain the title of "republic," Chukotka was now legally a sovereign entity within the Russian Federation.

Chukotka was the only autonomous region to succeed in legally separating from its parent province during the 1990s. Other autonomous regions followed Chukotka's example, but without the same success: The Khanty-Mansiiskii, Yamalo-Nenetskii, and Koriaksii autonomous regions each declared sovereignty from their parent provinces, but did not legalize their declarations with court approval.

The status of all of Russia's eighty-nine "subjects of the Federation" has remained a contentious issue in Russian politics and has been redefined several times since the collapse of the Soviet Union. The first attempt came in 1992, when Yeltsin signed three collective treaties with different groups of territories: The first was with the autonomous republics, such as Tatarstan and Yakutiya; the second was with territories and provinces; and the third was with Russia's single autonomous province and ten autonomous regions, including Chukotka. A year later, the new Constitution of the Russian Federation redefined the status of all of these territories, giving all of them – even the autonomous regions that had not gained legal independence from their parent provinces – equal rights in principle with one another in relation to the federal center.[11] Then, in 1995, a further redefinition was begun when Yeltsin signed the first in a series of bilateral power-sharing treaties with individual regions, beginning with the republics; by mid-1997, Russia had signed thirty-one such agreements.[12]

When Vladimir Putin became president of the Russian Federation in 2000, a new series of policy shifts began.[13] In May 2000, Putin distributed the eighty-nine subjects of the Federation into seven "federal districts," each headed by a "presidential representative."[14] In 2001, the Russian legislature began considering a plan to reduce the total number of regions in Russia (from eighty-nine to perhaps fifty), primarily by absorbing the autonomous regions once and for all into their parent provinces or territories, thus giving them no federal status whatsoever. In a story titled "Weapons against the Districts," in the 23 January 2001 issue of the Russian newspaper *Vedomosti*, Duma Deputy Irina Khakamada neatly summed up in the following statement the small regard given the interests of the indigenous population in this process:

> There are, for example, national autonomous regions, in which a very insignificant number of the indigenous population lives, for which this territorial-administrative division all the same plays no role whatsoever. [The indigenous population] is dying out, and these regions are being mercilessly used by financial groups and are becoming the basis for pumping out money to some kind of company or another.

As of the year 2004, discussions of the restructuring of the subjects of the Federation continued, unabated and unresolved.

Dvoevlastie in Chukotka

The period of greatest administrative change that occurred within Chukotka – change that had far-reaching implications for the indigenous population – began in 1991, the year that the Soviet Union collapsed. In August of that year, Yeltsin tried to regain more control over the Communist-controlled regional soviets by personally appointing a head of administration *(glava administratsii)* in each region, a position also known as governor *(gubernator)* (Sakwa 1993:183). These were appointed alongside the existing regional leaders, which created a brief and disorienting period of *dvoevlastie*, or dual power, in Chukotka. To understand the significance of this move, it is necessary to understand what the structure of local government had looked like in Chukotka (and in virtually every region in Russia) in the late Soviet period.

The core of local government had been the Soviet of Workers' Deputies, a large elected body that met four times a year. From this body, one deputy was elected chair of the Soviet. Attached to the Soviet was an Executive Committee *(ispolnitel'nyi komitet*, or *ispolkom)*, and this also had a chair presiding over it. While the Soviet convened infrequently, the Executive Committee was a full-time body (Hahn 1988:115). By design, the Executive Committee was subordinate to the Soviet, although at the same time it was also subordinate to – and took directives from – all the Executive Committees above it, in what has been called the "vertical line of executive power" (Postnikov 1996:278). For a village in Chukotka, the superordinate Executive Committees stacked above it included those at the district, regional, provincial, and federal levels.

In theory, the Executive Committee existed to carry out the laws and decrees issued by the Soviet (Kotok and Kuprits 1950:144), which meant that it handled the hands-on running of affairs in the region on behalf of the Soviet. However, some have argued that Executive Committees acted quite independently of the Soviets, taking their orders instead from Communist Party organs higher up (e.g. Meyer 1965:283–4). While this was likely true in local Soviets of European Russia, power dynamics in the autonomous regions must be considered in the light of nationality issues. For example, although Jeffrey W. Hahn (1988:248) viewed the Executive Committee as being superior to the Soviets, his assessment is based on the assumption that Executive Committees were "typically made up of middle-aged men with a higher education." In Chukotka, not only were the Regional Executive Committee chairs always Chukchis, they were often women.

John H. Miller (1992) studied varying combinations of indigenous and Russian first and second Party secretaries in a sample of union republics and autonomous republics, and found that the patterns remained fairly consistent within particular regions (for example, the Chechen-Ingush Republic consistently had a Russian first secretary and indigenous second secretary, while Yakutiya typically reversed these roles). His conclusion was as follows:

> The top party leadership in nationality areas is a carefully designed system in which Russian and indigenous officials act as a check on one another. The Russian presence is built in for political reasons and is no longer a consequence of lack of non-Russian expertise (ibid. 202).

The same assessment could be made of the pattern found in Chukotka's Soviets and Executive Committees through the years. While the chair of the Executive Committee at the regional level was *always* a Chukchi man or woman (with a Russian deputy), the chair of the Soviet was *always* a Russian man (the Soviet itself typically included a handful of indigenous deputies). The reasons for this pattern are without doubt the very ones Miller cites for the patterns he observed. In this case, however, the Executive Committees in Chukotka were most likely not as independent of the Soviets as Miller and Hahn indicate. Given the almost universal attitude among Russians of "benevolent chauvinism" toward the peoples of the North, it seems a fair assumption that, in Chukotka, there was a strong check on the indigenous chair of the Executive Committee by both the Russian deputy chair and the Russian chair of the Soviet.

This pattern of an indigenous chair of the Executive Committee and a Russian chair of the Soviet held constant until 1990, when for the first time a Chukchi (Etylin) was elected chair of the Soviet. In synchrony with the traditional ethnic balancing act, but in reverse, a Russian (Aleksandr Nazarov) was concurrently appointed chair of the Executive Committee – in this period of *perestroika*, the long-established patterns in Chukotka were also being restructured. By 1991, local government reflected the changes in the July 1991 Law of the RSFSR "On Local Self-Government in the RSFSR." Thus in addition to the regular Soviet, which met only four times a year, a smaller group of deputies – the *malyi sovet* or "Small Soviet" – was elected, and this body met about twice a month, presided over by Etylin. This gave the Soviet a much more active role in day-to-day governing, rivaling the role of the Executive Committee (Postnikov 1996:278).

Nazarov, the new Executive Committee chair, was a relative new-comer to Chukotkan politics at the time, whereas Etylin had long been entrenched in the local Party cadres. The two remained dominant fig-ures in local politics throughout the 1990s. Etylin had been groomed as part of the indigenous intellectual elite; he was born in Omolon in 1944 to a family of reindeer herders that worked for the Omolon state farm, where his mother and other family members remained after he moved on to pursue his education. He began his political career in 1969, at the age of twenty-five, when he was elected a deputy from Chukotka to the Magadan Province Soviet. He went on from there to hold a series of Party positions in the cities of Pevek and Lavrentiya, taking a degree from the Khabarovsk Higher Party School along the way. By 1983 he was holding a position in the regional Party in Anadyr'. In 1987 he went to Moscow to pursue graduate studies in economics, but in 1989 got swept up in the campaign for elections to Mikhail Gorbachev's newly created, *glasnost'*-era Congress of People's Deputies of the USSR. He never finished the graduate degree, but in 1990 he won a seat in this Congress, which lasted less than two years (until it dissolved when the Soviet Union ceased to exist in December 1991). Also in 1990, he concurrently became chair of the Chukotka Regional Soviet – the first indigenous person to hold this position.

Nazarov, a Russian and an incomer to Chukotka, was born in north-ern Kazakhstan in 1951. He began his career in construction, eventu-ally getting a technical degree in construction engineering. He did not come to Chukotka until 1973, when he arrived to work construction at the Bilibino nuclear power plant, subsequently traveling around the North helping to construct other power plants. In 1983, he be-came the deputy chair of the Bilibino District Executive Committee, and finally advanced to regional politics in 1987, when he became the deputy chair of the Chukotka Regional Executive Committee (under its chair, Nadezhda Otke, a Chukchi woman). In 1990, he advanced to chair the Regional Executive Committee, becoming the first Russian in Chukotka to hold a position that had been delegated to Chukchis throughout the Soviet period.

These career histories are given not for the sake of understanding the particular individuals so much as because they represent a pattern that was typical of such careers throughout the Soviet period, in Chukotka as well as in other autonomous regions. An elite group of locally raised indigenous intellectuals, beginning with Tevlianto in 1937 and ending with Etylin in 1990, were groomed to assume a top leadership position in the region as loyal Party members; they were balanced by a set of Russian incomers who also worked their way up through the regional Party to their eventual position of leadership. Everyone knew the system and knew his or her role in it. Party experience could complicate the otherwise typical "colonizer-colonized" power relationship; Sofia Rybachenko pointed out to me that Etylin, who had a much longer history in the Party politics of the region, at first served as a sort of collegial mentor to Nazarov, the relative newcomer. Publicly, the two leaders had nothing but praise for one another during their years of collaboration. However, because of the ambiguousness of the new structure of local government, the two were ultimately pitted against one another in a federally aggravated power struggle of a kind that Chukotka had never before experienced.

When Yeltsin appointed his heads of administration in all the regions of Russia, seeking reform-minded candidates (as opposed to Communist Party faithfuls), the man he chose in Chukotka was Nazarov. Although Etylin himself remained ambiguous on the point, several indigenous consultees indicated that Etylin could have had this position himself if he had fought for it.[15] The general consensus among these consultees was that Etylin decided to gamble on the future of the Soviets, and he simply miscalculated. However, given that Yeltsin's motivation behind appointing the heads of administration was to consolidate regional support for his reform-oriented government, it seems unlikely that he would have chosen a born-and-bred local Party politician over one who had his deepest roots outside of the local region. Moreover, Etylin for his part still openly avowed the strengths of a socialist system (as a deputy in the Soviet Congress of People's Deputies, he was referred to in one newspaper article as "the hard-line deputy from Chukotka with a knack for saying what everyone is thinking"),[16] while Nazarov claimed to wholeheartedly embrace democratization and privatization.

The net result was that after 1991, the power structure in Chukotka became very ambiguous, with no one knowing who to look to as the ultimate authority. This new, active division of power (as opposed to a more theoretical division of authority) between the Chair of the Soviet and the head of administration was an unfamiliar concept to everyone. Evidently, the transition in Chukotka was not made smoothly. A 1991 article in the local newspaper (then still called *Sovetskaia Chukotka*) alluded to a "war of words and petty discussions of who is more important – the deputies or the administration" (29 August 1991, page 1). By mid-1992, the newspaper (now called *Krainii Sever*) printed a front-page interview with the two leaders, titled "Two in the Same Boat" (20 June 1992, page 1). The preface to the interview alluded to "sharp growing pains" being experienced by the new power structures: "we are beginning to see a tendency toward a worsening of relations between the Soviet and the administration." By December, the two organs of power were issuing admonitory resolutions directed at one another and publishing them in the newspaper.[17]

Chukotka's conflict was not entirely unique: Local Soviets and newly appointed heads of administration in regions all across Russia were experiencing similar difficulties (Sakwa 1993:183–9). A key factor at the root of these conflicts was that, in most cases, the Soviets were dominated by Communists who were suspicious of post-Soviet democratic reforms, and for their inspiration they looked to the federal Soviet (resulting in a nascent "vertical line of *representative* power" as opposed to executive power – cf. Postnikov 1996:278). The Executive Committees, on the other hand, were led by heads of administration who had been nominated by Yeltsin, and he had chosen pro-reform allies where he could. Nazarov filled this role well, remaining a loyal member of the "party of power."[18]

Chukotka's escalating conflict, along with the others across the country, was resolved cataclysmically when Yeltsin issued a decree in 1993 that summarily called for the dissolution of all local Soviets. He did this in the wake of his own irresolvable conflict with the federal Soviet, the RSFSR Congress of People's Deputies, with which he had been at loggerheads for most of that year. This impasse led to a crisis when Yeltsin ordered the Congress to be dissolved, but the recalcitrant deputies refused to adjourn, instead barricading themselves into the Russian "White House" (the federal parliament building in Moscow). Yeltsin ended the conflict by opening tank fire on the building and forcing the deputies to surrender (Dunlop 1993:322). Since most of the local Soviets across Russia had supported the resistance of the federal deputies, Yeltsin called for their dissolution as well.

Reflecting on this moment in Chukotka's history, Etylin said he personally decided to resign his post as chair of the Chukotka Soviet as a protest against Yeltsin's behavior. "It was very unpleasant," he recalled; "I decided I didn't want to be a party to that kind of thing."[19] However the events unfolded, the net result was that Chukotka no longer had a Soviet of Workers' Deputies, or a *malyi sovet*, and the head of administration alone remained the main governing power in Chukotka. Eventually a new legislative body, called the Duma, was elected in Chukotka, just as a new Duma was elected on the federal level, but in Chukotka, this organ was very weak compared to the old Soviet. In the end, it was the head of administration who clearly emerged as the victor.

The role of the head of administration continued to evolve over the next two years. In December 1995, a decree of Yeltsin's went into effect that changed the upper house of the federal assembly, the *Sovet federatsii* or Federation Council (the Duma is the lower house), from an elected body to one automatically comprised of two representatives from each region: the head of administration and chair of the local Duma. The head of administration now served both at the local level and at the federal level. At this point, the Russian president still appointed the head of administration in Chukotka; but Yeltsin finally decreed that all regions should hold elections for the position of head of administration, and such an election was held in Chukotka in December 1996. Nazarov, the incumbent, won the election and retained his seat. He remained in power until January 2001, making his tenure nearly a decade long.

Thus, the weight of administrative authority in Chukotka gradually shifted from an indigenous chair of the Soviet to a Russian head of administration. In light of this, it is important to revisit Chukotka's separation from Magadan Province, which was proceeding apace during the initial period of transformation from 1991 to 1993. Etylin signed Chukotka's initial declaration of independence. The preamble to the draft declaration[20] prominently mentioned the welfare of the less-numerous peoples of Chukotka:

> The Supreme Soviet of the Chukotka Autonomous Republic
>
> * expressing the will of the people of the Chukotka Autonomous Republic,
> * realizing the historical responsibility for the fate of Chukotka,
> * supporting the respect, dignity, and rights of the less-numerous peoples, and people of all nationalities residing on the territory of Chukotka,
> * caring for the political, economic, social, and spiritual development of the people of Chukotka,
> * testifying to the respect toward the sovereign rights of all peoples of the RSFSR and the USSR,
>
> triumphantly declares the state sovereignty of the Chukotka Soviet Autonomous Republic. . . .

Shortly afterward, in February 1991, Etylin issued two pieces of legislation in Chukotka that were unabashedly pro-indigenous: "On the Nationalities Policy of the Soviet of Peoples Deputies of the Chukotka Soviet Autonomous Republic" and "On the Draft of the Status of Communal (Clan, Family) Lands of the Less-Numerous Peoples of the North."[21] Both pieces of legislation together outlined a progressive vision of indigenous priority in the region, including land rights, that was anything but fulfilled in the decade that followed. The preamble to the resolution on nationalities policy includes the following statement: " . . . taking note that the less-numerous peoples of Chukotka, by comparison with the incomer population, have ended up in a more difficult social and economic position. . . . " This assertion is a far cry from the rhetoric of "we're all in the same boat" that later became the dominant theme of Nazarov's administration (as discussed in Chapter 2).

However, by the time the separation from Magadan was legally accomplished in 1993, Etylin was already losing the struggle for ultimate authority in Chukotka, and by the fall of that year, he was out of the government altogether. Thus, the interpretation of Chukotka's newly independent status was left in the hands of the new head of administration, Nazarov. In the next few years, it became clear that his interpretation did not give such prominent place to the interests of the indigenous population.[22]

Etylin, now effectively exiled from politics, took refuge by returning to his academic career. He was taken on at the Russian Academy of Sciences research institute in Anadyr' as the head of a division called the Laboratory of Traditional Resource Use and Ethnosocial Research, and he turned his attention to advocating the interests of indigenous peoples, particularly from an economic perspective. In later years, he admitted that doors were clearly shut to him in local Chukotkan politics and activism, so he focused his attention on the national level, participating on several Duma committees to help draft federal legislation concerning indigenous peoples (such as the law on *obshchina* that was signed into law by Russian President Putin in 2000), and helping to establish a national Union of Reindeer Herders (which he later helped to connect to the World Association of Reindeer Herders). He began to travel internationally, and became quite well known abroad among advocates of indigenous rights. He continued to make attempts to reenter local politics, running for governor of Chukotka twice in opposition to Nazarov, but as was seen in Chapter 1, there was a price to be paid for opposing Nazarov.

The "New Russian" Style of the New *Gubernator*

By the time Nazarov won election to his post in December 1996, he was referring to himself as *gubernator* (governor) as opposed to the official term *glava administratsii* (head of administration), a practice that became common throughout Russia. The first task of the new

Duma and the existing head of administration was to hammer out a new charter for Chukotka (autonomous regions were disallowed by federal law from writing their own constitutions, but could write their own charters), and the two organs struggled over how their powers would be defined in that charter. In the draft charter, written in 1995, the *gubernator* is definitively made the ultimate power and authority in the region. Article Twenty-Seven outlines the three branches of government in Chukotka – the state Duma, the administration, and the Court – and then adds a second clause that reads:

> The highest official in the Chukotka Autonomous Region is the governor of the autonomous region, leading the executive power of the Chukotka Autonomous Region. The governor of the Chukotka Autonomous Region possesses the right to veto [*otkloniat'*] laws of the Chukotka Autonomous Region passed by the state Duma of the autonomous region.

When I arrived in the fall of 1995, I heard much discussion of the struggle between the Duma and the governor, because the director of the research institute in Anadyr', where I was affiliated, was at that time also a deputy in the regional Duma. He complained bitterly that the governor had been ruling by authoritarian decree, and said that a faction of deputies was struggling to rewrite the charter so that the rule of law took precedence over the governor. However, this faction was ultimately not powerful enough to push through the changes that the director had hoped for, and he was eventually driven not only out of Chukotkan politics, but also out of his position as director of the research institute, and out of Chukotka altogether.

Comments about the governor and his policies surfaced in nearly every conversation I had with indigenous residents about current conditions in Chukotka, and with precious few exceptions, those comments ranged from cautiously critical to venomously angry. The exceptions were consistently individuals (either indigenous or incomer) whose position and/or livelihood could be threatened by a public display of disloyalty – such as the president of the regional association of indigenous less-numerous peoples, who defended the administration's policies both in my interviews with him and in the meeting of the City Association of Indigenous Peoples discussed in Chapter 1. But for most indigenous residents, the governor and the new administration emerged as a central focus of their frustrations about their predicament. The administration was seen as having completely turned its back on the indigenous peoples and their needs; the less charitable among my consultees accused the governor of outright belligerence toward indigenous residents. It was suggested that he misappropriated federal funds earmarked for indigenous needs (in spite of his bold statements that he was too generous with funds for the indigenous population) and that he allocated those funds to construction or development projects that he personally benefited from, or worse, that he was using them to build palatial homes for himself both in the "mainland" and abroad.

It is not as though Governor Nazarov's less-than-pristine profile was unique in post-Soviet Russia. His reputation was at least partly structured simply by the unprecedented process through which he came to power, and the shock this process produced in the population at large. However, by the mid-1990s, many regional governors were similarly being accused of shady dealings, and while these accusations were politically loaded, it is highly likely that in all of these accusations there was some truth. In the financial crisis that began in 1995, when people's salaries were routinely delayed, the federal government began to accuse regional leaders of misdirecting the federal funds sent to them to pay back wages.[23] However, although Nazarov was accused locally in many kitchen conversations, and although many corrupt governors were accused by name in national mass media, it was only in October 2000, when Nazarov was investigated for tax fraud,[24] that his name appeared in national media reports about this alleged corruption. This "federal cleanliness" perhaps speaks to Nazarov's cozy position at the time as a Moscow insider – on friendly terms with Moscow's powerful mayor, Iurii Luzhkov (discussed more fully in Chapter 7) – and as a reliable pillar of support in the president's political party, Our Home Is Russia.

Aside from the criticism he received at home, Nazarov also had tense relationships in his international contacts. At first, Nazarov actively pursued relationships with U.S. businesspeople, particularly in the states of Alaska and Washington. In the fall of 1994, after years of planning and negotiation, the administration of Chukotka opened a representative office in Anchorage (and in so doing became the first Russian region to open an office anywhere in the United States). The office was opened in conjunction with Chukotka's acceptance in the Northern Forum, a cooperative organization of governments in the North organized by former Alaskan Governor Steve Cowper. The administration also created a trading company called "Chukotka, Inc.," which was said to have branch offices in Moscow and New York; the company was used to facilitate the import of consumer goods, especially foods, from Alaska and Washington State to Chukotka. A special Western-style grocery store was opened in Anadyr' in 1995, and its shelves were stocked with American brands of canned goods, pasta, cooking oils, and other staples, as well as candy bars, cigarettes, and soft drinks. Nazarov even became involved in negotiations with former Alaska Governor Walter Hickel[25] on plans for a tunnel under the Bering Strait, a scheme that envisioned providing an interhemispheric transportation link for worldwide delivery of products like timber and minerals.[26]

But good foreign relations were short-lived. Chukotka fell behind on its dues to the Northern Forum and was expelled, and its "branch office" in Anchorage was closed. After an initial avalanche of enthusiastic articles in *Krainii Sever* lauding the new era of international exchange in the early 1990s,[27] articles suddenly began to appear in 1995 that attacked the activities of foreigners in the region. Visiting foreigners were accused of an attitude of cultural imperialism, and it was implied that they only wanted to snatch away artifacts of Chukotka's cultural heritage; in some cases, it was suggested that scholars who came to work in Chukotka had ulterior commercial motives. Those who were specifically attacked by name were people who had made public their criticism of the Chukotkan administration, and this criticism was virtually always in regard to the indigenous population.

One issue of *Krainii Sever* in 1996, devoted an entire page to such attacks on foreigners. Two reports by outsiders were printed: One was a translation of an article by a French journalist for the newspaper *Le Monde* that reported on conditions in Chukotka's villages and openly criticized the Chukotka administration's treatment of indigenous residents; the other was a reprint of a report on the death of ethnographer Aleksandr Pika and several other American anthropologists in a boating accident off the coast of Chukotka in 1995 (the report was written by Olga Murashko and Dmitrii Bogoyavlensky and originally printed in *Zhivaya Arktika*, a newsletter published by the Moscow branch of the International Work Group for Indigenous Affairs).[28] Each of these reports was followed up by a local commentary that attacked people and activities written about sympathetically in the outsiders' articles. In the very center of the page was a box filled with text in all capital letters that set the tone of the entire presentation:

IN THE LAST FEW YEARS SEVERAL ZEALOTS OF "NATIONAL INTERESTS OF THE INHABITANTS OF CHUKOTKA" HAVE APPEARED – IN SCIENTIFIC AND PSEUDOSCIENTIFIC CIRCLES, AMONG JOURNALISTS, FOR THE MOST PART FOREIGNERS, POLITICIANS, AND BUSINESSMEN. REPRESENTED ON THIS PAGE ARE SMALL EXAMPLES OF THIS ZEAL, AND THEY WOULD NOT BE WORTH THE ATTENTION OF THE COMMUNITY IF THEY DID NOT BETRAY A CLEAR-CUT SYSTEM OF CREATING OPPOSITION BY ONE NATIONALITY AGAINST ANOTHER, LAYING "MINES" OF LACK OF FAITH IN RELATION TO POWER, FRENZIED ACCUSATIONS OF SEPARATISM AND INCOMPETENCE. THE COLOSSAL POWERS OF THE FEDERAL AND REGIONAL PROGRAMS OF THE SUPPORT OF REINDEER HERDING, NATIONAL VILLAGES, "CHILDREN OF THE NORTH," AND SUPPORT FOR STUDENTS ARE COMMONLY KNOWN. THE BILL RUNS TO BILLIONS AND BILLIONS OF RUBLES. LESS KNOWN ARE THE FACTS OF THE UNFOUNDED ACCUSATIONS DIRECTED AGAINST CHUKOTKA ON THE PART OF THE AFOREMENTIONED ZEALOTS. TODAY WE PULL BACK THIS CURTAIN JUST A BIT, WE NAME A FEW NAMES. . . .

Although such views about the activities of foreigners were indeed held by a segment of Chukotka's population, that segment appeared to be quite small. What must mainly be kept in mind is the fact that the newspaper *Krainii Sever* was owned and financed solely by the regional administration, and as the paper's publisher, the governor of the region was able to set the paper's editorial agenda. Individuals were frequently attacked in the pages of the paper, usually in ways that sought to damage more through insinuation than outright accusation, relying on the rhetorical device of implying that the negative conclusions were inevitable from the facts at hand (when the facts were usually scanty and/or misrepresented). What the individuals under attack typically had in common was having traveled abroad (especially to Alaska), having had contacts with visiting foreigners, or being foreigners themselves. These not-so-subtle clues in the pages of *Krainii Sever* telegraphed the administration's unwritten policy that all foreign activity in Chukotka was suspect, and repercussions could be expected.[29]

Chukotka as a Closed Border Zone

The greatest chilling effect on foreign relations was Chukotka's restrictive interpretation of federal border zone policy. During the Soviet period, Chukotka had been a closed military zone. Not only were foreigners absolutely forbidden to set foot inside of Chukotka, but even Soviet citizens had to have special permission to travel there. This particularly restrictive policy was motivated by the uncomfortable closeness of America, just kilometers away from the tip of the Chukotka Peninsula. Lonely border guard outposts, huts big enough for just one or two guards, were set up along the coast facing out across the Bering Strait; such a post also stood on Cape Dionysius, just a few kilometers outside of Anadyr', with a training camp for border guards nearby.

Gorbachev's period of *glasnost'* loosened things up considerably, fostering the Chukotka–Alaska friendship exchanges of 1989–90 and the U.S.–USSR agreement on visa-free travel between Alaska and Chukotka for indigenous residents. In what was called the "melting of the Ice Curtain," access to Chukotka became remarkably open between 1990 and 1994, and even groups of tourists began to pour into Chukotka for hiking, river rafting, hunting, and gazing at the exotica of tundra plants, wildlife, and indigenous culture. In 1993, the Russian Federation approved a new constitution that included articles guaranteeing freedom of movement within and beyond Russia for both Russian citizens as well as for foreigners.[30] By the time I arrived in Chukotka in 1995, the border guard post at Cape Dionysius stood abandoned, used mainly as a warming hut by spring and fall goose hunters. However, because of the ambiguity of the legal framework governing relations between the center and periphery in Russia, as well as the lack of effective mechanisms of enforcement for laws that did exist, regional governments within the Russian Federation by default had a great deal of leeway in interpreting constitutional rights in local legislation in the 1990s.[31] By mid-decade, Chukotka began implementing policies that placed greater restrictions on movement into and within the region.[32]

In March 1994, the administration of Chukotka passed a resolution called "On the Border Regime in the Territory of the Chukotka Autonomous Region,"[33] which was in response to a federal law called "On the State Border of the Russian Federation."[34] In the federal law, the concept of closed border *zones* no longer exists; only a five-kilometer strip directly along the international border is subject to special border controls. In fact, another federal law regarding closed administrative-territorial formations – meaning areas containing military objects or where nuclear waste is stored – expressly forbids a closed area to have boundaries that coincide with any subject of the Federation or with administrative districts within such a subject.[35] The Chukotka resolution, however, through loopholes within the wording of the resolution itself, effectively maintains all of Chukotka as a closed border zone.

According to the Chukotka resolution, the movements of all persons within the 5 kilometer border strip were to be closely monitored by federal border guards, the Federal Counterintelligence Service *(federal'naya sluzhba kontrrazvedki*, or *FSK)*, and the Ministry of Internal Affairs *(ministerstvo vnutrennykh del*, or *MVD)*. Entrance to this zone was to be granted only by permission from the MVD, and a complete itinerary of movements had to be submitted in advance (Article 2.5). Moreover, residents of the zone wishing to conduct any kind of "mass social-political, cultural or other measures" (how many participants qualifies as "mass" is not indicated) had to apply for permission one month in advance, and were required to supply information about the place, time, number of expected participants, and the name of the person responsible for the event (Article 3.1).

In a 1994 interview in *Krainii Sever* (appropriately published on Border Guard Day, one of many professional holidays in Russia), a lieutenant colonel in the Chukotka Border Guard explained the new resolution thusly:

> It's no secret that the large influx of diverse adventure seekers to Chukotka has the adverse effect of creating a criminal atmosphere. Therefore, not long ago, the administration of the region, in agreement with us, passed a resolution concerning the rules of the border regime regarding the movement of citizens in the border strip. According to this resolution, arrivals to Anadyr', Mys Shmidt, and Pevek are possible without permission, but for the right to further movement, they should receive from the border guards a special pass.[36]

Since Chukotka is so heavily settled along its coast, the 1994 resolution names thirty-five towns and villages – roughly half the number of towns and villages in the entire region – to which these rules apply. Although the resolution specifies only a 5 kilometer strip along the border in which these rules are active, a clause in the resolution (in Article 3.3) states that outsiders are forbidden without the permission of border guards to travel more than 50 kilometers from a populated point. This loophole extends the restrictions of the border regime far beyond the delineated 5 kilometer strip, and amounts to maintaining Chukotka as a closed border zone.

Enforcement in the 1990s was nowhere near as strict as in Soviet times, but the law was selectively enforced to suit the whims of the local administration – and one of those whims was clearly demonstrated to be keeping close tabs on the activities of outsiders in Chukotka, where "outsiders" included both foreigners and Russian citizens from outside the borders of Chukotka. For example, in the summer of 1995, two "outsider" scholars (one from Australia and one from St. Petersburg) were detained (in separate incidents) upon their arrival in Anadyr' and threatened with deportation on the grounds that they did not have the city of Anadyr' listed on their visa as one of the places they intended to visit.[37] This ostensibly violates the clause in the law stating that all itineraries must be preapproved. The Russian scholar did not intend to stay in Anadyr' – he was merely passing through on his way to conduct research elsewhere, and he had permission to visit that place. However, since Anadyr' is located on an inlet of the Bering Sea, it is technically within the border zone. Most incoming flights to the region come to the Anadyr' airport, making a stopover in that city hard to avoid. In fact,

Chukotka in the 1990s had very few flights that arrived at airports in its interior, beyond the border zone. Since nearly everyone arrived from the outside to a coastal town or city, and since movement inland from any point on the coast required permission, unmonitored movement anywhere within Chukotka rarely occurred.

In practice, there were even more restrictions, which remained on the level of oral lore until September 1998, when a "Procedure for the Entry of Foreign Citizens and Persons Without Citizenship into the Chukotka Autonomous Region" was finally published.[38] This document followed a few months after an amendment to a federal governmental resolution that added Chukotka to an already existing list of regions in Russia with special regulations for visits by foreigners, an amendment that I suspect was made as a result of Nazarov's lobbying at the federal level.[39] Chukotka had in practice been imposing such special regulations since 1994, as I personally experienced. The 1998 published procedures clarified that, for a foreigner to gain entry into Chukotka, a letter of request had to be addressed to the governor, not by the individual, but by a "responsible organization." If approved, the governor's office would issue a *rasporiazhenie* ("order" or "decree") granting the request and specifying certain conditions (by 2000, a condition began appearing on these decrees requiring researchers to present a copy of all research materials to relevant agencies of the Chukotkan administration). Having a Russian visa was not sufficient for entry to Chukotka – one had to have a decree from the governor as well. Eventually, having the governor's decree was no longer sufficient either – in 2000, a final step was added (in practice) of obtaining a special pass from the Chukotka border guard *prior* to arrival in Chukotka. Without all of these documents in hand upon arrival, visitors could be turned back at the Anadyr' airport, even if they had flown in from elsewhere within Russia. All domestic flights coming to Anadyr' were forced to wait on the tarmac while a border guard inspected the passport of each passenger. Foreign passports were collected, taken to the border guard station at the airport, and registered.

In conversations with Chukotkans, I occasionally pointed out that federal law prohibited an entire region from being a closed zone, but few believed me – it was clear that virtually all Chukotkans believed that the region remained closed as it had been in the Soviet period, only with a more liberal policy for allowing visitors. While I personally chafed against the border restrictions, I occasionally heard them defended, as often by indigenous residents as by incomers. The general consensus was that the tight controls protected the inhabitants of Chukotka from the various rabble that might otherwise slip in – and the examples of such rabble most often cited were criminals, Chechens, drug dealers, and "Gypsies."[40] However, for locals, the border controls had the potential to deeply disrupt daily life. The stipulation in the resolution that the border guard must first approve all public "cultural gatherings" effectively disallowed spontaneous performance of culture in communal gatherings and inserted the government into the practice of culture. This was a rather disconcerting tangible manifestation of the attitude expressed in the newspaper articles quoted in Chapter 2 – that indigenous residents had no need to do anything that was exclusive of other nationalities.

Conclusion

Before mid-century in Chukotka, it was the development of the indigenous peoples that was nominally the focus of attention in the region; but when the post-Stalinist thaw opened the way for development of industries like gold mining, express concern for the indigenous peoples began to be pushed aside. This was manifested not only in the change of the region's name from "national" to "autonomous," but also in the changing character of Chukotka's ever-increasing incomer population, which became less romantic and more utilitarian. Indigenous peoples still had a role in Chukotkan social and political life, but they were increasingly expected to "keep up" with their incomer counterparts.

Chukotka experienced a radical transformation in its political structure and character beyond even the overall transformation that resulted from the collapse of the Soviet Union. Seen from a distance, the Chukotkan administration of the 1990s appeared rather schizophrenic. On the one hand, it seemed to encourage and actively foster open interaction and exchange with interested parties from abroad, as evidenced by the opening of the administration's "branch office" in Anchorage and its membership in the Northern Forum. But on the other hand, it seemed to foster xenophobia and hostility toward outsiders, as evidenced by the border zone law and the practice of harassing visiting foreigners, as well as the discourse of articles in its regional newspaper. After the first successful "friendship exchanges" of 1989–90, many more groups interested in tourism, business, scientific research, and aid missions began to organize and prepare to undertake projects in Chukotka; most of them gave up after a few years of struggle with local authorities. Chukotka's administration seemed to be torn between the desire for the material benefits of capitalist enterprise and the loathing of forfeiting any measure of control over the activities occurring in the region. Having dozens of outsiders roaming freely about the region ultimately proved too threatening, and the region was locked down.

For the indigenous peoples of Chukotka, the net result of the transformation of local government and politics in Chukotka was twofold. First, it brought about an overall process of "reverse indigenization" of cadres in the region. As discussed in Chapter 4, Lenin's policy of indigenization *(korennizatsiya)* placed members of local national groups in positions within government and industry. Although this policy was implemented inconsistently (flagging the most during the Stalin period), in Chukotka it had resulted in a very stable pattern of indigenous representation in administrative positions at the federal, regional, and village levels. When the principle of democracy (that is, "majority rules") edged out the principle of indigenization in the 1990s, indigenous representation was very quickly swept away from federal and regional positions, and Russians predominated. The effect was not as severe at the district and village levels, and this is most likely related to the process of outmigration (discussed in Chapter 7) that removed so many incomers from the personnel pool.

The second effect on indigenous residents was that they had to look all the more beseechingly to the federal government for protection, since in relative terms the most progressive policy regarding indigenous peoples in Russia was coming from the federal. This, however, placed indigenous residents in a "catch-22" situation. Getting precedents set at the federal level was the most feasible approach for building a consistent policy, but federal laws were useless unless their implementation could be enforced at the local level. Yet legal reform in Russia was proceeding very slowly, and enforcement mechanisms were weak, if they existed at all. Nevertheless, many indigenous activists (and nonindigenous advocates) continued to push for the passage of federal laws that reflected indigenous rights, reasoning that a foundation had to be laid for the future. In the meantime, the predicament for indigenous residents was clear: How do you define a space for yourself when your role in the system is no longer supported by law, or by precedent, or by the willingness of the dominant population to share space and resources with you? Moreover, the political situation in Chukotka was only half the story. There were also deep socioeconomic problems that were wearing down everyone in Chukotka, but which had the most devastating effect on the indigenous population. These problems are addressed in Chapter 7.

1996

Malina eased her heavy frame into a kitchen chair with a sigh. She put on her reading glasses and again took up the telegram from her daughter in St. Petersburg. "Mama – please send 2 mil. rubles – stipend delayed again – kisses – Nadia." Malina shook her head and sighed again. Another 2 million rubles? A month's pay, for heaven's sake. She hadn't seen a paycheck in two months; it seemed like nobody was getting paid anymore. And yet we all keep trudging to work, she thought; but what else could you do? At least her pension came through every month, and her husband's, but that was barely enough to feed the two of them. Who knew when the construction boss would ever pay him his back salary? They still had 5 million rubles in their savings account, but little by little they were nibbling it away. Her husband Yuri was a generous man; she knew he would let her send Nadia the stipend money from their savings, even though Nadia wasn't his daughter.

Of course, she couldn't refuse Nadia the money. She was glad Nadia had gotten so far in college. Nadia's life had been so easy for her – but that is how Malina had wanted it for her daughters. They were born and raised in a Russian world – they had none of the naiveté that she had when she was growing up. They already knew things about Russian ways that it had taken her a lifetime to figure out, and she hoped that meant they would not experience the shocks that she had in her own encounters with the incomers. And they were half-Russian themselves. "Live among wolves and you'll howl like a wolf," as the saying went. Yes, Nadia could make it in St. Petersburg, and Malina was glad of it – what future was there for her back home in Chukotka anyway? Oi, things had gotten so hard! It had been hard when the Soviets were in power – who would have thought it could get even worse?

How long these Russian guests had stayed! How long she had tolerated them, bitten her tongue, turned the other cheek. And now at last many of them were leaving. For a moment she had been afraid Yuri would leave, too, and she hinted this to him one day. "Malinochka," he had said tenderly, "Wherever you are is my home. I'm not going anywhere." He was a good man. She was lucky. Malina sighed and reached for her purse. She found her little bankbook inside and flipped through its pages. If she went down to the telegraph office right now, she could wire the money to Nadia in time for her to get it the next day. She got up to get her coat.

7

SOCIOECONOMIC CONDITIONS
IN POST-SOVIET CHUKOTKA

IN THE SOVIET period, although living conditions in the North were difficult and good housing was often in short supply, at least everyone – indigenous and nonindigenous – could count on receiving a regular paycheck and having access to staple foods (that is, the foods were available on the shelves of shops *and* people could afford to pay for them). Health care was not of the best quality, but everyone had access to it, and even reindeer herders in the tundra could be flown to the central hospital in Anadyr' for treatment. The system had many imperfections, but people at least felt there was a comprehensible logic to it, and they knew how to navigate through it. In the 1990s, access to food, housing, and health care had become progressively more unequal and unpredictable. People no longer perceived any order to the system, but saw it rather as a free-for-all, and those with the most power got the goods. I often heard both incomers and indigenous residents use the phrase "*Vse sami po sebe*" to describe this atmosphere: "It's everyone for himself."

The 1990s were a difficult time for everyone in post-Soviet Russia. Nationwide economic crises wore down all segments of the population:

raging inflation and the failure of salaries to keep pace; the break-down in the supply of consumer goods resulting in nearly empty shop shelves in the late 1980s, to be remedied by the subsequent return to the shelves of consumer goods at prices hardly anyone could afford; and then the delays in the payment of salaries to state-sector workers, sometimes for months on end or even years. Moreover, many Soviet citizens felt demoralized by watching the country they had grown up in, the only country they had ever known, dissolve before their eyes, and then watching an already corrupt political system become much worse. From the perspective of ethnic Russians, the demoralization was compounded by the sense that the "Great Russians" of the past were no longer great, but had to go begging to the West for alms and for moral permission to rebuild their entire system anew according to an alien design.

On the other hand, if those at the "top of the heap" – the Russians – had plummeted this far, how much farther fell indigenous peoples, who had always been relegated to the bottom as "little brothers" in the fraternity of Soviet peoples? With only token exceptions, incomers had consistently occupied the top tier in all social spheres. They were the top management in the Party, in government positions, in indus-try, on collective farms, and in all important cultural institutions. As virtually everyone in the country scrambled to grab a share of a rapidly shrinking pie of opportunities, incomers were in the best position to get a slice. They could more successfully start business ventures be-cause they had the reserve capital (from their stronger earning power) and/or because they were better plugged into a network of recipro-cal relationships, the very patron-client networks they had used under the Soviet system to fulfill the otherwise impossible economic plans handed down from above (Hendley 1996). They could also use their connections to pursue higher education that led to greater employa-bility and earning potential. If they wanted to relocate to take greater advantage of opportunities elsewhere, as relatively recent immigrants they still had the kin networks in other parts of Russia to facilitate the transition.

Indigenous residents, on the other hand, lacked the training, ex-perience, connections, and financial resources to take advantage of the new capitalist rules in Russia (Bond 1994:304; Humphrey 1991). Although the achievements of the indigenous intelligentsia were publicly emphasized, it was actually only a tiny fraction of indigenous residents who successfully "made it" into top positions, whether in administration (such as the handful of Chukchi chairs of the Regional Executive Committee), economic management (such as the odd indigenous collective farm manager or state-sector geologist), or cultural enlightenment (such as the celebrated Chukchi writer Iurii Rytkheu). Most educated indigenous residents were tracked into postsecondary training programs resulting in low-paying jobs in culture and education. A report on indigenous employment in Chukotkan administrative and legislative organs, distributed at the 1997 Congress of Indigenous Less-Numerous Peoples of Chukotka,[1] showed that only 8.5 percent of employees in regional administrative organs were indigenous, and only 3.2 percent of employees in local organs of the federal government in Chukotka were indigenous. In district administrative organs, the figure was higher, 16.4 percent; however, when one factors out positions in the "national villages" (where indigenous residents were the majority population) and includes only positions in the higher administration of the districts, the figure drops to 4.6 percent. This was at a time when indigenous residents comprised nearly 20 percent of the overall population of Chukotka (see Table 3.1).

In general, Chukotka's indigenous residents experienced greater unemployment and decreased earning potential after 1991. The state farm system that had accounted for a majority of indigenous employment was falling apart in the wake of privatization. The once officially valorized (and relatively well-paid) reindeer herder was now looked upon with pity and often derision as government subsidies were abruptly withdrawn from reindeer enterprises. Those whose jobs had disappeared (or whose jobs still technically existed but no longer paid them any cash salary) had a difficult time finding employment elsewhere. Many moved to the cities in search of new jobs, but as will be discussed later in this chapter, most of them ended up unemployed or underemployed and either crammed in small apartments with relatives or relegated to poor housing (or both).

David G. Anderson (1996) proposes the idea of the citizenship regime to describe how one's place in Soviet society was in part defined by the particular bundle of rights that came with one's nationality as defined by the state (cf. Humphrey 1999). The less-numerous peoples of the North were a special category of Soviet citizen whose social position was in many ways officially privileged, not only by Lenin's policy of indigenization, but also by the many special rights that were granted to them by virtue of being less-numerous peoples. However, with the collapse of the Soviet system and the introduction of principles of democracy and the market into the Russian political and economic system, citizen regimes were changing. Writing of Evenkis and Dolgans in the Taimyr Autonomous Region, Anderson argues that the democratic reforms "impoverished their position materially, socially, and also in terms of the capacity to participate in a wider division of labor" (1996:111). Similarly, Chukotkan indigenous residents were experiencing a kind of erasure of the ideologically enfranchised position in society they once had. A prominent component of the new public transcript in Chukotka was that in a democratic system, the majority rules, and that meant indigenous residents had to fight their way along on footing that was supposedly the same for everyone.

In this chapter, I present an overview of the social and economic conditions in Chukotka in the mid-1990s, such as crumbling infrastructure, population shifts, demographic crises, and interethnic tensions that went along with a growing gap between rich and poor. In my conversations with indigenous residents, they continually raised the same set of problems as the most troublesome and of the greatest concern to the indigenous population – alcoholism; economic and social collapse in the villages; poverty stemming from the latter; and the deteriorating psychological state of the indigenous population, which was leading to more and more suicides. It is a bleak picture. While the public transcript trumpeted the idea that all Chukotkans were in the same boat and had to work together to solve their common problems, the indigenous hidden transcript articulated the suspicion that the Russian-dominated administration was deliberately trying to do away with them.

Material Conditions of Life in the 1990s

The physical infrastructure of Chukotka was disastrously crumbling in the 1990s. Everything from buildings to roads to electrical and energy systems was in need of renovation or complete reconstruction. The communication infrastructure was a particular problem, ranging from very poor in the cities to completely broken down in rural areas. Most Anadyr' and Tavaivaam apartments had telephones, but by no means did they all, and the waiting period to have a telephone installed was estimated to be anywhere from months to years. The startup costs were prohibitive for many residents, so they simply made do without telephones. Direct dialing was possible within Chukotka, although connections between towns often failed unpredictably. Long-distance calls within or beyond Russia's borders had to be placed through an operator, and the caller might wait an hour for the call to go through. Consequently, telegrams – something that seems rather old-fashioned in the West – were a quick and cheap alternative that was used often. Postal mail was also a reliable method of communication, but moved very slowly and stopped altogether if air transportation was grounded due to storms or budget shortfalls. Electronic mail began to appear in Chukotka by the mid-1990s, and was used by a select few residents, but users were hindered by antiquated telephone lines, which also made browsing Internet sites impractical.

One thing Anadyr' had no problem with in the 1990s, surprisingly, was retail commerce. Residents often commented incredulously on the number of shops per capita that existed in the city and speculated on how long they all could last. Over the years, I saw many new shops open, and saw a few close down as well. Although some shops specialized in food items, most were identical to one another – they all carried the same maddeningly mixed array of goods, from shampoo to clothing to electronics. One department store at least had enough physical space to sort these items out into various sections, but most shops were tiny and therefore crammed everything together on shelves behind a counter or in glass display cases. A few shops stocked household appliances, from coffee makers to refrigerators, and the city had two computer stores. A common topic of conversation and gossip was the presumed greediness of many of these shop owners, who were be-coming noticeably enriched by their retail businesses. Profit making was easy, since goods were purchased in Moscow, flown in relatively cheaply, and sold at a 300–500 percent markup. Many of my consul-tees insisted there was an agreement among merchants to keep prices consistently high in all shops.

Many Russian-produced food products were available in Chukotka, but in 1996, I saw an increasing representation of imported products from Europe, Asia, and the United States. Late in that year, near the end of my first research trip, I experienced a kind of inside-out culture shock when I walked into Anadyr's one department store and saw that Honey Maid graham crackers had suddenly appeared on the shelf, along with Blue Bunny ice cream, Famous Amos cookies, and honey in plastic bears. The apples I bought there bore Washington State stickers, and the eggs were actually sold in an egg carton, rather than being placed gingerly in a plastic bag by the store clerk, as was the usual practice. It was clear from the company names on the produce boxes that there had been shipments from the Pacific Northwest of the United States, and I later learned that a trade agreement had recently been made between Seattle-area distributors and several regions of the Russian Far East. All of these goods were generally more expensive than Russian products, but people were still lining up to buy them, evidence that at least a segment of the population was earning enough salary to have discretionary income. It must be said that shopping anywhere in Russia in the mid-1990s was a bit surreal, since one had to tote wads of cash to do it. Because of the inflation that ravaged the Russian economy after the collapse of the Soviet Union, the ruble was greatly devalued. The ruble–dollar exchange rate in 1995–6 (before the redenomination that knocked three zeroes off the ruble) was about five thousand to one. Consequently, most prices were marked in thousands and tens of thousands of rubles. The extra-high prices in Chukotka only exac-erbated this. In 1996, a roll of toilet paper cost 7,000 rubles in Anadyr', a carton of milk 22,000 rubles, a kilogram of apples 32,000 rubles. A shopper had to carry literally hundreds of thousands of rubles in hand to accomplish the day's shopping. Although a few stores in Anadyr' had purchased electronic cash registers, many store clerks still added up customer purchases on a wooden abacus – and to see them tally figures in the thousands on these devices was rather awe-inspiring.

The cost of living in Chukotka in the 1990s was unequivocally the highest in the country. While the minimum monthly living wage (that is, the minimum amount on which a person could supposedly survive) in Russia as a whole was 254,300 rubles in 1995, in Chukotka it was 818,000 rubles – more than triple the national average.[2] Actual salaries were correspondingly high. A law passed in 1932[3] entitled people working in the North to receive a 10 percent increase on their salaries for every year of work in the North, up to 100 percent of the original salary. This formula has been tinkered with over the years, but in 1995–6, there were still salary increases for working in the North, in the form of percentage bonuses and a supplement known as the "district coefficient." Northerners were also entitled to special privileges, such as having all moving expenses to and from the North paid for, receiving early retirement, and being guaranteed a state-provided apartment in central Russia upon their retirement from work in the North.[4] There was a time when these high salaries lured workers to Chukotka because prices remained relatively low in comparison, but in the 1990s, it began to be hardly profitable to work in the North. Moreover, paychecks in both public and private sector professions were delayed, sometimes for several months. It was commonly understood that regional administrators delayed salary payments of public employees in order to invest the funds and pocket the interest – as people often said to me, *"Den'gi kriutiatsia"* ("The money is circulating").

This fact of salary delays, as well as increasing unemployment as many enterprises failed (especially in rural areas), meant that many Chukotkans for the first time experienced real poverty. Statistics on unemployment were first gathered in 1992.[5] At first, many were able to rely on savings they had built up through their working years in the Soviet period; but after several bank crises that routinely wiped out savings accounts all over Russia, those who found themselves unemployed were left truly destitute. With the reorganization and nominal privatization of the entire state farm system throughout Russia, even those who were technically employed by former state farms in Chukotka (and these were overwhelmingly indigenous residents) in fact stopped receiving any cash salary by 1992 or 1993. Increasingly, extended families in villages collectively relied on the only sources of cash they had, which were various forms of government pensions (for retirees, for single mothers, for disabled children, and so on), and occasional profits from the sale of poached wildlife. If incomers found themselves in need of cash, they were more likely to turn to blackmarketing of alcohol in villages. All too often, pension payments went straight from the hands of despondent villagers to alcohol peddlers, while families went hungry or unclothed (this situation is discussed further later in this chapter).

While signs of poverty were visible in the 1990s, even in Anadyr', signs of wealth were just as visible – some people did have jobs, and some of those jobs paid well. The highest-paying positions in Chukotka were those in sea transport, the legislative-judicial system, mining and energy work, and banking (Ivanov 1996). Although the buildings in Anadyr' were dingy and uninviting from the outside, with dark and graffiti-covered stairwells, behind some of the apartment doors lay beautifully appointed and comfortable homes outfitted with washing machines and kitchen appliances (the most popular brands being Tefal and Bosch), name-brand Japanese television sets and stereos, and Pentium computers. On the streets, wealthier people appeared impeccably dressed in the latest Moscow styles, men in glossy leather coats, and women draped in fur from head to toe with perfectly coordinated gloves, purses, and boots.

The identity of the city's elite seemed almost desperately tied to Moscow, so much so that I came to refer to Anadyr' as "Little Moscow." Marina Peliave, my Chukchi colleague at the research institute, observed that "Muscovite airs" were especially strong in the fall, when families were returning from their vacations to the *materik* (the "mainland") and had just flown in from Moscow, but by the middle of winter they had begun to wear off. Ties between Anadyr' and Moscow were quite strong. Nonstop jet flights traveled between the two cities several times a week. The governor, Aleksandr Nazarov, was very much a Moscow insider during his tenure, and in his position as governor was obliged to travel to Moscow often, since regional governors simultaneously served in the federal upper house of legislation.[6] Nazarov was personal friends with the mayor of Moscow, Iurii Luzhkov, and in August 1996 Luzhkov paid a three-day visit to Chukotka, during which the two signed an agreement on mutual cooperation.[7] One of the first tangible manifestations of that cooperation came in November 1996, when Luzhkov helped Nazarov stage the ostentatious "Days of Chukotka Culture in Moscow," described in Chapter 5. Chukotkans, indigenous and incomer alike, were annoyed when public money was spent on what they saw as frivolous occasions and junketing, while obvious signs of poverty were only increasing around them, and in many conversations I heard Nazarov reviled for this.

Perhaps the most offensive manifestation of what was considered Nazarov's ostentatiousness was an expensive gift made to Luzhkov on the occasion of Moscow's 850th anniversary in 1998. Nazarov commissioned a china factory in the Moscow suburb of Likino-Dulevo[8] to custom-manufacture a large set of fine china for the gift. Moreover, he ordered a smaller, duplicate set to be put on display at the regional museum in Anadyr', where it covered a large, round table. A placard accompanying the display read: "This service was presented as a gift to the city of Moscow in honor of her 850th anniversary by Governor Aleksandr Viktorovich Nazarov on behalf of the people of Chukotka with wishes of prosperity and well-being." The irony of this gift's opulence was not lost on anyone, and was only reinforced by the fact that, upon exiting from the museum, one saw buildings falling to ruin, and went home to hear radio news reports of villages going without heating fuel and food deliveries as a result of budget shortfalls.

Privatization and Outmigration

As discussed in Chapter 6, Chukotka experienced a massive influx of immigrants from the temperate zones of the Soviet Union, primarily Russians and Ukrainians, over a period of about thirty-five years (the second half of the Soviet period). Although the rate of immigration proceeded gradually after an initial jump, when compared to the rates of population growth in the first half of the Soviet period, the overall increase in population during the twentieth century seemed cataclysmic. The population peaked at almost 160,000 by the time of the 1989 census. Over the next few years, Chukotka experienced another dramatic demographic shift as that number began to drop. As Russia tailspinned into economic crisis, people who had migrated to Chukotka in response to the offer of lucrative material benefits no longer had any incentive to stay. Many had always despised the harsh climate anyway, and felt a sense of isolation from what they considered the centers of culture back in the "mainland" (Kotov et al. 1995:225). Non-Russian incomers to Chukotka began to feel the siren call to return to their own homelands – to Ukraine, Belarus, Armenia, and so on. Beginning in 1990, the population of Chukotka began to decline, and its fall was far more rapid than its rise. In 1995 alone, 4,620 people immigrated, while 13,925 emigrated, for a net loss of 9,300 people – virtually all of them incomers (Ivanov 1996). By 1996, the peak population in the region had been reduced by almost half, to around 90,000. While the population of Anadyr' was 17,000 in 1991, by 1996 it had dropped to 12,875 (Goskomstat-SSSR 1991; Petrenko 1998).

Chukotka was not the only region of Russian experiencing population shifts at this time; people were relocating all over the former Soviet Union. Russians began returning from the former Soviet Republics, especially from Central Asia (Chinn and Kaiser 1996), and this was accompanied by a great deal of internal migration within Russia. Most people relocated to the central and southern regions of European Russia – to the Black Earth and Volga regions especially. The Russian Far East in general was the largest donor of internal migrants during this time, but Chukotka had by far the largest percentage change in population of any region in the entire country. Chukotka experienced a 48.3 percent drop due to outmigration between 1989 and 1996, while the next highest percent drops were found in Magadan Province with 36.8 percent and the Evenkiiskii Autonomous Region with 20.5 percent (Heleniak 1997:86–8). This mass exodus of incomers meant that, for the first time, indigenous residents began to see a slight gain in the relative proportion of their population in Chukotka (see Figure 6.2). In 1989, indigenous residents comprised only 10 percent of the total population of Chukotka, but throughout the 1990s that figure climbed steadily. Outmigration was still continuing at the end of the decade, although at a slower rate.

The immediate effect of this outmigration was the vacating of professional and managerial positions, especially in the villages (Vakhtin 1994:8–10). The first to leave were those with the most available resources to make the move – those with cash and connections back in European Russia – and it was the recently arrived managers and professionals in the cities who were in the best position to get out (as discussed in Chapter 5, incomers in general had the most control over their own mobility). These first outmigrants were followed in droves by others, while those who could not manage to leave the region altogether endeavored to at least get out of the harsh living conditions of the villages and move into the cities. This left a patchwork of vacant positions in Chukotka's villages, and created a sense of constant movement in Anadyr'. The entrances to shops were plastered with fliers advertising vacant apartments, as well as furniture, televisions, and other household items for sale, as those who were leaving sought to lighten their load.

This massive outmigration was not entirely spontaneous. The Russian federal government recognized that, given that it had to subsidize the high salaries paid in the North (and correspondingly high pensions), it would never be able to support all of the pensioners living there and have any hope of developing the economy further. In 1993, the Russian Federation passed a law that essentially reaffirmed the system of privileges for workers in the North, but also provided financial assistance to state-sector workers who wanted to relocate outside of the North (Bond 1994). This assistance included payment for all expenses associated with moving oneself and one's belongings, as well as the promise of a government-provided house or apartment back in the Russian "mainland." The issue of getting the local administration to deliver on this federal promise was one of the most commonly reported items in Anadyr's newspaper, *Krainii Sever*, and one of the most frequent features of the governor's campaign speeches was to review the numbers of apartments already provided and make promises to deliver more until all outmigrants were accommodated. Nevertheless, some incomers who desperately wanted to leave remained unable to do so, and in my conversations with such residents, I often heard the phrase *"My zalozhniki Severa"* ("we are hostages of the North").

My consultee Sofia Rybachenko offered an ironic perspective on this arrangement that highlights the unintended consequences that federal policies so often have for the indigenous population (but which sometimes seem to indigenous residents to be a willful intention to keep them down and out – and to the extent that ignorance and omission can be willful, they may be correct). All apartments in the Soviet Union had been provided by the government up until the collapse of the Soviet Union, after which a sweeping privatization program was implemented in Russia beginning in June 1992 (Boycko et al. 1995). One aspect of that program allowed residents of apartments to become the owners of those apartments cost-free simply by registering some documents with the city administration, and inhabitants of Anadyr' took advantage of this opportunity in droves. Since the population of Anadyr' was predominantly nonindigenous, very few indigenous residents became owners of desirable city apartments. When Sofia's eighteen-year-old daughter was ready to move into an apartment of her own in 1992, Sofia had to purchase it for her from a Russian family that was leaving the area for two million rubles – which at the time seemed like an impossible sum, but which she could take out of her still-intact savings.

What was ironic to Sofia was the fact that, at the same time as all of this was occurring, there was a general discourse among the incomer population about the "dependent nature" of indigenous residents – a phenomenon given the label *izhdivenchestvo*, which evoked an image of parasitism (as was mentioned in Chapter 3 – see footnote 19). In the first place, Sofia argued, indigenous residents were hardly to blame for the position they found themselves in, after the Soviet government had come in and taken over virtually every aspect of their lives. But what goaded her most of all was the refusal of incomers to characterize their own position as one of dependency. As she saw it:

> The incomers get to sell their apartments, and then they get free containers[9] to transport their belongings, and they get houses built for them back in the mainland. And what is that? That's not dependency? Why? In what sense are they better? Please!

From Sofia's point of view, there was a desperate need among the indigenous residents for housing in the city, as great a need as there was for housing back in the "mainland" for emigrating incomers. In many cases, large extended families were living together in one-room apartments, and in Tavaivaam, many of these had no plumbing at all. Given this state of affairs, she said, the government could have easily taken back the apartments that they had given to incomers for free and passed them along to needy indigenous families.

In fact, the need for housing for indigenous families in Anadyr' had reached an unprecedented intensity by the mid-1990s, and it was directly related to the chain reaction that the process of outmigration had triggered – a process that was in turn triggered by the difficult economic conditions that prevailed in the Russian North in the early 1990s. As incomers vacated positions in the cities, people living in the villages began to flock to fill those positions. Life in the city seemed incomparably better than life in the village, where any plumbing at all was rare, and even rarer were the fresh fruit, vegetables, and dairy products that were so common in the Soviet period. Those leaving the villages included many indigenous residents, but incomers were the most likely to leave (inversely, while indigenous residents were the most likely to stay behind in the villages, some incomers did also, for a wide variety of reasons). Departing incomers vacated the top tier of management positions in the village. For example, in Snezhnoe, the head clerk in the village administration, the head economist in the state farm, and the bank clerk had all gone, and it was difficult to find trained replacements for them. In fact, the economist remained unreplaced, while the administrative clerk was replaced by an indigenous woman who had not been sent to Anadyr' for the training necessary to maintain village records properly. The village bank branch was simply closed, forcing villagers to travel 18 kilometers to the town of Ust'-Belaia in order to manage their finances. Many other technical and laboring positions were also vacated in the village.

The 1992 privatization program resulted in the withdrawal of most federal subsidies for the state farms – they were expected to reform themselves into small business and make their own profit to support themselves, just as other commercial enterprises throughout the country were doing. The former state farm itself was expected to at least be self-supporting and pay salaries to its employees out of its own profits. The only things the state delivered were certain supplies for the reindeer herders, and even these became increasingly sparse (Gray 1997). State farm employees, accustomed simply to putting in their day of work and receiving their paycheck, waited in vain for salaries to appear, having no idea what else they could do. By 1996, they had not received a paycheck for three years; they and their families survived by taking groceries on credit from the village store (when the store was willing) and supplementing this with reindeer meat ("sold" to them on credit by the state farm), fish caught in nets in the Anadyr' River, and berries, mushrooms, and pine nuts gathered in the tundra around the village. A few villagers kept gardens and greenhouses with vegetables like tomatoes, cucumbers, carrots, potatoes, cabbages, and greens.

Those on the budget of the village administration (known as *budzhetniki*), on the other hand, received a more regular and substantial salary, since the administration was not dependent on any kind of market principle but was still simply part of the state sector. These were workers in the school, the medical station, the mayor's office, the bathhouse, and so on. Because their salary was more reliable, the village store was more willing to extend credit to the *budzhetniki* than to state farm employees, knowing that payment was more likely to follow before long. This provided a strong incentive for those working in the already crumbling tundra reindeer brigades to abandon their positions and fill the many vacant positions in the village administration, which in turn contributed to the even more rapid downfall of reindeer herding in Chukotka.

For example, one couple in Snezhnoe, Ivan and Zoia Tevliatval, had worked together in one of the state farm reindeer brigades, she as a *chumrabotnitsa* (a "tent worker," meaning a woman who cooked and did household maintenance at the camp), he as a *pastukh* (a herdsman). By the time I visited Snezhnoe in the summer of 1996, Zoia had taken a job in the village mayor's office, and Ivan was working as a stoker in the coal plant. Ivan in particular was not pleased about the arrangement – he enjoyed living in the tundra and said that he missed

PLATE 7.1. Two reindeer herders pose in Snezhnoe's diesel electric plant, where one of them has taken a job

it – but the couple had two adolescent boys to support and could not simply ignore the fact that a job in the village would give them a much more steady income, plus allow them to live with their children during the school year.

The Tevliatvals' story was typical of many other indigenous residents in the village (see Plate 7.1). The village's only Koriak family was headed by elder siblings (the parents had both died some years before) who each had dreams of leaving the village altogether. The sister, a young and competent elementary school teacher, dreamed of life in St. Petersburg; but her heart went out to the village children who would be without a teacher if she left, and so for the time being she remained. Her brother wanted to study veterinary science at a school in Nizhnii Novgorod; by early 1998 he had made it as far as Anadyr', where he managed to get a job as a security guard and planned to save his money to go further. He lived in one of Anadyr's run-down communal apartments. His sister followed in 2000, managing to get both a private apartment in the city and a job at one of the city's elementary schools.

The increasing migration to Anadyr' prompted Governor Nazarov to issue a resolution that attempted to prevent immigration from the villages.[10] The resolution ordered city officials to refuse to register documents regarding the sale or transfer of an apartment unless the person receiving the apartment could show an official stamp of residency in the city. However, no one could obtain official residency without proof of employment in the place of residence. Thus, a person coming from a village would have to arrange for employment before coming to live in the city – a task that was virtually impossible for villagers given the difficulties of communication and transportation between city and village. The only way out of this catch-22 was if the villager knew a relative or friend who had an apartment in the city and would permit the villager to stay temporarily in that apartment. In principle, one could then get a job, obtain official residency, and go back to the housing office to request an apartment of one's own. But in the interim, this exacerbated the crowded conditions in many dwellings. To make matters worse, as city residents outmigrated or were encouraged to move to other housing, entire apartment blocks were systematically emptied out and then mothballed by the city to save the costs of sending heat to these buildings from the central power plant. Some smaller buildings were demolished.

Nevertheless, there were many inhabitants of Snezhnoe and other villages living in Anadyr'. All of this placed an undeniable burden on the city to solve the problem of housing for indigenous residents. This led to the very problem described above by Sofia: a long waiting list of indigenous residents clamoring for housing in the city, expecting that it should be provided to them for free just as it always had been in the Soviet period. Because the earning power of indigenous residents was on the average so much less than that of incomers, most of these families could never dream of having adequate living space with hot water and a bathroom if they had to buy a privatized apartment on their own. The agency responsible for dealing with this issue was the Division on National Questions and Migration of the Anadyr' city administration. This office maintained, in cooperation with the City Association of Indigenous Less-Numerous Peoples of Chukotka, a waiting list of indigenous families needing apartments – that is, a special list was maintained separately from any nonindigenous families that might be in need of housing.[11]

In the summer of 1996, seventy-two entries were on the waiting list, and the family at the top had signed onto the list in 1985. Apartments were given to families as they "became available," although what that meant was never clarified altogether. Presumably, the administration could buy up the apartments of departing incomers, and federal funds (related to *Goskomsevera* economic development programs) were supposedly earmarked to subsidize housing for the indigenous population. The governor in fact often made statements in the media about how much money had been given for the housing needs of the indigenous population. Nevertheless, there was very little movement on this waiting list. Most of my indigenous consultees were cynical about the funds the administration had supposedly paid on their behalf, and rumors of misappropriation and outright embezzlement were rife. Nikita Suslov quipped, "if they had really given us as much money as they claim to have given, we'd all be millionaires by now!" He added bitterly that it was not as though the indigenous population were the greatest drain on the budget: "Altogether, what are we, fifteen thousand people? Surely it wouldn't break them to give us the money we need."

Demographic Crisis and Alcohol

Thanks in large part to the painstaking demographic research of the late Aleksandr Pika (Pika 1993; Pika and Bogoyavlensky 1995),[12] a profile of the demographic processes unique to indigenous residents in the Russian North is available – and the profile is disturbing. For his study of violent death (meaning accidents, homicides, and suicides) among the indigenous peoples of the Russian North, Pika gathered data between 1987 and 1990 in seven regions of the North, including the Chukotka Peninsula. In Chukotka, of 136 violent deaths he recorded, 79 were accidental, 35 were suicides, and 22 were homicides. Pika found that the level of violent deaths among indigenous residents in the Russian North far exceeded that in both industrialized countries and Third World countries. By the late 1970s, the average life expectancy of northern indigenous peoples was eighteen years lower than for the rest of the USSR. In the 1990s, all of these indicators became substantially worse. Statistics, however, cannot reveal the repercussions each of these deaths has in the communities where they occur. It is a very bitter irony that the story of many of the problems experienced by indigenous residents in Chukotka in the 1990s can be told through a series of deaths that occurred in 1996.

Two deaths occurred in the village of Snezhnoe during the two-month period I was staying there. The first occurred the day after I arrived, when an elderly Chukchi reindeer herder went down to the river's edge, tied a rope around his neck, attached a boulder to the other end, and threw himself into the river. The incident came up later in many conversations I had with villagers, as well as with the mayor; the consensus was that he had been depressed of late, that he had told family members that he could see no future anymore, and that he had ended his life out of despair. He was mourned as one of the last *stariki* ("respected old men") in the village, making his loss all the more significant. Over and over, indigenous residents in Snezhnoe said that things were far worse for them than in other villages because most of their *stariki* had died off, and they had no link to their traditions. They often pointed to the more successful reindeer state farm in the neighboring town of Ust'-Belaia as an example of the best-case scenario, saying that the reason the farm was more successful was because its *stariki* were still actively involved in the reindeer brigades. This man's death was more than just a tragic but isolated event; it signaled the passing of an institution that was seen as a key source of strength and direction for the village, and it evoked even deeper despair among the survivors. In a village of only about 375 people, the loss of any individual is keenly felt.

The second death came when a Chukchi woman in her fifties succumbed to a respiratory disease that appeared to be emphysema. This second death became an object lesson in how the dynamics of village management could lead to ethnically tinged tension. The woman died on a Sunday morning, and her daughter wanted to notify relatives in other towns immediately by telephone. In the past, almost every village apartment had a telephone, and residents could call to any other town or village in Chukotka directly; if they had no phone, there were two telephone operators in the post office who could place their call for them. In 1996, because of the general breakdown in services that had been occurring all over Chukotka since the late 1980s, Snezhnoe was reduced to a single telephone line, and the telephone operators were laid off. Those wishing to make a call had to go to the post office during business hours and ask the Russian postmistress to place the call for them. However, due to budget cuts, business hours at the post office had been reduced to about two hours a day, only on weekdays. Thus when the daughter went on Sunday to the postmistress's home (which was attached to the post office itself), the postmistress told her that it was not a working day and she would not place the call for her, death or no death.

I had gotten to know this family particularly well during my stay in the village, because the daughter was a childhood friend of the colleague from the research institute with whom I was traveling, Marina Peliave. Marina and I had interviewed the mother before she had died, and we had visited the family many times, so we were urged to attend the funeral and to sit with the body in the days preceding it. It was during one of these sittings that the story of the denied phone call was told; the daughter burst into tears as she told it, and another woman from the village turned to me and said, "Yes, we have all kinds of people here; some are good, and some are evil." The daughter recovered somewhat and, turning to Marina, she cried, "Marina! Write it, write about how we are out of control here!" She used the phrase *bez predel*, which translates as "without limits," but in context, the meaning seemed to evoke the complete lack of any kind of control over what people could get away with. The ethnic component of this conflict should not be overplayed, since the ethnicity of the postmistress was not mentioned, and the daughter was half-Russian herself. But the postmistress was the face of the grinding bureaucracy that rose above the village and remained distant and disinterested in the painful realities of the everyday life of the predominantly indigenous villagers, and that bureaucracy was overwhelmingly Russian.

Shortly after I left Snezhnoe, I received word that a young man from another family I had gotten to know had died. At first, it was thought that the death might be a homicide; he had been out drinking with friends, and had gotten into a brief fight with one of the other young men in the village. However, several witnesses said he had seemed fine after the fight, and a medical examiner concluded that the death was alcohol-related. Such deaths are not uncommon among indigenous residents in the Russian North. In his 1993 study, Pika's sample showed that 65 percent of all violent deaths were accidental, and of these, 25.1 percent were alcohol-related. Moreover, deaths from exposure, which constituted 18.6 percent of accidental deaths, were often alcohol-related in that the deceased had passed out in the open air after having become intoxicated (Pika 1993:66).

Alcohol-related deaths are part of the very complicated problem of alcohol use in the village. It is quite likely the young man overdosed on *spirt*, a kind of pure-grain alcohol. Because *spirt* tastes rather like vodka but is far more potent, and because drinkers often switch from vodka to *spirt* at some point during a drinking bout, it is easy to ingest unintentionally far more alcohol than one expects to or realizes. Intoxication was common in the village, and was likely to occur at any time during the day or night. This does not mean that everyone was drunk all of the time, although I often encountered Anadyrites who had this impression of village indigenous residents. In fact, many residents of Snezhnoe were conscientious teetotalers and despaired over the alcoholism that plagued some of their friends and family members. In some cases, alcohol abuse led to fights among young men or domestic violence between couples, but not always. It was clear from my observations and conversations with villagers that many who drank did so to escape the painful realities of their everyday lives.

Alcohol abuse is a contentious issue throughout Chukotka today, and in much the same way that the idea of *izhdivenchestvo* has arisen in the incomer discourse, so too has the idea that indigenous residents are somehow naturally (biologically or genetically) predisposed to become alcoholics. In its less charitable form, this manifests as the racist assertion that all indigenous residents will prove themselves to be irresponsible drunkards, an assertion that is unfortunately not unfamiliar to U.S. and Canadian citizens, since it appears in the discourse about Native Americans and Eskimos. Even among indigenous residents in Chukotka, I often heard the self-depreciating comment that the indigenous "organism" was weak because it could not process alcohol. These opinions seem to be based on comparisons of indigenous and incomer drinking patterns – indigenous residents are observed to become drunk much more quickly and easily. This is coupled with vague popular awareness of alcohol consumption research (some of it based in the Russian North) that has demonstrated a genetic component to the way alcohol is metabolized in some Asian populations.[13] However, the genetic factors in this research were observed only in *some* individuals among Japanese, Chinese, and Korean populations, and in fact these factors mitigated *against* alcohol overconsumption and developing alcoholism. The little research that has been conducted among Alaskan and Chukotkan populations has provided no evidence that indigenous residents are genetically more likely to become alcoholics than nonindigenous residents, and in fact, the researchers explicitly warn that social and cultural factors are highly likely to be implicated in further research as factors influencing drinking patterns.[14]

In spite of this discourse about indigenous people as alcoholics, I found that alcohol abuse and alcoholism were by no means ethnicity specific problems in Chukotka. Many Russians I encountered placed great importance on alcohol as a component of Russian culture, and alcohol was prominently featured at virtually every Russian gathering I attended, both public and private. I knew several Russians who clearly suffered from alcoholism and who frequently were found to be intoxicated at work. Ironically, I never heard anyone opine that Russians had trouble processing alcohol or were predisposed to become alcoholics; on the contrary, drinking and drunkenness among Russians was far more likely to be not only approved of, but even encouraged. One Russian acquaintance, who had become a teetotaler after struggling with alcoholism most of his life, told me that whenever he attended social gatherings with Russian friends, he always felt like "a spy in the enemy camp," being held slightly suspect as the only one not drinking. A story told to me by Nikita Suslov further reveals the degree of alienation between drinkers and nondrinkers in Chukotka:

> People think I'm weird because I don't drink. They stare at me.... When I worked construction, one woman at the company came up to me specially. "You're Nikita Suslov?" "Yeah, that's me." "You're a

non-drinker?" "Yes, I don't drink." "Why?" "Just because." You know, I was raised amid this terrible system of alcoholism, my own mother drank and I suffered from that. This woman just looked at me. "Huh. You're probably crazy [*bol'noi*]," and she walked away. Practically all Russian society drinks, and if you don't, you are abnormal.

This seemed like a bitter injustice to indigenous residents – amidst the strongly pro-alcohol society of Russians, to be pigeonholed as born alcoholics incapable of rising above drunkenness if they drank too much, and to be castigated as abnormal if they refused to drink at all.

The dominant incomer discourse on alcohol abuse by indigenous residents for the most part ignored the associated social factors. Yet it was apparent that a key catalyst influencing indigenous residents to overuse alcohol was depression resulting from the negative impact that current social and economic conditions were having on their lives (and the same may be said of Russian alcoholics). Another key factor that becomes especially important in concert with the first is the change in the availability of alcohol. The mayor of Snezhnoe explained that alcohol was strictly rationed during the *glasnost'* period of the late 1980s (cf. Kerttula 2000:117). He said that a predetermined number of bottles of vodka would appear on the store shelves on Friday afternoons, which would quickly be bought up. On Friday night and Saturday, revelers (who were by no means limited to the indigenous population) would consume the vodka and be drunk for a day, and by Sunday, everyone would be sobering up and preparing to begin the work week. This resulted in a specific drinking pattern: All available alcohol would be immediately consumed (cf. Avksentyuk et al. 1995:198). Alcoholism was prevented simply by virtue of the limited supply. In the 1990s, alcohol became more readily available, and combined with the established binge-drinking pattern, this availability resulted in higher rates of alcohol abuse.

By the mid-1990s, although the regional government had issued resolutions condemning the abuse of alcohol, and the governor spoke against alcohol abuse in speeches and in newspaper editorials (which many Chukotkans saw as almost laughable hypocrisy, since the governor was observed getting drunk in Anadyr's bar-casino whenever he was in town), vodka and *spirt* were available at virtually any time. The supply was limited in the village shop in Snezhnoe, but buyers had many other options. Russian President Boris Yeltsin issued a decree on 29 January 1992 regarding free trade in Russia that, in the North, was "for all intents and purposes a decree lifting all controls on the trade in alcohol" (Vakhtin 1994:19). After that, a new class of entrepreneurs emerged, known as *kommersanty*, who routinely obtained a supply of alcohol, transported it to the villages (primarily on river barges and *vezdekhody*) and sold it out of private apartments. In this way, alcohol was available to villagers twenty-four hours a day, seven days a week, and the only challenges were finding enough cash to make the purchase and waking up the *kommersant.* Cash was obtained through a wide variety of means, from squandering pension checks, to selling personal belongings, to selling wild reindeer meat and grizzly bear furs poached during trips to the tundra.

Some Chukotkan indigenous residents were aware that some Alaskan indigenous residents had declared their villages dry, and they had heard that this drastically curtailed the abuse of alcohol in those villages. Consequently, indigenous activists in Anadyr' began to discuss the idea of implementing dry laws in Chukotkan villages. However, what seems a relatively simple task in Alaska – to declare a dry law – becomes nightmarishly bureaucratic in Chukotka. Since Chukotkan villages are subject to the district administrations above them, such legislation would have to be passed down from above, through the chain of command that rises above the village mayor to the district administration and on up to the regional administration, relations that are ultimately regulated by Russian federal law.[15] Even if a dry law were to be passed in an indigenous village, it would be extremely difficult to enforce such a law. If *kommersanty* could somehow be prevented from selling alcohol out of private apartments in Snezhnoe, for example, those who were determined to drink would take a motorboat 18 kilometers upriver to Ust'-Belaia, a larger town, and buy alcohol there. Thus, battling alcoholism through supply would require a fundamental change in the structure of local government to be carried out at the federal level.

Virtually every indigenous Chukotkan I interviewed either volunteered or admitted that alcohol abuse was one of the most severe problems indigenous residents faced. Several consultees adamantly insisted that it was *the* most important problem for indigenous residents. Sofia, in her pointed way, said that if indigenous residents did not drink, they would have no other problems – that is, they would have enough competent people available to handle their own problems. Another teetotaling consultee, Lidia Neekyk, lamented that an entire generation of indigenous residents was being lost to alcoholism, and that these people were greatly needed. She said alcohol took their best young people and ruined their lives, and ended the lives of old people before their time.

Several indigenous consultees went so far as to say that the regional administration was directly and willfully responsible for the easy accessibility of alcohol to indigenous residents and the subsequent alcohol-related social problems, and I saw evidence of this myself. In one case, I was told a story – independently confirmed by several sources – of district bosses bringing vodka on a visit they made to a remote reindeer herding village in Bilibinskii district and offering it as a gift to villagers. Once the free vodka was gone and the villagers were drunk, the helicopter pilots who brought the bosses pulled out more bottles – but these were not for free. In the end, the villagers had traded away most of the furs they had hunted over the winter for vodka. I also often heard the rumor that the administration and/or the military profited from alcohol sales by buying it directly off incoming ships and selling it for a profit in the villages. Even if such a rumor proved to be untrue, what remains significant is what it reveals of the level of distrust among indigenous residents for the regional administration. These rumors were a component of the hidden transcript that was being circulated among indigenous residents. Perhaps the strongest statement of this is the following assertion of Nikita Suslov:

> [The governor] *needs* us to be drunkards [*emu nado, chtoby my pili*]; otherwise we would demand things from him. But as long as we are all drunk, and sick, and dying, he knows we will be useless. So it is profitable to him if we drink.

Whether the governor had such a plot up his sleeve or not, this presented itself as a plausible explanation for the seemingly willful neglect of the alcohol problem in Chukotka.

Conclusion

The 1990s were a time of dizzying transformation for all Chukotkans, during which no aspect of life was left unaffected. It was a time of striking, almost incomprehensible contrasts. Basic infrastructure crumbled at the same time as the shiny visage of merchant capitalism was manifested in the appearance of new shops offering imported Western goods. The new and perplexing experience of unemployment plunged some into poverty, while others paraded the outward signs of their newfound wealth, and rich and poor alike were shocked by the high prices in the shops of Anadyr'. Privatization was a powerful force that separated the haves from the have-nots, giving greater security in finances, housing, and mobility to some as it relegated others to a desperate search for a salary and a place to live. Coupled with massive migration shifts, this left Chukotka in a state of demographic chaos throughout the decade. The most alarming symptom of these stresses was the disturbing rate at which Chukotkans – the vast majority being indigenous residents – fell prey to the increasingly easy availability of alcohol. It is perhaps little wonder that in the midst of these fundamental crises, it was difficult to imagine what use there might be in organizing a movement for indigenous rights and interests – people were perhaps simply too busy burying their dead.

2002

Malina trudged up Otke Street past the new, marble-faced bank building, squinting her eyes at the sun glinting off its spotless windows. Up ahead, she could see that the renovation of the old Hotel Chukotka on the corner was nearly completed – although she hoped they would come to their senses and repaint that garish purple trim. She reached the corner and waited for several sleek foreign-make cars to pass, followed by one battered Russian car that rattled and squeaked as it rounded the corner. She could not help but chuckle to herself at the contrast.

As she neared the outdoor market, she passed a small group of men talking and laughing in a foreign language. What is that? she thought. Must be Turkish – she knew half the construction workers they brought in were Turkish, although for the life of her she couldn't understand why Chukchis couldn't do the work just as well. Another pair of men passed her, walking with quick strides and deep in conversation. Ah, that's English, she thought, no mistaking that one. She had learned a little English in school, but nowhere near enough to understand what they were saying. Good grief! She couldn't keep track of the foreigners here anymore. Even the newly arrived Russians brought in by the new governor seemed foreign, those "Friends of Roman," as they called them, so young and businesslike and at the same time so naïve, so wet behind the ears, thinking they had all the answers for Chukotka's problems. It was all certainly interesting, but it gave her an odd sort of feeling inside, a sort of melancholy . . . or no, it was like homesickness. She didn't really feel at home here anymore, she missed the days when a walk up Otke Street meant stopping every 50 meters to chat with another friend, to laugh and joke and gossip in the relaxed and intimate atmosphere of one's own neighborhood. But now everything looked and sounded different, and somehow the intimacy had been lost. Maybe she was just old. Old and tired. Walking up this hill got a little harder every year. . . .

"Yetti, Lina."

It was her friend Tonia, greeting her in Chukchi. "Yetti," she replied, and felt a smile spread across her face. But as she stopped to chat she was bumped from behind by a man hurrying past and speaking into a mobile phone in god-knows-what language. Malina glared at him and then looked at Tonia. They both burst into laughter.

Epilogue

REWRITTEN TRANSCRIPTS?

THIS BOOK BEGAN with a glimpse at the emergence of Russia's indigenous peoples in the early 1990s on the international radarscope of indigenous activism. I will conclude by considering briefly what the national scene looked like at the end of the decade (indeed, at the turn of the century), before turning to consider the future prospects for Chukotka's indigenous peoples.

In May 2000, the Association of Indigenous Lesser-Numbered Peoples of the North, Siberia, and the Far East celebrated its ten-year anniversary with a "Jubilee Conference" in Moscow. Indigenous leaders produced a volume of articles summing up the state of Russia's indigenous movement to commemorate the event (Suliandziga and Murashko 2000).[1] A full week of activities was organized, beginning with a plenary session held in the large assembly hall of the Russian government's Council of the Federation building on Novyi Arbat Street in Moscow. In attendance were indigenous leaders both from the regions of Russia and beyond Russia, as well as government representatives from Russia, Scandinavia, and North America, all of whom made decorous speeches. Honorary certificates and congratulatory gifts were handed out liberally. The plenary was presided over by the Association's new president, Sergei Nikolaevich Khariuchi, but Khariuchi ceremoniously invited to the stage the two past presidents of the Association – Vladimir Sangi and Eremei Aipin – in a significant moment that emphasized the mending of past rifts in the leadership of Russia's indigenous peoples. The situating of this event in the halls of government power was reminiscent of the founding congress of the Association that was held in the Kremlin in 1990. Indeed, Eremei Aipin began his speech to the plenary by commenting that he suspected about 80 percent of the people present in the room were also in attendance at that founding congress.

Yet the Association appeared much changed at this juncture, both in superficial appearances as well as in its fundamental modus operandi. It had now adopted a new acronym for its English-language name: RAIPON, Russian Association of Indigenous Peoples of the North (far from an accurate translation of the Russian, but also a far more catchy and pronounceable name – so much so that this name was being pronounced in Russian-language conversations to refer to the Association). Whereas when I had visited Aipin at the offices of the Association in 1996 I had found them dishearteningly empty and quiet, RAIPON's new offices in southwest Moscow (in a government building where the former *Goskomsevera* was also housed) were full of people and buzzing with activity. RAIPON now had a website – www.raipon.org – packed with pages outlining the Association's many programs, and listing the regional organizations affiliated with RAIPON – thirty-four in all. And there was a very active youth group that was developing a whole array of projects of its own.

It very quickly became clear that one thing had been the main catalyst in this transformation of the Association: the infusion of funds and activities from foreign nongovernment organizations (NGOs). The Inuit Circumpolar Conference (ICC) was the first on the scene in 1996 with its project, Institution Building for Northern Russian Indigenous Peoples, funded by the Canadian International Development Agency (CIDA).[2] In 1999, the United Nations Environment Programme/Global Resource Database Information Centre in Arendal, Norway (UNEP GRID-Arendal),[3] provided space on its Internet server for the creation of the RAIPON website, which came online in January 2000. But in May 2000, it was obvious that this was only the tip of the iceberg. One of the many events subsumed under the umbrella of RAIPON's tenth anniversary jubilee was a Roundtable with Partners and Donors held in the *Goskomsevera* conference room upstairs from RAIPON's offices. NGOs from all of the circumpolar countries as well as several European countries were represented at the table, and each presented its own project that it wanted RAIPON to consider. In fact, a bit of tension was in the air as the different groups began to sense each other as competitors for RAIPON's attention, and some quibbling ensued about how much information they were willing to share with one another around the table. A mere six months before, no NGOs had been interested in RAIPON aside from the founding partners mentioned previously, and the Association's two first vice-presidents, who were presiding over this meeting, were visibly taken aback by the aggressive nature of these new contenders. It seemed as though RAIPON was stepping into a new era, but it was a step that required some caution.

Chukotka's indigenous leaders were quite visible amid all of the events of the Jubilee. Maia Ettyryntyna, who had been Chukotka's elected representative to the Council of the Federation in the early 1990s and was now working on the staff of the Council, opened the initial plenary session in the Council's assembly hall, and was later praised by her fellow indigenous leaders and presented with an enormous bouquet of roses. Nina Vaal, the only indigenous representative among Chukotka's many lieutenant governors, made a brief speech at the plenary session and brought greetings from Governor Nazarov. Larisa Abriutina, a former deputy in the Chukotka Duma and current vice-president of RAIPON on health issues, was actively present at the Roundtable of Donors and Partners and presided over a workshop on the problems of Russia's indigenous peoples, sponsored by the International Arctic Science Committee and held at the offices of *Goskomsevera* and RAIPON. Liudmila Ainana, the diminutive and extremely activist chair of the Society of Eskimos was in attendance at the larger gatherings, telling all who would listen to her about how Nazarov had recently canceled the official registration of her organization on a technicality. And Vladimir Etylin was typically omnipresent at all events, representing his many different capacities – vice-president of RAIPON on issues of traditional economy, founder and promoter of the Russian Reindeer Herders' Association, co-drafter of many of the pieces of legislation relating to indigenous peoples that were then being considered by the federal government, former deputy in the Congress of Peoples' Deputies, and all-around activist extraordinaire.

Yet the one Chukotkan indigenous leader who was significantly *not* visible, and indeed not in attendance at all, was the president of Chukotka's indigenous association, Aleksandr Omrypkir. One of the events of the week was a gathering of the Coordinating Council of the Association, which consisted of all the presidents of the regional associations across Russia or their proxies. During a long afternoon-into-evening session, this council heard arguments on a list of pressing questions, including petitions by various new regional associations to be officially recognized by RAIPON, and many votes were taken and officially recorded. At one point, Mikhail Todyshev, one of RAIPON's two first vice-presidents, took a roster of all the regional associations. All were represented, save one: Chukotka. Abriutina, Ainana, and Etylin each stood up and said they could not account for why none of them was given a proxy vote by Omrypkir. Their frustration was palpable, and yet none of them expressed surprise, nor even belabored the issue. The voting went on without them, although each in turn contributed actively to the intervening discussions.

Of course, the echoes of the vibrant and boisterous discussions of these gatherings were barely carried back to the ears of Chukotka's indigenous population. Even if Etylin had been able to saturate every form of media outlet in Chukotka with his message, the same old problems prevented that message from reaching the ones for whom it was most intended, the indigenous people living in the villages and the tundra beyond: The radio broadcasts did not reach them anymore, they could no longer afford to subscribe to the newspaper, and the television sets they had access to did not carry local Chukotkan programming. The Administration of Governor Nazarov continued to stracize Etylin publicly, and he was unofficially thwarted at every turn when he tried to pursue his activist agenda locally. Even by the year 2000, it was difficult to connect Chukotka to this whirlwind of internationally observed activity being organized by indigenous peoples in Moscow.

By 2002, with the ousting of Nazarov and the appearance of Roman Abramovich as governor, the potential for radical change seemed very real. Because of Abramovich's reputation as an oligarch and a Yeltsin insider, Chukotka was in the national spotlight far more than it perhaps ever had been in its history, and moved into the international spotlight as Abramovich was featured in articles in the *Washington Post*, the *Seattle Times*, and *Der Spiegel*.[4] The bedraggled appearance of the city of Anadyr' was transformed, to the amazement and delight of its residents, as Abramovich demolished decrepit buildings and constructed new ones. The Chukotkan administration even launched its own website for the first time – www.chukotka.org. And Abramovich's staff, through his outreach offices all over the region, continued to solve everyday problems demonstratively for Chukotkan citizens. Not surprisingly, Abramovich's approval rating among Chukotkan residents after his first year in office reached 96 percent.[5]

Yet at the time of this writing, in early 2004, it remained to be seen what this change in official power from above might portend for the agenda of Chukotka's indigenous activists, and for Chukotka's indigenous population in general. Certainly, from the perspective of villagers, meeting basic needs for food, clothing, and heating pretty much covers everything on their agenda, and for them there might indeed seem to be little point in promoting a separate indigenous movement when these needs are being met. And yet, all of the systemic problems described in this book had yet to be addressed, and not all of them were likely to disappear simply as a result of the appearance of a (seemingly) benevolent governor. Moreover, in 2002 Abramovich announced that he would not seek a second term as governor, and might not even "sit out" the duration of his current term.[6] One could only speculate who might follow him – Etylin, or someone from Abramovich's circle, or a returnee from the Nazarov circle.

But if the period of prolonged crisis continues to pass and a sense of normalcy returns to Chukotka's villages (as indeed seems possible), it is likely that other issues will return to the table – such as rights to land for the practice of subsistence activities like hunting, fishing, and most important, reindeer herding. If reindeer herding stabilizes and reindeer head counts begin to rise again, surely the issue of ownership of reindeer and other assets will emerge. This is a matter that became hopelessly obfuscated as Soviet state farms were transformed to supposedly privatized farms, which were subsequently transferred back into a form of municipal ownership, all while reindeer herders themselves simply struggled to survive (Gray 2000). Even in regions with not-so-corrupt governors, these issues, as well as the more general issue of local self-government for indigenous peoples, have often been addressed specifically through the vehicle of indigenous activism.[7]

But I suspect Chukotka will take a slightly different course from the rest of the regions in the Russian North where indigenous peoples live, and this has to do partly with its delayed arrival in the arena of effective local activism, and partly with its proximity to Alaska. As mentioned previously, a wide variety of groups waited many years to begin working more closely with Chukotkans on "development issues," broadly defined, such as establishing reliable channels for delivering emergency aid, setting up exchanges of experience among indigenous communities, assisting in the reconstruction of basic infrastructure, providing business training for local reindeer enterprises, to name just a few desired projects. As they bided their time just outside of Nazarov's "ice curtain," these groups had the opportunity to study the solutions found in other regions of the Russian North and to plan for the future on the basis of others' experiences. The two most visible and mobile Chukotkan activists – Etylin and Liudmila Ainana – had long been in contact with many of these groups through their frequent visits to Alaska, and Ainana had been working already for several years with Alaska's North Slope Borough on a project of support for sea mammal hunters (Krupnik and Vakhtin 2002:20). Etylin had shared with me ideas and plans for many projects that he would pursue if only he were not hindered by the restrictive policies of the Chukotkan administration. Already in 2001, aid had begun to reach Etylin in the form of grants from NGOs eager to execute development projects in Chukotka. Etylin himself finally fulfilled a long sought-after dream when he filled the seat in the federal Duma that was vacated by Abramovich when he became governor, and thus he had obtained the influence he sought to carry out his plans.

The question is, will this foster a waxing of grassroots indigenous activism in Chukotka, or will it obviate the need for such activism, even sweep the momentum out of the hands of indigenous Chukotkans? Several recent studies have observed the growth in the number of NGOs operating at the local level and linking with both international development agencies and government agencies.[8] Some studies question whether the activities of such NGOs really do bring benefits for the lives of the local inhabitants they target (Escobar 1995). NGO staff are criticized for being insufficiently knowledgeable of local conditions, for favoring solutions imposed from the top down in a way that smothers existing grassroots activity, and for being more concerned with presenting short-term "success stories" to their financial donors than with the long-term well-being of local communities. Nevertheless, this moment of potential change is exciting for indigenous Chukotkans. As important as the last decade of the twentieth century was for most of Russia, the first decade of the twenty-first century promises to be even more pivotal for Chukotka.

APPENDIX

TABLE A.1. Ethnicity of Deputies in the USSR Soviet of Nationalities and Congress of People's Deputies (CPD), 1959–91, from Autonomous Regions in the North

Region	1958–61 5th Session	1962–9 6th Session	1966–9 7th Session	1970–3 8th Session	1974–8 9th Session	1979–83 10th Session	1984–8 11th Session	1989–91 CPD
Koriaksii	Orlov RUSSIAN	Orlov RUSSIAN	Orlov RUSSIAN	Koerkov KORIAK	Koerkov KORIAK	Tynentek'ev KORIAK	Akeev KORIAK	Kosygin KORIAK
Nenetskii	Ledkov NENETS	Ledkov NENETS	Ledkov NENETS	*Ledkov NENETS*	Vyucheiskii NENETS	Bobrikov NENETS	Bobrikov NENETS	Vyucheiskii NENETS
Taimyrskii	Mikhailov SAKHA	Chuprina DOLGAN	Portniagin DOLGAN	*Portniagin DOLGAN*	Spirodonov DOLGAN	Chuprin DOLGAN	Silkin NENETS	Pal'chin NENETS
Khanty-Mansiiskii	Sagandukova KHANTY	Kosiakova MANSI	Grigor'eva KHANTY	*Grigor'eva KHANTY*	Kiseleva MANSI	Mukhina KHANTY	Ovsiannikova MANSI	Aipin KHANTY
Chukotkskii	Rul'tytegin CHUKCHI	Nutetegryne CHUKCHI	Nutetegryne CHUKCHI	Tynel' CHUKCHI	Tynel' CHUKCHI	*Tynel' CHUKCHI*	Otke CHUKCHI	Etylin CHUKCHI
Evenkiiskii	Koinachenok EVENK	Uvachan EVENK	Uvachan EVENK	Uvachan EVENK	Uvachan EVENK	*Uvachan EVENK*	Cheronchina EVENK	Mongo EVENK
Yamalo-Nenetskii	Vanuito NENETS	Khoralia NENETS	Laptander NENETS	Kuznetsov RUSSIAN	Kuznetsov RUSSIAN	*Kuznetsov RUSSIAN*	Okotetto NENETS	Rugin KHANT

Note: Italics indicate that the person named probably served during that session, but data were unavailable or ambiguous. Also elected to the Soviet of Nationalities of the Congress of People's Deputies of the USSR in 1989 was the Nanai ethnographer Evdokiia Aleksandrovna Gaer. She was elected from a district in Primorskii Krai; the Nanai have no autonomous territorial formation of their own, and thus she does not appear in this table.

TABLE A.2. Ethnicity of Deputies in the RSFSR Congress of People's Deputies (CPD), 1990–3, and in the Federal Assembly of the Russian Federation, 1993–9, from Autonomous Regions in the North

Region	RSFSR CPD	Federal Assembly 1993–5			Federal Assembly 1996–9		
	State Duma	Council of the Federation		State Duma	Council of the Federation		
Koriaksii	Solodiakova KORIAK	Leushkin RUSSIAN	Oinvid KORIAK	Popov KORIAK	Bronevich ITEL'MEN	Mizinin RUSSIAN	Oinvid KORIAK
Nenetskii	Vyucheiskii KOMI	Komarovskii RUSSIAN	Sablin RUSSIAN	Chilingarov ARMENIAN	Butov (unknown)	Vyucheiskii KOMI	Chilingarov ARMENIAN
Taimyrskii	Maimago DOLGAN	Nedelin RUSSIAN	Filatov RUSSIAN	Vasil'ev RUSSIAN	Nedelin RUSSIAN	Zabievorota UKRAINIAN	Piskun UKRAINIAN
Khanty-Mansiiskii	Sondykov KHANTY	Filipenko RUSSIAN	Shafranik RUSSIAN	Aipin/Medvedev KHANTY/RUSSIAN	Filipenko RUSSIAN	Sobianin RUSSIAN	Medvedev RUSSIAN
Chukotskii	Etyryntyna CHUKCHI	Kotesova RUSSIAN	Etyryntyna CHUKCHI	Nesterenko RUSSIAN	Nazarov RUSSIAN	Nazarenko UKRAINIAN	Nesterenko RUSSIAN
Evenkiiskii	Uvachan EVENK	Sturov RUSSIAN	Uss RUSSIAN	Gaiul'skii EVENK	Bokovikov RUSSIAN	(unknown)	Gaiul'skii EVENK
Yamalo-Nenetskii	Yar NENETS	Neelov RUSSIAN	Korepanov RUSSIAN	Goman UKRAINIAN	Neelov RUSSIAN	Korepanov RUSSIAN	Goman UKRAINIAN

Note: In 1998, Nesterenko resigned her post as Duma deputy to take a position in the Ministry of Finance. A by-election was scheduled for 31 May 1998, and Vladimir Etylin opted to try again for a role in national politics. He was defeated by V. S. Babichev, who took 61 percent of the vote to Etylin's 21 percent (in third place was "against all" with 13 percent). A regular election was held in December 1999, and Babichev was ousted by Roman Abramovich, who was elected governor of Chukotka a year later.

NOTES

Preface

[1]For insight into the activities of Berezovskii and Abramovich, see Corwin 2000, Fossato 1999, and Lambroschini 1999.

[2]See, for example, *Radio Free Europe/Radio Liberty Newsline*, 17 July 2000 ("Berezovskii To Give Up Immunity?"), and 19 July 2000 ("Berezovskii Says Goodbye to Lower House"), Internet edition.

[3]See "Oligarch to Battle Incumbent for Governor's Seat?" *Radio Free Europe/ Radio Liberty Russian Federation Report*, 18 October 2000 Internet edition.

[4]Aleksei Germanovich, "Iskusstvennyi Otbor Gubernatora" (Artificial Selection of a Governor) in *Vedomosti*, 25 October 2000. See also "Another Incumbent Governor Faces Federal Pressure," *Radio Free Europe/Radio Liberty Russian Federation Report*, 25 October 2000 Internet edition.

[5]See www.strana.ru for 30 October 2000 on Nazarov's insistence of innocence.

Chapter 1

[1]The first research trip in 1995–6 lasted fourteen months, nine of which were spent in Chukotka, with the other five spent in St. Petersburg and Moscow. This was followed by additional research in Chukotka: four months in the

fall of 1998, three months in the summer of 2000, and three months in the spring of 2001.

[2]The Gwich'in Steering Committee has a website at www.alaska.net/~gwichin/index.html.

[3]See, for example, the story "People from the Other Shore" in Rytkheau's 1956 collection *Stories from Chukotka* (Rytkheu 1956).

[4] "Gazeta Meniaet Nazvanie" (A Newspaper Changes Its Name), *Sovetskaia Chukotka*, 19 June 1990, p. 3.

[5]"Old rubles" refers to rubles as they were before the 1 January 1998 redenomination of the ruble, which knocked three zeroes off the end.

[6]"A Esli Bez Ambitsii?! Rezonans na Rezonans: Marginaly "Murgin Nutenut" o Perspektivakh ee Sushchestvovaniya" (And What If Ambition Is Lacking?! Response to a Response: Marginal notes on *Murgin Nutenut* Regarding the Prospects for Its Survival), *Krainii Sever*, 14 August 1993, p. 4.

[7]"Tak Umiraiut Gazety" (Thus Do Newspapers Die), *Sovetskaia Chukotka*, 8 July 1993, p. 2.

[8]This was the basic assessment expressed in an article about a party that was thrown for the staff of *Murgin Nutenut* at the *Iaranga*. Ironically, the party was given a slogan: "*Murgin Nutenut* – the newspaper that is always with us." See *"Murgin Nutenut v Iarange"* (*Murgin Nutenut* in the *Iaranga*), *Krainii Sever*, 29 November 1994.

[9]The quotation is taken from an appeal to the Chukotka Duma written by members of the *Murgin Nutenut* staff in 1995, typescript in the author's possession.

[10]The exception was Chechnya, which remained engaged in an unresolved military conflict with the Russian government.

[11]"Sel'skie skhody Vankarema i Khatyrki, Sovet Veteranov i AMNCh: Podderzhivaem Kandidaturu Nazarova" (Village Meetings of Vankarem and Khatyrka the Union of Veterans and AMNCh: We Support the Candidacy of Nazarov), *Krainii Sever*, 12 October 1996.

[12]I attended the meeting, and all quotes are transcribed and translated from a tape recording I made there with permission from Serekov.

[13]The Council of Elders is designated in the Association's charter as the "higher ethical-spiritual organ of the Association," and thus it makes sense that its members should be kept apprised of important Association activities. The Council also has veto power over Association decisions.

Chapter 2

[1] For a useful explanation of how the United Nations system operates, including the role of NGOs, see Roulet 1999.

[2] In Canada, the phrase most often used to describe indigenous peoples collectively is "First Nations." For discussions of the term "Fourth World," see Graburn 1981; Leksin and Andreyeva 1995; Manuel and Posluns 1974; McFarlane 1993:160.

[3] *United Nations Draft Declaration on the Rights of Indigenous Peoples*, approved by the United Nations Working Group on Indigenous Populations in 1994, and also approved by the United Nations Sub-Commission on Prevention of Discrimination and Protection of Minorities (Doc. E/CN.4/Sub.2/1994/2/Add.1). The document continues to move through the UN approval process.

[4] See, for example, Aipin 1991a, 1991b; Etylen 1989a, 1989b, 1990; Gaer 1989b; Mongo 1989.

[5] Typical examples include Achirgina-Arsiak 1992; Aipin 1989, 1994; Gaer 1989a; Nemtushkin 1988; Rytkheu 1988a, 1988b, 1989; Sangi 1988, 1990.

[6] "Bolshie Problemy Malykh Narodov" (The Big Problems of Small Peoples), *Kommunist* 16 (November) 1988, pp. 76–83. Also found in translation in IWGIA 1990.

[7] See also "Association of Peoples of the North," *Current Digest of the Soviet Press*, Vol. XLII, No. 13, 1990, p. 34. Apparently Sangi created his organization prior to the congress in 1990; the newspaper *Pravda* reported on 9 August 1989 that an Association of Less-Numerous Peoples of the Soviet North had been created. See "Association of Small Peoples," *Current Digest of the Soviet Press*, Vol. XLI, No. 32, 1989, p. 28.

[8] The Association's charter and program are published in translation in IWGIA 1990; see also "Convention of the 26," *IWGIA Newsletter*, No. 2 (September/October 1991), pp. 17–18. A Russian version of the charter, revised in 1999, can be found on the Association's website, www.raipon.ru.

[9] For reports on the congress, see Glebov and Crowfoot 1989; Has and Zaochnaia 1993; Kaapcke 1994; Korobova 1991; Luk'iachenkho and Novikova 1991; Schindler 1992; Vakhtin 1993, 1994. See also "Native Northern Peoples Eye their Rights," *Current Digest of the Soviet Press*, Vol. XLII, No. 29, 1990, p. 20.

[10] See *Radio Free Europe/Radio Liberty News Briefs*, 23–7 August 1993, p. 4. See also Pika and Prokhorov 1994:40; Tkachenko and Koriakhina 1995.

[11]See Asch 1997; Feit 1989; Freeman 2000; Minority Rights Group 1994; Nuttall 1998; Scott 2001.

[12]The decree mentioned is from 22 April 1992, *"O Neotlozhnykh Merakh po Zashchite Mest Prozhivaniya i Khoziaistvennoi Deiatel'nosti Malochislennykh Narodov Severa"* (On Urgent Measures for the Protection of the Places of Residence and Economic Activity of the Less-Numerous Peoples of the North). For an excellent compendium (in Russian) of recent legislation affecting indigenous peoples, see Kriazhkov 1994 and its follow-up volume, Kriazhkov 1999. This decree is included on page 199 of the first volume.

[13]Constitution of the Russian Federation of 12 December 1993. Article 69: "The Russian Federation guarantees the rights of the indigenous less-numerous peoples in accordance with the universally recognized principles and norms of international rights and the international agreements of the Russian Federation." Article 72.1: "Under the joint authority of the Russian Federation and the subjects of the federation fall:... m) The defense of the primordial dwelling places and the traditional way of life of the less-numerous ethnic communities."

[14]*Federal'nyi Zakon Rossiiskoi Federatsii No. 82-FZ ot 30 Aprelia 1999 g. "O Garantiyakh Prav Korennykh Malochislennykh Narodov Rossiiskoi Federatsii"* (Federal Law of the Russian Federation No. 82-FZ of 30 April 1999 "On Guarantees of the Rights of Indigenous Less-Numerous Peoples of the Russian Federation").

[15]The address of the Association's website is www.raipon.ru. RAIPON stands for Russian Association of Indigenous Peoples of the North, which is now the official English-language title of the organization.

[16]Kolyma is essentially the region that was left in Magadan Province when Chukotka was taken away. The Association was created before the Magadan–Chukotka split, which is discussed in Chapter 6.

[17]The original charter and program of the Association of Indigenous Peoples of Chukotka are published in *Magadanskii Olenevod*, Vol. 42, 1990, pp. 15–22.

[18]Omrypkir was sensitive about this point, which led me to believe he was often criticized for it. He was later named the Chukotkan representative to the federal-level State Committee of the North *(Goskomsevera)*, and during our second interview he was careful to point out that this meant he did *not* receive money from the local administration.

[19]I later learned that there was a city-level Association in addition to the regional one that Omrypkir headed, and in the late 1990s Anadyr's indigenous activists increasingly saw this city Association as an alternative to Omrypkir's Association.

[20]See Arato 1991; Sedaitis and Butterfield 1991; Wedel 1998.

[21]*Obshchestvennyi Sovet po Rabote s Naseleniem iz Narodnostei Severa.* A similar organization was created at the same time in Pevek, which was then the only other populated point in the region that was recognized as a full-fledged city.

[22]Chukotka's Yup'iks were inducted into the Inuit Circumpolar Conference (ICC) in 1989. See "Soviet Inuit 'Reunited' with Arctic Family," United Press International wire story, 24 July 1989, accessed on LEXIS.

[23]For example, in 2000, after Ainana had made appearances in Alaska during which she openly criticized Nazarov, Nazarov canceled the official registration of the Society of Eskimos on what Ainana later claimed was a petty technicality. Ainana simply re-registered the society, and when I saw her in May 2000 at the ten-year jubilee of the national-level indigenous Association, she had now added this incident to her litany of criticisms of Nazarov.

[24]Since I never visited the Chakotka Peninsula, activism undertaken specifically by Eskimos is not as apparent in my account. For other accounts, see Kerttula 2000; Krupnik and Vakhtin 2002.

[25]The Cossack Semen Dezhnev is celebrated as the first Russian to sail around the Chukotka Peninsula, having embarked from a winter fortress at the mouth of the Kolyma River in 1648 (Dikov 1989:69).

[26]The writer is apparently unaware that the continental part of Chukotka is separate from the Chukotka Peninsula.

[27]"Statistika – Azbuka Glasnost': Kto My, Kakie My, Kak My Zhivem?" (Statistics – The Alphabet of Openness: Who Are We, What Are We, How Do We Live?), *Krainii Sever*, 4 April 1996, p. 3.

[28]"Otklik Na Odnu Nenauchnuyu Stat'iu" (Response to One Unscientific Article), *Krainii Sever*, 18 April 1996, p. 2.

[29]"Prodolzhaem Diskussiyu: Rasa, Plemia, Narod . . . " (We Continue the Discussion: Race, Tribe, People), *Krainii Sever*, 27 April 1996, p. 4.

[30]Two years later, Dallakian would be promoted to a position high within the Chukotkan administration and very close to the governor, and would be called colloquially "Nazarov's right-hand man." He would later be supplanted in this role by others, as various personalities rose to, and fell from, grace with the governor. Dallakian rose again, however, when Roman Abramovich became governor in 2000 and Dallakian was appointed to his inner circle.

[31]"Pered S"ezdom Stoiat Bol'shie Zadachi . . . " (Major Problems Stand Before the Congress . . .), *Krainii Sever*, 7 April 1994, p. 2; "Smena Orientirov" (A Change of Orientation), *Krainii Sever*, 26 April 1994, p. 2.

[32]Although I am quoting a newspaper version of this interview, it is highly likely
that the piece underwent editorial review by Dallakian personally, since the
newspaper was controlled by the regional administration.

[33]Panaugve is a direct transliteration of the name as it was printed in Russian
in the newspaper article. The person being referred to is Caleb Pungowiyi
of Kotzebue, a former president of the Inuit Circumpolar Conference.

[34]"Nishcheta na fone frantsuzskikh dukhov" (Destitution Against the Background of French Perfume), *Krainii Sever*, 28 April 1994, p. 2.

[35]For scathing critiques of the Soviet government, see Pika and Prokhorov 1994;
Rytkheu 1988a; Sangi 1988; Schindler 1990; Vakhtin 1994. For more sympathetic views, see Bartels and Bartels 1995; Graburn and Strong 1973.

Chapter 3

[1]In the United States, the term "Eskimo" has come to be considered inaccurate
or even derogatory by some (but by no means not all), who prefer to refer to
groups instead by their specific ethnonyms: Inuit, Iñupiaq, Yup'ik, or Aleut.
In Russia, however, there is little consciousness that "Eskimo" might be an
inappropriate designation, and Yup'iks are called, and refer to themselves
as, *eskimosy*. The exception is among Eskimo intellectuals in Chukotka who
have international contacts, and there is an Eskimo society that bears the
name "Yupik."

[2]The Chuvans, or *chuvantsy*, were once considered a subgroup of the Yukagirs
(Levin and Potapov 1964:788).

[3]Since Soviet ethnographers came to consider Kereks merely the subdivision of
the Koriaks living within Chukotka (Levin and Potapov 1964:852), they were
defined out of existence by Soviet administrative categories that recognized
only twenty-six indigenous groups in the Russian North. They were later
defined back into existence with the introduction in 1998 of a new census
tallying form by the State Committee of the Russian Federation on Statistics, which listed thirty-two indigenous groups. See *Postanovlenie Gosudarstvennogo Komiteta Rossiiskoi Federatsii po Statistike No. 57 ot 14 Avgusta
1997 Goda "Ob Utverzhdenii formy Federal'nogo Gosudarstvennogo Statis-
ticheskogo Nabliudeniya za Izmeneniem Chislennost' Malochislennykh
Narodov Severa v Sel'skoi Mestnosti Raionov ikh Prozhivaniya."* (Resolution of the State Committee of the Russian Federation on Statistics No. 57
of 14 August 1997 "On the Confirmation of the Form of Federal State Statistical Observation of Changes in the Number of Less-Numerous Peoples
of the North in Rural Localities of the Districts Where They Reside"). In
March 2000, the peoples of the North were folded into a broader category
that included all "less-numerous" *(Malochislennye)* peoples of Russia (not

limited to the North), reflecting new trends in Russian federal policy. See *Postanovlenie Pravitel'stva Rossiiskoi Federatsii No. 255 ot 24 Marta 2000 g. "O Edinom Perechne Korennykh Malochislennykh Narodov Rossiiskoi Federatsii."* (Resolution of the Government of the Russian Federation No. 255 of 24 March 2000 "On the Single Common List of Indigenous Less-Numerous Peoples of the Russian Federation").

[4]Some key sources on Chukotka and the Chukchi include Bogoras 1904–9; Dikov 1989; Kerttula 2000; Krupnik 1993; Leontev 1973; Schindler 1990; Vdovin 1965.

[5]On Siberian Eskimos, see Arutiunov 1969; Bogoras 1913; Hughes 1984; Kerttula 2000; Krupnik 1980, 1993; Krupnik and Vakhtin 2002; Menovshchikov 1988, 1990; Mikhailova 1977; Schweitzer 1990; Vakhtin 1994.

[6]On the Chuvans, see D'iachkov 1992:202; Levin and Potapov 1956:788–98; on the Evens/Lamuts (not exclusively within Chukotka), see Bogoras 1918; Nikolaev 1964; Popova 1981; Tugolukov 1985; Vitebsky 1992; on the Kereks, see Leontev 1976, 1983; on the Koriaks (in Chukotka and in the Koriak Autonomous Region), see Bogoras 1917; Jochelson 1905–8; on the Yukagirs (not exclusively within Chukotka), see Bogoras 1918; Gogolev 1975; Kreinovich 1982; Tugolukov 1979.

[7]See entry for "Chukcha" on page 326 in the Chukchi-Russian/Russian-Chukchi dictionary by P. I. Inenlikei (1982).

[8]Personal communication with Michael Krauss, Alaska Native Language Center, University of Alaska Fairbanks.

[9]Sources in English include Anisimov 1963; Cherkasov 1982; Dolgikh 1972; Gurvich 1962, 1969; Levin and Potapov 1964; Shimkin and Shimkin 1975; Uvachan 1960.

[10]Examples of indigenous Siberian ethnographers include Vasilii Nikolaevich Uvachan, an Evenk; Chuner Mikhailovich Taksami, a Nivkh; Evdokiya Aleksandrovna Gaer, a Nanai. See Kuoljok 1985; Slezkine 1994.

[11]In 1998, the Russian Federation moved to delete Line 5 from Russian passports, drawing an outcry from many large national groups within Russia once the new passports began to appear. The strongest opposition came from the Republic of Tatarstan, which refused to issue the new Russian passports, resolving instead to issue its own Tatarstani passports and to allow for dual Tatar/Russian citizenship for the republic's citizens (see Graney 2001).

[12]For discussions of the Committee of the North, see Kuoljok 1985; Slezkine 1994. See Taracouzio (1938:473) for an English translation of the original law creating the Committee. The original Committee of the North *(Komitet Severa)*, created in the 1920s, was disbanded in 1935, and its function was given over to the industrial entity *Glavsevmorputi (Glavnoe Upravlenie*

Severnogo Morskogo Puti, Main Administration of the Northern Sea Route), created in 1933 (Slezkine 1994:280–1). *Glavsevmorputi* was disbanded in 1969, and there was no agency overseeing the peoples of the North until 1988, when *Goskomsevera* was created (*Gosudarstvennyi Komitet Rossiiskoi Federatsii po Voprosam Razvitiya Severa,* the State Committee of the Russian Federation on Questions of the Development of the North). In 1991, *Goskomsevera* was subsumed under the Ministry of Nationalities, but in 1996 it was reestablished as a separate State Committee within the Russian government. In May 2000, the new Russian President Vladimir Putin signed a decree abolishing *Goskomsevera* again and dividing its functions among two new ministries, the Ministry for Economic Development and Trade *(Ministerstvo Ekonomicheskogo Razvitiya i Torgovli)* and the Ministry for the Affairs of the Federation, Nationality, and Migration Policy of the Russian Federation *(Ministerstvo po Delam Federatsii, Natsional'noi i Migratsionnoi Politiki Rossiiskoi Federatsii).* See *Ukaz Prezidenta Rossiiskoi Federatsii No. 867 ot 17 Maia 2000 g. "O Strukture Federal'nykh Organov Ispolnitel'noi Vlasti"* (Decree of the President of the Russian Federation No. 867 from 17 May 2000 "On the Structure of Federal Organs of Executive Power"); see also *Radio Free Europe/Radio Liberty Newsline,* 19 May 2000, Internet edition.

[13]"Small peoples" is a holdover from the former official designation, which was *malye narody Severa,* where the word *malye* means "small" or "minor." In the course of *glasnost'*-era indigenous activism, indigenous intellectuals considered the term *malye* demeaning, and it was replaced by *malochislennye* in common usage as well as in legal documents (Slezkine 1994:378n26). Just to drive this point home, a book of essays by indigenous activists was published in 1991 under the title *Narodov Malykh Ne Byvaet* (There Are No Minor Peoples) (Korobova 1991).

[14]For discussions of Soviet nationalities policy, see Agarwal 1969; Connor 1984; Conquest 1967; Pipes 1964.

[15]The "classics" in this literature include Blumer 1951; Cohen 1985; Maheu 1995; McAdams et al. 1996; Melucci 1989; Mouffe 1984; Tarrow 1994; Touraine 1992.

[16]See, for example, cultural anthropology textbooks by Harris and Johnson 2003; Haviland 2002; Kottak 2002; and Peoples and Bailey 2003; as well as Lewellyn's (1992) political anthropology text. One exception to this trend is Schultz and Lavenda (2001).

[17]See Balzer 1999 for a recent example of this tendency.

[18]For critiques of this tendency, see Abu-Lughod 1990; Brown 1991, 1996; Ortner 1995.

[19]There is a subtle slippage in word play here; the term *izhdivenstvo* simply means "dependence," while the term *izhdivenchestvo* escalates the concept to "parasitic smugness." That simple infix *che* changes the concept from a situation over which the subject probably has no control to one in which the subject is thought to be willfully exerting an attitude.

[20]An entire book similar to this one could be written on the predicament of the environmentalist movement in Chukotka. There is one environmentalist group in Chukotka, Kaira Club, and its founders were also persecuted by the Nazarov administration.

[21]This erasure did have roots in the late Soviet period; for example, as discussed in Chapter 6, a 1980 law changed the designation "national region" to "autonomous region," undermining the original purpose of these territorial formations, which ostensibly was to provide a titular homeland for less-numerous peoples. However, I would argue that Soviet-era erasure was less deliberate than post-Soviet erasure.

[22]One of the first such forays into Chukotka was the multidisciplinary, multinational LASPOL-IMSECO (Leningrad Association of Soviet Polar Scientists–Institut du Monde Soviétique et de l'Europe Centrale et Orientale) expedition led by the formerly Soviet, Sorbonne academic Boris Chichlo (Chichlo 1993).

[23]Personal communication with Russel Barsh, A.B., J.D., Adjunct Professor of Law, New York University School of Law.

[24]Urban intellectuals might be more likely simply to arrange with the newspaper personally to write an article or editorial to be printed in the paper.

[25]See Dmytryshyn et al. 1985 for several examples of such letters written to Russian Tsars.

[26]See "Native Northern Peoples Eye Their Rights" *Current Digest of the Soviet Press*, Vol. XLII, No. 29, 1990, p. 20.

[27]*Krainii Sever*, 17 December 1996, p. 5.

[28]*AKB* stands for *agitno-kul'turnaia brigada*, or agitation-culture brigade. This institution was placed in each village and charged with bringing socialist enlightenment – usually in the form of books, newspapers, and movies – to Soviet citizens in remote locations, such as reindeer herders.

Chapter 4

[1]Again, the caveat here is that the Society of Eskimos was also quite active on the Chukotka Peninsula, but along rather different lines, and is beyond the purview of this book.

[2]See, for example Bobrick 1992; Dmytryshyn et al. 1985, 1986, 1989; Forsythe 1992; Slezkine 1994; Wood 1991.

[3]Such sources include Fitzhugh and Crowell 1988; Kozlov 1988; Levin and Potapov 1964; Pika and Prokhorov 1994; Vakhtin 1993. Historical works exclusively dealing with the indigenous peoples of Chukotka include Bogoras 1904–9; D'iachkov 1992; Dikov 1989; Krupnik 1989, 1993; Leontev 1973; Menovshchikov 1977; Odulok 1954; Schindler 1990; Vdovin 1965.

[4]Pronounced *SYO-mush-kin.*

[5]While there is great hype about literacy levels in Soviet sources, when I visited a reindeer brigade in 1996 and settled into the tent graciously vacated for me, I did find a stash of novels underneath my reindeer-skin mattress. Later that evening, one of the herders stopped by to retrieve from the stash the book he was reading.

[6]See also the following sources on the history of Chukotka: Bush 1872 (an account by an American surveyor for the Russian–American telegraph line, a project that took him through Chukotka in the 1860s); D'iachkov 1992 (a prerevolutionary snapshot of Chukotka in the 1880s); Dikov 1974 (a comprehensive survey from prehistory until 1989), and Dikov 1989 (an updated version of the same); Kaminskii 1973 (the history of the introduction of aviation to Chukotka in the 1930s); Krushanov 1987 (a history of the Chukchi covering the seventeenth through the twentieth centuries, similar to Vdovin 1965 but written in the light of contemporary ethnicity theory in Soviet ethnography); Leontev 1973 (history of the Nikita Khrushchev and early Leonid Brezhnev years in Chukotka, 1958–70); Obruchev 1957 (an account of a geological expedition in Chukotka in the 1930s); Semushkin 1934, 1952, 1954 (fictionalized accounts of Soviet Chukotka in the 1920s and 1930s); Sverdrup 1978 (memoirs of a Norwegian geophysicist on a polar expedition that took him through Chukotka); Vdovin 1965 (an older history of the Chukchi covering the seventeenth through the twentieth centuries); Zhikharev 1961 (a general history of the Russian Northeast that provides a colorful account of the revolutionary period in Chukotka, pp. 37–69).

[7]The eleven *Revkomtsy* buried at the site, in the order in which their names appear on the memorial plaques, are Mandrikov, Berzin', Bulatov, Kulinovskii, Arens Val'ter, Titov, Mefodii Galitskii, Ignatii Fesenko, Iosif Buchek, Iakub Mal'sagov, and Semen Grinchuk, all killed in 1920 (the eldest at the time of their murder in 1920 was Mal'sagov, age forty-four, the youngest was Berzin', age twenty-one). Mikhail Kurkutskii and Vasilii Kleshin died in 1938 and 1973 respectively, and their bodies were added later to the site.

[8]For discussions of collectivization in the North, see Anderson 2000; Balzer 1999; Grant 1995; Kerttula 2000; Schindler 1997; Slezkine 1994; Vakhtin 1994.

[9]See Buckley 1995; Gambold-Miller 2002; Hivon 1995; Humphrey 1995.

[10]The lengths of the terms were irregular for various reasons, not the least of which was World War II, but most were four years long. The 1990 session was a new form, the Congress of Peoples' Deputies, and only one session of it was ever held. It was cut short when the Soviet Union was dissolved.

[11]For a colorful description of this 1937 election "campaign," see Dikov 1989: 228–9.

[12]The Soviet-era Russian Soviet Federated Socialist Republic (RSFSR) also had its own Supreme Soviet, a unicameral body with no special platform for representing indigenous nationalities. While representatives from the peoples of the North sometimes did get elected to the Supreme Soviet of the RSFSR, their seats were not virtually guaranteed in the same way the seats in the USSR Supreme Soviet were.

[13]See also I.S. Gurvich (1987), who wrote "K Sotsializmu, Minuya Kapitalizm" (To Socialism, Skipping Capitalism).

[14]See Slezkine (1994:152) for background on the Committee of the North.

[15]See Dikov (1989:256, 282) for details on how the Faculty changed over the years. In 2001, the Faculty was reorganized and renamed Institute of the Peoples of the North *(Institute Narodov Severa)*, and the Institute now has a website at http://www.herzen.spb.ru/htmlrus/inst8.html.

[16]Soviet kindergarten *(detskii sad)* resembled what Americans would call a day care center – a place where working parents could leave their preschool age children for a half or full day – except that the Soviet version was subsidized by the state.

[17]See, for example, Balzer 1999:164; Grant 1995:72; Kerttula 2000:14; Rethmann 2001:55; Vakhtin 1994:60.

[18]Semushkin also describes such a bell being used in the residential school from the very beginning, in the 1920s (Semushkin 1934: 37; cf. Rethmann 2001:56).

[19]Bruce Grant collected a similar narrative in his interview with a Nivkh district administration employee in Sakhalin: "[In the last twenty years] the dark side of the state boarding school system came out. It produced a whole generation of young people completely unable and uninterested in caring for themselves" (Grant 1995:153).

[20]Slezkine (1994:236) offers a similar quote: "When I stepped ashore wearing my Komsomol outfit, everybody walked away from me . . . 'you're not one of us anymore,' they said. 'Now you're one of the bosses.'"

Chapter 5

[1]These roads are found between Pevek and Komsomol'skii in Chaunskii district; between Keperveem, Bilibino, and Vstrechnyi in Bilibinskii district; and between and Iultin and Ozernyi in Iultinskii district.

[2]Indigenous inhabitants nevertheless found ways to subvert the boundaries occasionally. Reindeer herders in Snezhnoe told me stories of meeting herders from neighboring brigades at the border of their state farm territories, and playing card games to gamble for the right to pasture their herd on the other brigade's territory.

[3]The first "Friendship Flight" in June 1988 brought eighty Alaskans to the coastal city of Provideniya. It was followed in February 1989 by the first Soviet delegation to Alaska, which brought one hundred people to Anchorage, many of whom stayed as guests in private homes. For accounts of these early exchanges see Beaudry 1990; Berliner 1989; Gras 1989; Krauss 1994; Sheldon 1989.

[4]This is the figure of the Committee for State Statistics of the Chukotka Autonomous Region for 1 January 2001. My description of Anadyr' reflects its state in the 1990s; since Abramovich took office in 2001, much new construction has been undertaken in the city.

[5]"Belyii gorod, etazhami voskhodiashchii v sinevu!" From the poem *Kontrasty* (Contrasts), first published in the 8 April 1978 issue of *Magadanskaya Pravda*, also published in his collection of poems titled *Net Luchshego Lekarstva, Chem Liubov'* (There's No Better Medicine Than Love), Anadyr': Izdatel'skii dom "Chukotka," 1998, p. 53.

[6]These pipeways should not be confused with utilidors. A *utilidor* is a large, underground tunnel housing a pipe large enough to allow a human to enter for utility purposes. Pipeways are aboveground concrete housings laid over small, insulated heating pipes.

[7]It has long been the practice in Russia, both during the Soviet period and today, to close down summarily towns and villages that are deemed to be "without prospects" and to compel their residents to relocate to other towns (cf. "Census to Confirm Disappearance of Hundreds of Villages?" *Radio Free Europe/Radio Liberty Russian Political Weekly*, 15 May 2002, Internet edition). In 1995, Governor Aleksandr Nazarov issued a resolution that summarily closed down several of Chukotka's industrial towns. The

move was particularly controversial because heat and electricity were cut off to the town before all of the residents had been relocated. The resolution is titled *Postanovlenie Glavy Administratsii Chukotskogo Avtonomnogo Okruga No. 311 ot 13.09.95 g. "Ob Uprazdnenii i Ob"edinenii Naselennykh Punktov v Chukotskom Avtonomnom Okruge"* (Resolution of the Head of the Administration of the Chukotka Autonomous Region No. 311 of 13.09.95 "On the Abolition and Unification of Population Points in the Chukotka Autonomous Region"). See also *Postanovlenie Pravitel'stva Rossiiskoi Federatsii No. 1188 ot 4 Dekabria 1995 g. "O Merakh po Stabilizatsii Sotsio-Ekonomicheskoi Obstanovki v Chukotskom Avtonomnom Okruge i Sotsial'noi Zashchite Naseleniya Poselka Iultin"* (Resolution of the Government of the Russian Federation No. 1188 of 4 December 1995 "On Measures for Stabilizing the Socioeconomic Situation in the Chukotka Autonomous Region and the Social Support of the Population of the Town of Iultin"), published in *Rossiiskaya Gazeta*, 14 December 1995, p. 4, with the headline "SOS! Poselka Iultin Uslyshan Pravitel'stvom V. Chernomyrdina" (The SOS! of the Town of Iultin Is Heard by the Government of V. Chernomyrdin).

[8]See *Postanovlenie Pravitel'stva Rossiiskoi Federatsii No. 1237 ot 16 dekabria 1995 g. "O Realizatsii Regional'noi Programmy Obustroistva Natsional'nykh Sel – Mest Kompaktnogo Prozhivaniya Malochislennykh Narodov Severa Chukotskogo Avtonomnogo Okruga na 1996 g. i Blizhaishuyu Perspektivu"* (Resolution of the Government of the Russian Federation No. 1237 of 16 December 1995 "On the Realization of the Regional Program of Reconstruction of National Villages – Places of Compact Residence of Less-Numerous Peoples of the North of the Chukotka Autonomous Region for 1996 and the Near Future"), published in *Rossiiskaya Gazeta*, 25 January 1996, p. 6.

[9]The Twenty-Second Communist Party Congress is historic because it was at this congress that Khrushchev ordered Stalin's body to be removed from Lenin's tomb, a very public acknowledgment of Stalin's fall from reverence.

[10]*Vezde* means "everywhere," and *khod-* is the root of the verb *khodit'*, "to go." Thus, a *vezdekhod* is a "go-everywhere." Some Chukotkans called them "ATVs" (they knew this stood for all-terrain vehicle), but I usually protested that an ATV was more often thought of as a lightweight, three-wheeled vehicle – nothing whatsoever like the huge, rumbling, smoke-belching behemoths that were *vezdekhody*.

[11]For an overview of Russia's privatization program, see Wegren 1998. For an overview of the reorganization of state farms in Chukotka, see Gray 2000.

[12]"Podvodia pervye itogi – Tavaivaam segodnia" (The First Summing-Up: Tavaivaam Today) *Krainii Sever*, 15 December 1994, pp. 2, 7.

[13]President Yeltsin renamed this holiday "Day of Accord and Reconciliation" in 1996, but Chukotkans either ignored the new appellation or rolled their eyes at the mention of it.

[14]*Postanovlenie Gubernatora Chukotskogo Avtonomnogo Okruga No. 14 ot 22 Ianvaria 1998 g. "O Provedenii Meropriatii v Dni Natsional'nykh Prazd-nikov i Znamenitel'nykh Dat"* (Resolution of the Governor of the Chukotka Autonomous Region No. 14 of 22 January 1998 "On the Conducting of Activities on the Days of National Holidays and Important Dates").

[15]*Ergyron* is Chukchi for "sunrise."

[16]The performers use the word "amateur" (*liubitel'skii*, from the verb *liubit'*, "to love") to distinguish what they do from those who earn their living by performing – as do the members of *Ergyron*, a professional *(professional'nyi)* ensemble.

[17]For background on the Decade and the Day of Indigenous People, see related pages on the website of the United Nations High Commissioner for Human Rights, http://www.unhchr.ch/indigenous/.

[18]The building was renamed Palace of Children's and Youth Arts in the post-Soviet period.

[19]The idea of cultural capital is, of course, attributable to Bourdieu 1986.

[20]"Krasnaia Ryba po Dostupnoi Tsene" (Red Fish at an Affordable Price), *Izvestiya*, 6 December 1995.

[21]The directors of these amateur ensembles were usually paid employees of village Houses of Culture. In 1996, a new precedent was set when Anadyr's amateur ensemble *Atasikun* performed at the annual winter carnival and, for the first time ever, was paid a fee by the administration to do so.

Chapter 6

[1]Since the prisoner population was not counted, this figure may be a distortion.

[2]*Zakon Verkhovnogo Soveta R.S.F.S.R ot 20 Noiabria 1980 g. "Ob Avtonom-nykh Okrugakh R.S.F.S.R"* (Law of the Supreme Soviet of the RSFSR of 20 November 1980 "On Autonomous Regions of the RSFSR").

[3]Yeltsin repeated this statement in several other speeches in 1990; for a full review of these, see Dunlop 1993:62–5. See also *Radio Free Europe/Radio Liberty News Briefs*, Vol. 2, No. 26, 14–18 June 1993, p. 1.

[4]In what has come to be called "asymmetrical federalism" (cf. Poelzer 1995), the various territorial formations within the Soviet Union did not share equal status in relation to the federal center. Autonomous republics were on the top of the hierarchy within Russia, whereas autonomous regions were unequivocally at the bottom. This has sometimes been called *matrioshka*

federalism (*matrioshki* are the little wooden nesting dolls that are such a popular tourist souvenir in Russia and Eastern Europe), because not only were autonomous regions at the bottom of the status hierarchy, they were also encompassed within larger territories – provinces or territories – which were in turn encompassed within the Russian Republic, which was in turn encompassed within the Soviet Union (Bremmer and Taras 1993).

[5]See the following issues of *Radio Liberty Report on the USSR* for 1990: No. 33, p. 39 (on Karelia's declaration); No. 36, pp. 30–1 (for the Komi Republic's declaration); No. 38, p. 40 (for Yeltsin's criticism of Gorbachev for not granting more independence to the republics). For continuing coverage of this phenomenon, see the following issues of *The Current Digest of the Post-Soviet Press* for 1993: No. 22, "Vologda Province Wants to be Vologda Republic"; No. 26, "Provinces, Republics Keep Jockeying for Position"; No. 31, "A Russian United States"; No. 34, "Yet Another Republic"; No. 37, "Urals Residents Want To Unite"; and also *Radio Free Europe/Radio Liberty News Briefs* in 1993: No. 25, "Autonomous Okrugs Acquire Same Rights as Krais and Oblasts"; No. 26, "Republics Insist on Sovereignty"; No. 28, "Sverdlovsk Oblast Declares Itself Ural Republic"; No. 31, "Amur Oblast Declares Itself Republic"; No. 41, "Regional Leaders Consider Creation of Siberian Republic"; No. 45, "Urals Republic Proclaimed."

[6]The "farce of sovereignties" assertion was made in the newspaper *Moskovskaya Novosti*. See *Current Digest of the Soviet Press*, Vol. XLV, No. 21 (1993), p. 18.

[7]*Reshenie Soveta Narodnykh Deputatov Chukotskoi Avtonomnogo Okruga XXI Sozyva ot 28 Sentiabria 1990 g. "O Provozglashenii Chukotskoi Sovetskoi Avtonomnoi Respubliki"* (Decision of the Soviet of People's Deputies of the Chukotka Autonomous Region of 28 September 1990 "On the Proclamation of the Chukotka Soviet Autonomous Republic"). See also "Chukchi Autonomous Republic Declared," *Radio Liberty Report on the USSR*, Vol. 2, No. 41 (1990), p. 28; "Chukotka Becomes a Republic," *Current Digest of the Soviet Press*, Vol. XLII, No. 39 (1990), p. 21.

[8]Interview with Vladimir Mikhailovich Etylin, Anadyr', 24 October 1996.

[9]*Zakon Rossiiskoi Federatsii ot 17 Iiunia 1992 Goda "O Neposredstvennom Vkhozhdenii Chukotskogo Avtonomnogo Okruga v Sostav Rossiiskoi Federatsii"* (Law of the Russian Federation from 17 June 1992 "On the Direct Inclusion of the Chukotka Autonomous Region in the Composition of the Russian Federation").

[10]*Postanovlenie Konstitutsionnogo Suda RF ot 11 Maia 1993 g. "Po Delu o Proverke Konstitutsionnosti Zakona Rossiiskoi Federatsii ot 17 Iiunia 1992 Goda 'O Neposredstvennom Vkhozhdenii Chukotskogo Avtonomnogo Okruga v Sostav Rossiiskoi Federatsii'"* (Resolution of the Constitutional

Court of the RF from 11 May 1993 "On the Matter of Verification of the Constitutionality of the Law of the Russian Federation from 17 June 1992 'On the Direct Inclusion of the Chukotka Autonomous Region in the Composition of the Russian Federation'"). See also Sharlet 1993:325; *Radio Free Europe/Radio Liberty News Briefs*, Vol. 2, No. 21, May 1993, p. 5.

[11]This is defined in Article 5 of the 1993 Constitution of the Russian Federation. The types of territorial formations listed include republics, territories *(krai)*, provinces *(oblast')*, cities of federal significance (meaning Moscow and St. Petersburg), autonomous provinces (there is only one in Russia – the Jewish Autonomous Province in the Russian Far East), and autonomous regions *(okrug)*. That order roughly reflects the former hierarchy among these types of territories. A smaller unit that is also found within all of these territorial formations is the district *(raion)*.

[12]See *Radio Free Europe/Radio Liberty Newsline* for 8 July 1997, Internet edition.

[13]For the development of Putin's policy on the regions, see "www.rferl.org/newsline" Julie A. Corwin, End Note ("The New Gang of Seven?"), *Radio Free Europe/Radio Liberty Russian Federation Report*, 17 May 2000, Vol. 2, No. 18. Internet edition.

[14]*Ukaz Prezidenta RF No. 849 ot 13 Maia 2000 g. "O Polnomochnom Predstavitele Prezidenta RF v Federal'nom Okruge"* (Decree of the President of the RF No. 849 of 13 May 2000 "On the Authorized Representative of the President of the RF in the Federal District"), published in *Rossiiskaya Gazeta*, 16 May 2000.

[15]There is a further complication that is not immediately relevant to this discussion. By a decree of 22 August 1991, Yeltsin also created the position of "presidential representative" in each region, in an attempt to consolidate his power further. Thus three loci of power – head of administration, chair of the local Soviets, and the presidential representative – each vied for power in the regions (Sakwa 1993:182–4). I occasionally heard the opinion that Etylin could have and/or should have tried to attain to the position of presidential representative, and that he had let an opportunity slip through his fingers.

[16]Gerald Nadler, "Two Rulers, No Cabinet, Little Food." *Washington Times*, 16 September 1991, accessed on LEXIS.

[17]Some examples are found on page 2 of the 15 December 1992 issue of *Krainii Sever.*

[18]At the party's fifth congress in April 1998, Nazarov was elected to the party's political council (see *Institute for East West Studies (IEWS) Russian Regional Report*, Internet Edition, Vol. 3, No. 17, 30 April 1998.

[19]Interview with Etylin, Anadyr', 24 October 1996.

20Photocopy of the draft declaration dated 28 September 1990, obtained from Etylin's personal files.

21Both pieces of legislation are published in *Resheniya Tret'ei Sessii Soveta Narodnykh Deputatov Chukotskoi Sovetskoi Avtonomnoi Respubliki* (7 Fevralia–11 Fevralia 1991 g.) (Decisions of the Third Session of the Soviet of People's Deputies of the Chukotka Autonomous Republic, 7 February– 11 February 1991), Anadyr': Sovet Narodnykh Deputatov Chukotskoi Sovetskoi Avtonomnoi Respubliki, 1991, pp. 113–15, 159–62.

22See Pika and Prokhorov (1994:86) for an insightful discussion of the implications of local sovereignty movements for the indigenous peoples living in the autonomous regions.

23See, for example, the following *Radio Free Europe/Radio Liberty Newsline* reports (Internet edition): "Yeltsin Blames Regions for Unpaid Debts" (23 January 1998); "Nemtsov Says Regional Leaders May Be Punished" (27 January 1998); "Ministry Reports on Misappropriation of Wage Funds" (25 February 1998).

24See "Another Incumbent Governor Faces Federal Pressure," *Radio Free Europe/Radio Liberty Russian Federation Report*, 25 October 2000, Internet edition. The item says Nazarov was also "suspected of involvement in the illegal sale of quotas for procuring water resources granted to local enterprises."

25Hickel was governor of Alaska 1966–9 and again 1990–4.

26Yereth Rosen, "Alaskans, Russians Envision Bering Strait Tunnel," Reuters, 23 February 1993, accessed on LEXIS. There is also a story on the proposed tunnel reprinted from *RIA Novosti* in the 13 August 1996 edition of *Krainii Sever*, p. 2. Although many considered the idea spurious, by 2001 its proponents were still pushing it, now trying to capture the ear of the new governor, Abramovich – see the story "Politekonomika: Beringova Susha" (Political Economy: Bering Land Bridge), *Vedomosti*, 18 January 2001. Apparently the idea for such a tunnel dates back to the beginning of the century – see Kolarz 1967.

27The titles of these articles are indicative of the general mood: 19 May 1992, "Beringiya, Nash Obshchii Dom" (Beringia, Our Common Home); 27 June 1992, "Aliaska–Chukotka – Problemy Obshchie" (Alaska–Chukotka – Common Problems); 9 November 1993, "Ia by Eshche v Ameriku s"Ezdil . . . " (I Would Go to America Again . . .); 30 August 1994, "Chukotka–Aliaska: My Stali Blizhe Drug k Drugu" (Chukotka–Alaska: We've Become Closer to One Another).

28*Krainii Sever*, 28 March 1996, p. 3. The pair of articles regarding the article in *Le Monde* were titled "Smeshno, no Neveselo . . . " (Funny, But Not Happy . . .), and "Kommentarii Korrespondenta: Zashorennye Gorizonty" (Correspon-dent's Commentary: Blinded Horizons). The pair of articles regarding Pika's expedition were titled "I Vnov' – Razygrysh 'Natsional'noi' Karty" (And Again – Drawing the 'National' Card), and "Kommentarii Nachal'nika Okruzhnogo Upravleniya Nauchno-Informatsionnogo Obespecheniya" (Commentary of the Head of the Department of Science and Information).

[29]Not surprisingly, Chukotka became infamous for its lack of press freedom. In a study sponsored by the Glasnost' Defense Fund in 2000, eighty-seven of Russia's regions (excluding Chechnya and Ingushetia) were rated accord-ing to a "media freedom index" that considered a variety of factors such as freedom of access to information and freedom to distribute informa-tion. Chukotka ranked eighty-sixth out of eighty-seven, second only to the Karachaevo-Cherkassia Republic. See "Each Region Violates Media Free-dom in Its Own Way," *Radio Free Europe/Radio Liberty Russian Federation Report*, 31 January 2001, Internet edition.

[30]Article 27.1: "Everyone who is legally located on the territory of the Russian Federation has the right to freely move about and to choose a place of sojourn and residence"; Article 27.2: "Everyone can freely depart across the borders of the Russian Federation. Citizens of the Russian Federation have the right to return unimpeded to the Russian Federation."

[31]A survey of over nine thousand laws adopted in the regions, condzucted in 1997 by Russian Minister of Justice Sergei Stepashin, found that more than one-third violated federal legal norms (see *Radio Free Europe/Radio Liberty Newsline*, 12 December 1997, Internet edition). In 2000, the new Russian President Putin proposed legislation that would allow him to re-move regional governors for violations of federal law (see the article in the Russian newspaper *Segodnia* for 18 May 2000, "Vernite Unesennyi Suverenitet: Putin Sobiraet Vlast', Rozdannuyu [sic] El'tsinym Guberna-toram" (Return Runaway Sovereignty: Putin Gathers Up the Power That Yeltsin Handed Out to Governors).

[32]Even in 1991 under Etylin, there was a law on the books that technically main-tained all of Chukotka as a border zone. However, the Chukotkan adminis-tration at that time was more liberal in allowing access to foreigners.

[33]*Postanovlenie Administratsii Chukotskogo Avtonomnogo Okruga No. 124 ot 29 Marta 1994 g. "O Pogranichnom Rezhime na Territorii Chukotskogo Avtonomnogo Okruga"* (Resolution of the Administration of the Chukotka Autonomous Region No. 124 of 29 March 1994 "On the Border Regime on the Territory of the Chukotka Autonomous Region"). Published in *Krainii Sever*, 17 May 1994. This resolution was superceded by a revised resolution with the same name, passed on 31 March 2000. The essential provisions of the resolution remain unchanged.

[34]*Zakon RF No. 4730-I ot 1 Aprelia 1993 g. "O Gosudarstvennoi Granitse Rossiiskoi Federatsii"* (Law of the RF No. 4730-I of 1 April 1993 "On the State Border of the Russian Federation").

[35]See Article 1.2 of *Zakon RF ot 14 Iiulia 1992 g. No. 3297–1 "O Zakrytom Administrativno-Territorial'nom Obrazovanii"* (Law of the RF of 14 July 1992 No. 3297–1 "On Closed Administrative-Territorial Formations").

[36]"Poka est' Gosudarstvo – est' Granitsy" (As Long as There Is a State – There Is a Border), *Krainii Sever*, 28 May 1994. Note that the speaker is not referring to permission to enter Chukotka, which had to be obtained from the administration, but to permission for traveling beyond the point of entry.

[37]Russian federal practice has since changed such that all Russian visas no longer need to include places to be visited.

[38]"Poriadok V"ezda Inostrannykh Grazhdan i Lits Bez Grazhdanstva v Chukotskii Avtonomnyi Okrug" (Procedure for the Entry of Foreign Citizens and Persons Without Citizenship into the Chukotka Autonomous Region), *Vedemosti: Zakonodatel'nye i Normativnye Akty* (Chukotka's legislative gazette, an insert in *Krainii Sever*), No. 12 (17), September 1998, pp. 7–8.

[39]*Postanovlenie Pravitel'stva RF No. 1641 ot 27 Dekabria 1997 g. "O Vnesenii Izmenenii v Perechen' Territorii Rossiiskoi Federatsii s Reglamentirovannym Poseshcheniem dlia Inostrannykh Grazhdan"* (Resolution of the Government of the RF No. 1641 of 27 December 1997 "On the Introduction of Changes into the List of Territories of the Russian Federation with Regulated Visitation for Foreign Citizens"). The full list, originally published in 1992, includes fifteen other regions, among them the northern regions of Kamchatka Province, Krasnoyarsk Territory, Murmansk Province, and Arkhangelsk Province.

[40]Chukotkans were not alone in these concerns. In 2002, the city of Novyi Urengoi in the Yamalo-Nenets Autonomous Region wanted to become an officially "closed city" for similar reasons. See "Magnitogorsk, Novyi Urengoi Want to Reduce Ranks of Immigrants and Become Closed Cities," *Radio Free Europe/Radio Liberty Russian Federation Report*, 2 May 2002.

Chapter 7

[1]*Svedeniya o Chislennosti Predstavitelei Korennykh Malochislennykh Narodov (Chislennost' i Protsentnyi Sostav) v Zakonodatel'nom Organe, Ispolnitel'nykh Organakh i Organakh Mestnogo Samoupravleniya Chukotskogo Avtonomnogo Okruga* (Information About the Number of Representatives of the Indigenous Less-Numerous Peoples (Numbers and Percentages) in Legislative Organs, Executive Organs, and Organs of Local Self-Government of the Chukotka Autonomous Region).

[2]*Previewing Russia's 1995 Parliamentary Elections*, a Carnegie Endowment, study edited by Michael McFaul and Nikolai Petrov, p. 131. These figures are in "old rubles," before the January 1998 redenomination.

[3]"Statute on Privileges for Persons Working in the Extreme North of the RSFSR of 10 May 1932," found in translation in Taracouzio 1938:491–5.

[4]See the following Russian laws published in Kriazhkov 1994: *Postanovlenie Pravitel'stva Rossiiskoi Federatsii No 572 ot 11 Avgusta 1992 g. "O Kompensatsii Raskhodov, Sviazhannykh s Vyezdom iz Raionov Krainego Severa i Priravnennykh k nim Mestnostei* (Resolution of the Government of the Russian Federation No 572 of 11 August 1992 "On Compensation for Expenses Connected with Leaving Districts of the Far North and Equivalent Locations"), p. 210; *Postanovlenie Pravitel'stva Rossiiskoi Federatsii No. 653 ot 1 Sentiabria 1992 g. "O Vozmeshchenii Predpriiatiyam, Uchrezhdeniyam i Organizatsiyam, Raspolozhennym v Raionakh Krainego Severa i Priravnennykh k Nim Mestnostiakh, Zatrat na Vyplaty po Raionnym Koeffitsientam i Protsentnym Nadbavkam"* (Resolution of the Government of the Russian Federation No. 653 of 1 September 1992 "On Reimbursement to Enterprises, Institutions, and Organizations Situated in the Districts of the Far North and Equivalent Locations for Expenditures on Payments of the District Coefficient and Percentage Bonus"), p. 211; *Postanovlenie Verkhovnogo Soveta Rossiiskoi Federatsii ot 19 Fevralia 1993 g. "O Poriadke Vvedeniya v Deistvie Zakona Rossiiskoi Federatsii 'O Gosudarstvennykh Garantiyakh i Kompensatsiyakh dlia Lits, Rabotaiushchikh i Prozhivaiushchikh v Raionakh Krainego Severa i Priravnennykh k nim Mestnostiakh'"* (Resolution of the Supreme Soviet of the Russian Federation from 19 February 1993 "On the Procedure for Bringing into Effect the Law of the Russian Federation 'On State Guarantees and Compensation for Persons Working and Living in the Districts of the Far North and Equivalent Locations'"), p. 223; *Postanovlenie Soveta Ministrov – Pravitel'stva Rossiiskoi Federatsii No. 1012 ot 7 Oktiabria 1993 g. "O Poriadke Ustanovleniya i Ischisleniya Trudovogo Stazha dlia Polucheniya Protsentnoi Nadbavki k Zarabotnoi Plate Litsam, Rabotaiushchim v Raionakh Krainego Severa, Priravnennykh k nim Mestnostiakh i v Ostal'nykh Raionakh Severa"* (Resolution of the Soviet of Ministers – Government of the Russian Federation No 1012 of 7 October 1993 "On the Procedure for the Establishment and Calculation of the Working Length of Service for Receipt of the Percentage Bonus and Salary by Persons Working in the Districts of the Far North, Equivalent Locations, and the Rest of the Districts of the North"), p. 249.

[5]See Goskomstat Rossii 1999; cf. Anderson 1996:107.

[6]This upper house is known as the *Sovet Federatsii*, or Council of the Federation. As of 1996, Russian election law was rewritten so that each of Russia's

eighty-nine regional governors automatically became a representative in the Council of the Federation.

7"Interv'iu u Aviatsionnogo Trapa. Iurii Luzhkov: Chukotka Ocharovala Nas!" (Interview at the Jet Way. Iurii Luzhkov: Chukotka Charmed Us!). *Krainii Sever,* 20 August 1996, p. 1

8The china factory in Likino-Dulevo is called *ZAO Tovarishchestvo Kuznetsovskii Farfor (fabrika "Dulevo").*

9These "containers" *(konteinery)* are no small matter; they are steel boxes the size of a backyard shed that are used to transport freight on steam ships.

10*Postanovlenie Gubernatora Chukotskogo Avtonomnogo Okruga No. 181 ot 16 Avgusta 1999 g. "O Vremennykh Ogranicheniyakh Registratsii Pribyvaiushchikh Grazhdan po Mestu Zhitel'stva v g. Anadyre i Raionnykh Tsentrakh Chukotskogo Avtonomnogo Okruga"* (Resolution of the Governor of the Chukotka Autonomous Region No. 181 of 16 August 1999 "On the Temporary Limitation of Registration of Incoming Citizens for Place of Residence in Anadyr and District Centers of the Chukotka Autonomous Region").

11The list was titled *"Grazhdan, Nuzhdaiushchikhsia v Uluchshenii Zhiloi Ploshchadi po Sostoianiyu na 1 Aprelia 1996 g. – iz Chisla Malochislennykh Korennykh Narodov Severa, Prozhivaiushchikh v g. Anadyre"* (Citizens Needing to Improve Their Living Space as of 1 April 1996 – from Among the Less-Numerous Indigenous Peoples of the North Living in the City of Anadyr').

12As Pika (1993:62) has pointed out, Russian statistical agencies do not compile separate demographic profiles for the less-numerous peoples of the North. To compile statistics on mortality for individual populations of indigenous peoples, Pika had to visit local offices of ZAGS (*Zapisi Aktov Grazhdanskogo Sostoianiya* – Registry of Acts of Civil Affairs) in villages across the North, from the Kola Peninsula to the Chukotka Peninsula.

13See Crabb et al. 1989; Li and Lockmuller 1989; Segal et al. 1991.

14See Avksentyuk et al. 1995; Kurilovitsch et al. 1994; Segal 1998; Segal et al. 1994.

15*Federal'nyi Zakon RF No. 154-FZ ot 28 Avgusta 1995 g. "Ob Obshchikh Printsipakh Organizatsii Mestnogo Samoupravleniya v Rossiiskoi Federatsii"* (Federal Law of the RF No. 154-FZ of 28 August 1995 "On General Principles for the Organization of Local Self-Government in the Russian Federation").

Epilogue

1An English translation was later produced by IWGIA; see Kohler and Wessendorf 2002.

[2]ICC's project is described on its own website, which can be accessed at the address www.inuitcircumpolar.com. A description of the project in Russian appears on the RAIPON website, www.raipon.org.

[3]The UNEP/GRID-Arendal website can be found at the address www.grida.no.

[4]Andrew Higgins, "It Isn't Always Normal To Discover a Mogul in the Arctic Snow," *Wall Street Journal*, Wednesday, 13 June 2001, p. A1; "A Fresh Wind Blows: A New Governor Brings Personal Wealth, Promise of Change to Destitute Russian Province," *Seattle Times*, Monday, 14 May 2001; "Messias in der Eiswüste" (Messiah in the Ice Desert), *Der Spiegel*, Vol. 52, 2000, pp. 144–6.

[5]"Oligarch/Governor Continues to Enjoy Popularity," *Radio Free Europe/Radio Liberty Russian Federation Report*, 20 February 2002. Internet edition.

[6]I first learned this in April 2002 from a Chukotkan consultee in St. Petersburg, who had attended a gathering Abramovich held with students from Chukotka. He told them he was leaving the future of Chukotka in their hands, since he did not intend to seek a second term. See also "Governors and Business in Putin's Russia," *EastWest Institute Russian Regional Report*, 8 May 2002.

[7]See Balzer 1999; Fondahl 1998; Novikova 2002; Sirina 1999.

[8]See, for example, Cellarius and Staddon 2002; Fisher 1997; Leve and Karim 2001.

REFERENCES

Abu-Lughod, Lila, 1990, "The Romance of Resistance: Tracing Transformations of Power Through Bedouin Women." *American Anthropologist* 17:41–55.

Achirgina-Arsiak, Tatiana, 1992, "Paianitok!" *Etudes/Inuit/Studies* 16(1–2):47–50.

Agarwal, N. N., 1969, *Soviet Nationalities Policy*. Agra, India: Sri Ram Mehra.

Aipin, Eremei, 1991a, comments made at the joint meeting of the Soviet of the Union and the Soviet of Nationalities, Supreme Soviet. In *Piataya Sessiya Verkhovnogo Soveta S.S.S.R., 20–25 Maia 1991 g., Stenograficheskii Otchet, Biulleten'*, No. 61. Pp. 126–7. Moscow: Verkhovnyi Sovet SSSR.

———, 1991b, comments made at the joint meeting of the Soviet of the Union and the Soviet of Nationalities, Supreme Soviet, 24 May 1991. In *Piataya Sessiya Verkhovnogo Soveta S.S.S.R., 20–25 Maia 1991 g., Stenograficheskii Otchet, Biulleten'*, No. 64. P. 227. Moscow: Verkhovnyi Sovet USSR.

———, 1994, "My Home Among the Snow. Arctic Peoples: What Are We?" In *AEPS and Indigenous Peoples' Knowledge: Report on Seminar on Integration of Indigenous Peoples' Knowledge*. B. V. Hansen, ed. Pp. 202–5. Copenhagen: Ministry for the Environment (Iceland), Ministry of the Environment (Denmark), and the Home Rule of Greenland (Denmark Office).

Aipin, Yeremei [Eremei], 1989, "Not By Oil Alone." *IWGIA Newsletter* 57:137–43.

Anderson, David, 2000, *Identity and Ecology in Arctic Siberia: The Number One Reindeer Brigade*. Oxford: Oxford University Press.

Anderson, David G., 1996, "Bringing Civil Society to an Uncivilised Place: Citizenship Regimes in Russia's Arctic Frontier". In *Civil Society: Challenging Western Models*. Chris Hann and Elizabeth Dunn, eds. Pp. 99–120. New York: Routledge.

Anisimov, A. F., 1963, "Cosmological Concepts of the Peoples of the North." In *Studies in Siberian Shamanism*. H. N. Michael, ed. Pp. 157–229. Toronto: University of Toronto Press.

Appadurai, Arjun, 1990, "Disjuncture and Difference in the Global Cultural Economy." *Public Culture* 2(2):1–24.

Arato, Andrew, 1991, "Social Movements and Civil Society in the Soviet Union." In *Perestroika from Below: Social Movements in the Soviet Union*. Judith B. Sedaitis and Jim Butterfield, eds. Pp. 197–214. Boulder, CO: Westview Press.

Arutiunov, S. A., 1969, *Drevnie kul'tury aziatskikh eskimosov (Uelenskii mogil'nyk)* (Ancient Cultures of the Asian Eskimos [The Uelen Burial Ground]). Moscow: Nauka.

Asch, Michael, 1997, *Aboriginal and Treaty Rights in Canada: Essays on Law, Equity, and Respect for Difference*. Vancouver: UBC Press.

Avksentyuk, Alexi V., et al., 1995, "Alcohol Consumption and Flushing Response in Natives of Chukotka, Siberia." *Journal of Studies on Alcohol* 56:194–201.

Balzer, Marjorie Mandelstam, 1999, *The Tenacity of Ethnicity: A Siberian Saga in Global Perspective*. Princeton, NJ: Princeton University Press.

Bartels, Dennis A., and Alice L. Bartels, 1995, *When the North Was Red: Aboriginal Education in Soviet Siberia*. Montreal: McGill-Queen's University Press.

Beaudry, Nicole, 1990, "A Week with Soviet Eskimo Singers and Dancers." *Canadian Folk Music Bulletin* 24(2):25–6.

Berliner, Jeff, 1989, "Siberians Fly to Alaska." United Press International, Fairbanks, AK.

Bloch, Alexia, 1996, Between Socialism and the Market: Indigenous Siberian Evenki Grapple with Change. Dissertation, University of Pittsburgh, Pittsburgh, PA.

Blumer, Herbert, 1951, "Social Movements." In *New Outline of the Principles of Sociology*. A. M. Lee, ed. Pp. 199–220. New York: Barnes and Noble.

Bobrick, Benson, 1992, *East of the Sun: The Epic Conquest and Tragic History of Siberia*. New York: Poseidon Press.

Bogoras, Waldemar [Bogoraz, Vladimir], 1904–9, "The Chukchee." *The Jesup North Pacific Expedition*, Vol. 7, Parts 1–3. *Memoirs of the American Museum of Natural History*, 11. New York: G. E. Stechert.

————, 1913, "The Eskimo of Siberia." *The Jesup North Pacific Expedition*, Vol. 8, Parts 3. *Memoirs of the America Museum of Natural History*, 12. New York: G. E. Stechert.

————, 1917, "Koryak Texts." *Publications of the American Ethnological Society,* Vol. 5. Leiden: E. J. Brill; New York: G. E. Stechert.

————, 1918, "Tales of the Yukaghir, Lamut and Russianized Natives of Eastern Siberia." *Anthropological Papers of the American Museum of Natural History* 20(1): 3–148.

Bond, Andrew R., 1994, "Outmigration, Economic Dislocation, and Reassessment of the Labor Resource in the Russian Far North." *Post-Soviet Geography* 35(5):299–308.

Bourdieu, Pierre, 1986, "The Forms of Capital." In *Handbook of Theory and Research for the Sociology of Education.* J. Richardson, ed. Pp. 241–58. New York: Greenwood Press.

Boycko, Maxim, Andrei Shleiter, and Robert Vishny, 1995, *Privatizing Russia.* Cambridge, MA: MIT Press.

Bremmer, Ian, and Ray Taras, eds., 1993, *Nations and Politics in the Soviet Successor States.* Cambridge, UK: Cambridge University Press.

Brown, Michael F., 1996, "On Resisting Resistance." *American Anthropologist* 98(4):729–35.

Brown, Michael F., 1991, "Beyond Resistance: A Comparative Study of Utopian Renewal in Amazonia." *Ethnohistory* 38(4):388–413.

Buckley, Cynthia J., 1995, "Back to the Collective: Production and Consumption on a Siberian Collective Farm." In *Rediscovering Russia in Asia: Siberia and the Russian Far East.* S. Kotkin and D. Wolff, eds. Pp. 224–39. Armonk, NY: M. E. Sharpe.

Burdick, John, 1995, "Everyday Resistance Is Not Enough: Anthropology and Social Movements." *Dialectical Anthropology* 20:361–85.

Bush, Richard J., 1872, *Reindeer, Dogs, and Snow-Shoes: A Journal of Siberian Travel and Explorations Made in the Years 1865, 1866, and 1867.* London: Sampson Low, Son, and Larston.

Cellarius, Barbara A., and Caedmon Staddon, 2002, "Environmental Non-governmental Organizations, Civil Society, and Democratization in Bulgaria." *East European Politics and Societies* 16(1):182–222.

Cherkasov, Arkadi, 1982, "The Native Population of the Soviet North: Language Education and Employment." *Musk-Ox* 30 (Summer):65–72.

Chernyshevsky, Nikolai, 1986, *What Is To Be Done?* Ann Arbor, MI: Ardis.

Chichlo, Boris, 1993, "1991 International Expedition 'World Scientists' Contribution to the Siberian Far North'." In *Questions Siberiennes. Sibérie III: Les Peuples du Kamtchatka et de la Tchoukotka* (Siberian Questions. Siberia III: The Peoples of Kamchatka and Chukotka). B. Chichlo, ed. Pp. 23–33. Paris: Institut d'Études Slaves.

Chinn, Jeff, and Robert J. Kaiser, 1996, *Russians as the New Minority: Ethnicity and Nationalism in the Soviet Successor States.* Boulder, CO: Westview Press.

Clemmer, Richard O., 1999, "Resistance and the Revitalization of Anthropologists: A New Perspective on Cultural Change and Resistance." In *Reinventing Anthropology*. D. Hymes, ed. Pp. 213–47. Ann Arbor, MI: University of Michigan Press.

Cohen, Jean L., 1985, "Strategy or Identity: New Theoretical Paradigms and Contemporary Social Movements." *Social Research* 52:663–716.

Comaroff, Jean, 1985, *Body of Power, Spirit of Resistance: The Culture and History of a South African People*. Chicago, IL: University of Chicago Press.

Comaroff, John, and Jean Comaroff, 1992, *Ethnography and the Historical Imagination*. Boulder, CO: Westview Press.

Connor, Walker, 1984, *The National Question in Marxist-Leninist Theory and Strategy*. Princeton, NJ: Princeton University Press.

Conquest, Robert, 1967, *Soviet Nationalities Policy in Practice*. London: Bodley Head.

Corwin, Julie, 2000, "End Note: Russian Oligarch's Pre-Election Asset Grab." *Radio Free Europe/Radio Liberty Russian Federation Report* 2(8).

Crabb, D. W., et al., 1989, "Genotypes for Aldehyde Dehydrogenase Deficiency and Alcohol Sensitivity." *Journal of Clinical Investigation* 83:314–16.

Daes, Erica-Irene A., 1989, "On the Relations Between Indigenous Peoples and States." *Without Prejudice* 2(2):41–52.

Das, Veena, 1995, *Critical Events: An Anthropological Perspective on Contemporary India*. Oxford, UK: Oxford University Press.

D'iachkov, A. E., 1992 [1893], *Anadyrskii Krai* (Anadyr' Territory). Magadan: Magadanskoe Knizhnoe Izdatel'stvo.

Diakonova, Natalia, and Ekaterina Romanova, 2003, "The Role of the Yakut Intelligentsia in the National Movement." In *Indigenous Ecological Practices and Cultural Traditions in Yakutia: History, Ethnography, and Politics*. Hiroki Takakura, ed. Pp. 13–22. Sendai: Center for Northeast Asia Studies, Tohoku University.

Dikov, N. N., 1974, *Ocherki Istorii Chukotki s Drevneishikh Vremen do Nashikh Dnei* (Sketches of the History of Chukotka from Ancient Times to the Present Day). Novosibirsk: Nauka.

———, 1989, *Istoriya Chukotki s Drevneishikh Vremen do Nashikh Dnei* (The History of Chukotka from Ancient Times to the Present Day). Moscow: Mysl'.

Dmytryshyn, Basil, E. A. P. Crownhart-Vaughan, and Thomas Vaughan, eds., 1985, *Russia's Conquest of Siberia, 1558–1700: A Documentary Record*. Vol. 1, *To Siberia and Russian America: Three Centuries of Russian Eastward Expansion, 1558–1867*. Portland, OR: Oregon Historical Society.

———, 1986, *Russian Penetration of the North Pacific Ocean, 1700–1797: A Documentary Record*. Vol. 2, *To Siberia and Russian America, Three Centuries of Russian Eastward Expansion, 1558–1867*. Portland, OR: Oregon Historical Society.

————, 1989, *Russian American Colonies, 1798–1867: A Documentary Record.* Vol. 3, *To Siberia and Russian America, Three Centuries of Russian Eastward Expansion, 1558–1867.* Portland, OR: Oregon Historical Society.

Dolgikh, B. O., 1972, "The Formation of the Modern Peoples of the Soviet North." *Arctic* 9(1):17–26.

Drucker, Philip, 1958, *The Native Brotherhoods: Modern Intertribal Organizations on the Northwest Coast.* Washington, DC: United States Government Printing Office.

Dunlop, John B., 1993, *The Rise of Russia and the Fall of the Soviet Empire.* Princeton, NJ: Princeton University Press.

Dunn, Michael, 2000, "Chukchi Women's Language: A Historical-Comparative Perspective." *Anthropological Linguistics* 42(3):305–28.

Edelman, M, 2001, "Social Movements: Changing Paradigms and Forms of Politics." *Annual Review of Anthropology* 30:285–317.

Eidheim, Harald, 1968, "The Lappish Movement: An Innovative Political Process." In *Local-Level Politics: Social and Cultural Perspectives.* M. J. Swartz, ed. Pp. 205–16. Chicago, IL: Aldine.

Escobar, Arturo, 1992, "Culture, Practice and Politics: Anthropology and the Study of Social Movements." *Critique of Anthropology* 12(4):395–432.

————, 1995, *Encountering Development: The Making and Unmaking of the Third World.* Princeton, NJ: Princeton University Press.

Etylen [Etylin], Vladimir Mikhailovich 1989a, speech made at the Second Congress of People's Deputies. In *Vtoroi S"ezd Narodnykh Deputatov S.S.S.R. 12–24 Dekabria 1989 g. Stenograficheskii Otchet,* Tom I. Pp. 612–15. Moscow: Verkhovnyi Sovet SSSR.

————, 1989b, speech submitted to the First Congress of People's Deputies. In *Pervyi S"ezd Narodnykh Deputatov S.S.S.R. 25 Maia – 9 Iiunia 1989 g., Stenograficheskii Otchet,* Tom IV. Pp. 433–9. Moscow: Verkhovnyi Sovet SSSR.

————, 1990, speech made at the Fourth Congress of People's Deputies. In *Pervyi S"ezd Narodnykh Deputatov S.S.S.R. 17–27 Dekabria 1990 g., Stenograficheskii Otchet,* Tom II. Pp. 374–5. Moscow: Verkhovnyi Sovet SSSR.

Fabian, Johannes, 1983, *Time and the Other: How Anthropology Makes Its Object.* New York: Columbia University Press.

Feit, Harvey, 1989, "James Bay Cree Self-Governance and Land Management." In *We Are Here: Politics of Aboriginal Land Tenure.* E. N. Wilmsen, ed. Pp. 68–98. Berkeley, CA: University of California Press.

Fienup-Riordan, Ann, 2000, *Hunting Tradition in a Changing World: Yup'ik Lives in Alaska Today.* New Brunswick, NJ: Rutgers University Press.

Fisher, William F., 1997, "Doing Good? The Politics and Antipolitics of NGO Practices." *Annual Review of Anthropology* 26:439–64.

Fitzhugh, William W., and Aron Crowell, 1988, *Crossroads of Continents: Cultures of Siberia and Alaska*. Washington, DC: Smithsonian Institution Press.

Flerov, V. S., 1973, *Revkomy Severo-Vostoka S.S.S.R.* (*Revkoms* of the Northeast of the USSR). Magadan: Magadanskoe Knizhnoe Izdatel'stvo.

Fliert, Lydia van de, ed., 1994, *Indigenous Peoples and International Organisations*. Nottingham, UK: Spokesman.

Fogel-Chance, Nancy, 1993, "Living in Both Worlds: 'Modernity' and 'Tradition' Among North Slope Inupiaq Women in Anchorage." *Arctic Anthropology*. 30(1):94–108.

Fondahl, Gail, 1998, *Gaining Ground? Evenkis, Land, and Reform in Southeastern Siberia*. Boston, MA: Allyn and Bacon.

Forsythe, James, 1992, *A History of the Peoples of Siberia: Russia's North Asian Colony 1581–1990*. New York: Cambridge University Press.

Fossato, Floriana, 1999, "Kremlin Players Vie for Political Power." *Radio Free Europe/Radio Liberty Weekday Magazine, Internet edition* (8 June 1999).

Fox, Richard G., and Orin Starn, eds., 1997, *Between Resistance and Revolution: Cultural Politics and Social Protest*. New Brunswick, NJ: Rutgers University Press.

Freeman, Milton M. R., ed., 2000, *Endangered Peoples of the Arctic: Struggles to Survive and Thrive*. Westport, CT: Greenwood Press.

Gaer, Evdokia A., 1989a, "I Ask For the Floor: A Chernobyl on Chukotka. The Peoples of the North Are Paying for Nuclear Tests." *Moskovskie Novosti* 34 (20 August):5.

———, 1989b, speech made at the First Congress of People's Deputies (also translated in Glebov and Crowfoot 1989). In *Pervyi S"ezd Narodnykh Deputatov S.S.S.R., 25 Maia – 9 Iiunia 1989 g., Stenograficheskii Otchet*, Tom III. Pp. 84–91. Moscow: Verkhovnyi Sovet SSSR.

Gambold-Miller, Liesl, 2002, "Communal Coherence and Barriers to Reform." In *Rural Reform in Post-Soviet Russia*. D. J. O'Brien and S. K. Wegren, eds. Pp. 221–42. Baltimore, MD: Woodrow Wilson Center Press.

Gazha, Andrei, 1998, *Net Luchshego Lekarstva, Chem Liubov'* (There's No Better Medicine Than Love). Anadyr': Izdatel'skii Dom "Chukotka."

Glebov, Oleg, and John Crowfoot, 1989, *The Soviet Empire: Its Nations Speak Out*. New York: Harwood Academic Publishers.

Gogolev, Z. V., et al., 1975, *Yukagiry: Istoriko-Etnograficheskii Ocherk* (The Yukagirs: Historical-Ethnographic Sketch). Novosibirsk: Nauka, Sibirskoe Otdelenie.

Goskomstat Rossii, 1994, *Rossiiskii Statisticheskii Ezhegodnik: Statisticheskii Sbornik* (Statistical Annual of Russia: Statistical Collection). Moscow: Goskomstat Rossii.

———, 1999, *Regiony Rossii: Ofitsial'noe Izdanie* (Regions of Russia: Official Publication), Vols. 1, 2. Moscow: Goskomstat Rossii.

Goskomstat RSFSR, 1991, *Kratkaya Sotsial'no-Demograficheskaya Kharakteris-tika Naseleniya R.S.F.S.R. (po Dannym Vsesoiuznoi Perepisi Naseleniya 1989 Goda)*, Chast' I (Brief Sociodemographic Characterization of the Population of the RSFSR [According to Data from the All-Union Census of the Population of 1989], Part I). Moscow: Respublikanskii Informatsionno-Izdatel'skii Tsentr.

Goskomstat SSSR, 1991, Chislennost' Naseleniya Soyuznykh Respublik po Gorodskim Poseleniyam i Raionam na 1 Ianvaria 1991 g.: Statisticheskii Sbornik (Population of the Union Republics by City and District on 1 January 1991: Statistical Collection). Moscow: Goskomstat SSSR.

Graburn, Nelson H. H., 1981, "1,2,3,4: Anthropology and the Fourth World." *Culture* 1(1):66–70.

Graburn, Nelson H. H., and Stephen Strong, eds., 1973, *Circumpolar Peoples: An Anthropological Perspective*. Pacific Palisades, CA: Goodyear.

Graney, K. E., 2001, "Ten Years of Sovereignty in Tatarstan – End of the Beginning or Beginning of the End?" *Problems of Post-Communism* 48(5):32–41.

Grant, Bruce, 1995, *In the Soviet House of Culture: A Century of Perestroikas*. Princeton, NJ: Princeton University Press.

Gras, Helle, 1989, "Soviet Inuit 'Reunited' with Arctic Family." United Press International, 24 July 1989, accessed on LEXIS.

Gray, Patty A., 1997, "Snezhnoe: Where East and West Collide." *Transitions: Changes in Post-Communist Societies* 4(6):96–100.

———, 2000, "Chukotkan Reindeer Husbandry in the Post-Socialist Transition." *Polar Research* 19(1):31–7.

Grichenkovaia, I., and Ivan Ivanovich Ivkev, 1990, "Interv'iu posle Uchreditel'noi Konferentsii Korennykh Narodov Chukotki i Kolymy: Uslyshat' i Poniat' Drug Druga" (Interview After the Founding Conference of Indigenous Peoples of Chukotka and Kolyma: Listen and Understand Each Other). *Magadanskii Olenevod* 42:10–13.

Gurvich, I. S., 1962, "Directions To Be Taken in the Further Reorganization of the Economy and Culture of the Peoples of the North." *Soviet Anthropology and Archaeology* 1(2):22–30.

———, 1969, "Socio-Economical Transformation and Modern Ethnical Development of the Inhabitants of the Siberian Polar Zones of the North-Eastern Regions." In *Circumpolar Problems: Habitat, Economy, and Social Relations in the Arctic*. G. Berg, ed. Pp. 53–60. New York: Pergamon Press.

———, 1987, "Vvodnyi Ocherk: K Sotsializmu, Minuya Kapitalizm" (Introductory Sketch: To Socialism, Skipping Capitalism). In *Etnicheskoe Razvitie Narodnost'ei Severa v Sovetskii Period* (Ethnic Development of the Peoples of the North in the Soviet Period). I. S. Gurvich, ed. Pp. 11–31. Moscow: Nauka.

Hahn, Jeffrey W., 1988, *Soviet Grassroots: Citizen Participation in Local Soviet Government*. Princeton, NJ: Princeton University Press.

Hann, Chris, and Elizabeth Dunn, 1996, *Civil Society: Challenging Western Models*. New York: Routledge.

Harris, Marvin, and Orna Johnson, 2003, *Cultural Anthropology*, 6th ed. Boston: Allyn and Bacon.

Haruchi, Galina, 2002, "The Indigenous Intelligentsia." In *Towards a New Millennium: Ten Years of the Indigenous Movement in Russia*. Thomas Køhler and Kathrin Wessendorf, eds. Pp. 86–93. Copenhagen: International Work Group for Indigenous Affairs.

Has, Michael, and Tyan Zaochnaia, 1993, "The Present Situation of Indigenous Peoples in Siberia." In *Amazonia and Siberia: Legal Aspects of the Preservation of the Environment and Development in the Last Open Spaces*. M. Bothe, T. Kurzidem, and C. Schmidt, eds. London: Graham and Trotman.

Haviland, William A., 2002, *Cultural Anthropology*, 10th ed. Belmont, CA: Wadsworth.

Heleniak, Timothy, 1997, "Internal Migration in Russia During the Economic Transition." *Post-Soviet Geography and Economics* 38(2):81–104.

Hendley, Kathryn, 1996, *Trying to Make Law Matter: Legal Reform and Labor Law in the Soviet Union*. Ann Arbor, MI: University of Michigan Press.

Hill, Jonathan D., 1988, *Rethinking History and Myth: Indigenous South American Perspectives on the Past*. Chicago, IL: University of Illinois Press.

Hivon, Myriam, 1995, "Local Resistance to Privatization in Rural Russia." *Cambridge Anthropology* 18(2):13–22.

Hodgson, Dorothy L., 2002, "Introduction: Comparative Perspectives on the Indigenous Rights Movement in Africa and the Americas." *American Anthropologist* 104(4):1037–49.

Hughes, Charles C., 1984, "Siberian Eskimo." In *Handbook of North American Indians*, Vol. 5, *Arctic*. D. Damas, ed. Pp. 247–61. Washington, DC: Smithsonian Institution Press.

Humphrey, Caroline, 1991, "" 'Icebergs', Barter, and the Mafia in Provincial Russia." *Anthropology Today* 7(2):8–13.

———, 1994, "Remembering an 'Enemy': The Bogd Khaan in Twentieth-Century Mongolia." In *Memory, History, and Opposition Under State Socialism*. R. S. Watson, ed. Pp. 21–44. Santa Fe, NM: School of American Research Press.

———, 1995, "Introduction (to the special issue of *Cambridge Anthropology* titled "Surviving the Transition: Development Concerns in the Post-Socialist World"). *Cambridge Anthropology* 18(2):1–12.

———, 1999, "Traders, 'Disorder,' and Citizenship Regimes in Provincial Russia." In *Uncertain Transition: Ethnographies of Change in the Postsocialist*

World. M. Burawoy and K. Verdery, eds. Pp. 19–52. New York: Rowman and Littlefield.

Inenlikei, P. I., 1982, *Chukotsko – Russkii i Russko – Chukotskii Slovar': Posobie dlia Uchashchikhsia Nachal'noi Shkoly* (Chukchi – Russian and Russian – Chukchi Dictionary: Textbook for Pupils in Elementary School). Leningrad: Prosveshchenie.

Ivanov, Valerii, 1996, "Statistika – Azbuka Glasnost': Kto My, Kakie My, Kak My Zhivem?" (Statistics – The Alphabet of Openness: Who Are We, What Are We Like, How Do We Live?). *Krainii Sever,* 4 April 1996' p. 3.

IWGIA, 1990, *Indigenous Peoples of the Soviet North.* IWGIA Document No. 67. Copenhagen: International Work Group for Indigenous Affairs.

Jochelson, Waldemar [Vladimir], 1908, "The Koryak." *The Jesup North Pacific Expedition,* Vol. 6, Parts. 1–2. *Memoirs of the American Museum of Natural History,* 10. New York: G. E. Stechert.

Kaapcke, Gretchen, 1994, "Indigenous Identity Transition in Russia." *Cultural Survival Quarterly* Summer / Fall 1994:62–68.

Kaiser, Robert J., 1994, *The Geography of Nationalism in Russia and the USSR.* Princeton, NJ: Princeton University Press.

Kaminskii, M., 1973, *V Nebe Chukotki* (In the Skies of Chukotka). Moscow: Molodaya Gvardiya.

Kerttula, Anna M., 1997, "Antler on the Sea: Creating and Maintaining Cultural Group Boundaries Among the Chukchi, Yup'ik, and Newcomers of Sireniki." *Arctic Anthropology* 34(1):212–26.

———, 2000, *Antler on the Sea: The Yup'ik and Chukchi of the Russian Far East.* Ithaca, NY: Cornell University Press.

Kochan, Lionel, and Richard Abraham, 1962, *The Making of Modern Russia.* New York: Penguin Books.

Køhler, Thomas, and Kathrin Wessendorf, eds., 2002, *Towards a New Millennium: Ten Years of the Indigenous Movement in Russia.* Copenhagen: International Work Group for Indigenous Affairs.

Kolarz, Walter, 1967, "The Chukchi of the Soviet Far East." In *Beyond the Frontier: Social Process and Cultural Change.* P Bohannan and F. Plog, eds. Pp. 103–17. Garden City, NY: Natural History Press.

Korobova, E. S., ed., 1991, *Narodov Malykh Ne Byvaet* (There Are No Small Peoples). Moscow: Molodaya Gvardiya.

Kotok, V. F., and N. Ia Kuprits, 1950, *Konstitutsiya S.S.S.R.: Uchebnoe Posobie dlia Prepodavatelei Srednei Shkoly* (Constitution of the SSSR: Textbook for Teaching Middle Schools). Moscow: Gosudarstvennoe Uchebnoe Pedagogicheskoe Izdatel'stvo Ministerstva Prosveshcheniya RSFSR.

Kotov, A. N. et al., 1995, Chukotka: Prirodno-Ekonomicheskii Ocherk (Chukotka: Natural-Economic Sketch). Moscow and Anadyr': Izdatel'stvo Art-Liteks.

Kottak, Conrad Phillip, 2002, *Cultural Anthropology*, 9th ed. Boston, MA: McGraw-Hill.

Kozlov, V. I., 1988, *The Peoples of the Soviet Union*. Bloomington, IN: Indiana University Press.

Krauss, Michael, 1994, Crossroads? "A Twentieth-Century History of Contacts Across the Bering Strait." In *Anthropology of the North Pacific Rim*. W. W. Fitzhugh and V. Chaussonet, eds. Pp. 365–79. Washington, DC: Smithsonian Institution Press.

Kreinovich, E. A., 1982, *Issledovaniya i Materialy po Yukagirskomu Iazyku* (Research and materials on the Yukagir Language). Leningrad: Nauka, Leningradskoe Otdelenie.

Kriazhkov, V. A., 1994, *Status Malochislennykh Narodov Rossii: Pravovye Akty i Dokumenty* (The Status of the Lesser-Numbered Peoples of Russia: Legal Acts and Documents). Moscow: Iuridicheskaya Literatura.

———, 1999, *Status Malochislennykh Narodov Rossii: Pravovye Akty, Kniga Vtoraya* (The Status of the Lesser-Numbered Peoples of Russia: Legal Acts, Book Two). Moscow: Izdanie g-na Tikhomirova, M. Iu.

Krupnik, Igor, 1980, "Eskimosy (Pokhoronnaya Obriadnost')" (Eskomos [Funerary Rites]). In *Semeinaya Obriadnost' Narodov Sibiri: Opyt Sravnitel'nogo Izucheniya* (Family Ceremonials of the Peoples of Siberia: An Experiment of Comparative Study). I. S. Gurvich, ed. Pp. 207–15. Moscow: Nauka.

———, 1989, *Arkticheskaya Etnoekologiya: Modeli Traditsionnogo Prirodopol'zovaniya Morskikh Okhotnikov i Olenevodov Severnoi Evrazii* (Arctic Ethnoecology: Models of Traditional Use of Nature Among Marine Hunters and Reindeer Herders of Northern Eurasia). Moscow: Nauka.

———, 1993, *Arctic Adaptations: Native Whalers and Reindeer Herders of Northern Eurasia*. Hanover, NH: University Press of New England.

Krupnik, Igor, and Nikolai Vakhtin, 2002, "In the 'House of Dismay': Knowledge, Culture, and Post-Soviet Politics in Chukotka, 1995–1996." In *People and the Land: Pathways to Reform in Post-Soviet Siberia*. E. Kasten, ed. Pp. 7–43. Berlin: Dietrich Reimer Verlag.

Krushanov, A. I., 1982, *Sovety Severo-Vostoka S.S.S.R. (1941–1961 gg.): Sbornik Dokumentov i Materialov, Chast' 2* (The Soviets of Northeast USSR [1941–61]: Collection of Documents and Materials, Part 2). Magadan: Magadanskoe Knizhnoe Izdatel'stvo.

———, 1986, *Sovety Severo-Vostoka S.S.S.R. (1962–1982 gg.): Sbornik Dokumentov i Materialov, Chast' 3* (The Soviets of Northeast USSR [1962–82]: Collection of Documents and Materials, Part 3). Magadan: Magadanskoe Knizhnoe Izdatel'stvo.

———, 1987, *Istoriia i Kul'tura Chukchei: Istoriko-Etnograficheskiie Ocherki* (The History and Culture of Chukotka: Historical-Ethnograhic Sketches). Leningrad: Nauka.

Kuoljok, Kerstin Eidlitz, 1985, *The Revolution in the North: Soviet Ethnography and Nationality Policy*. Uppsala: Acta Universitatis Upsaliensis.

Kurilovitsch, S. A., et al., 1994, "Alcohol Drinking Among Chukotka Natives: The Myths and Reality." *Arctic Medical Research* 53(Suppl. 2):545–6.

Lâm, Maivân Clech, 2000, *"At the Edge of the State: Indigenous Peoples and Self-Determination."* Ardsley, NY: Transnational Publishers.

Lambroschini, Sophie, 1999, "Kremlin Maneuvers for Loyalty of Large Companies Before Election." *Radio Free Europe/Radio Liberty Weekday Magazine* (21 September 1999).

Lantis, Margaret, 1973, "The Current Nativistic Movement in Alaska." In *Circumpolar Problems: Habitat, Economy, and Social Relations in the Arctic*. G. Berg, ed. Pp. 99–118. New York: Pergamon Press.

Leatherbarrow, W. J., and D. C. Offord, 1987, *A Documentary History of Russian Thought from the Enlightenment to Marxism*. Ann Arbor, MI: Ardis.

Leksin, Vladimir, and Yelena Andreyeva, 1995, "The Small Peoples of the North: Ethnic Relations and Prospects for Survival Under New Conditions." *Polar Geography and Geology* 19(1):36–78.

Leontev, V. V., 1973, *Khoziaistvo i Kul'tura Narodov Chukotki (1958–1970 gg.)* (Economy and Culture of the Peoples of Chukotka, 1958–70). Novosibirsk: Izdatel'stvo "Nauka" Sibirskoe Otdelenie.

———, 1976, *Na Zemle Drevnykh Kerekov* (In the Land of the Ancient Kereks). Magadan: Magadanskoe Knizhnoe Izdatel'stvo.

———, 1977, "The Indigenous Peoples of Chukchi National Okrug: Population and Settlement." *Polar Geography* 1:9–22.

———, 1983, *Etnografiya i Fol'klor Kerekov* (Ethnography and Folklore of the Kereks). Moscow: Nauka.

Leontev, V. V., and K. A. Alekseev, 1980, *Chukotskii Iazyk: Uchebnik i Kniga dlia Chteniya v 3-m Klasse Chukotskoi Nachal'noi Shkoly.* (Chukchi Languge: Textbook and Reader for the Third Grade in Chukchi Elementary Schools) Leningrad: Prosveshchenie.

Leve, Lauren, and Lamia Karim, 2001, "Privatizing the State: Ethnography of Development, Transnational Capital, and NGOs." *Political and Legal Anthropology Review* 24(1):53–8.

Levin, M. G., and L. P. Potapov, 1956, *Narody Sibiri* (The Peoples of Siberia). Moscow: Akademiya Nauk.

———, 1964, *The Peoples of Siberia*. Chicago, IL: University of Chicago Press.

Lewellen, Ted C., 1992, *Political Anthropology: An Introduction*. Westport, CT: Bergin and Garvey.

Li, T-K., and J. C. Lockmuller, 1989, "Why Are Some People More Susceptible to Alcoholism?" *Alcohol Health and Research World* 13(4):310–15.

Liarskaya, Elena, 2001, "Kul'turnaya Assimiliatsiya ili Dva Varianta Kul'tury?" (Cultural Assimilation or Two Variants of Culture?). In *Antropologiya.*

Fol'kloristika. Lingvistika: Sbornik Statei, Vypusk 1 (Anthropology. Folk-loristics. Linguistics: Collection of Articles, Vol. 1). A. K. Baiburin and V. B. Kolosova, eds. Pp. 36–55. St. Petersburg: European University of St. Petersburg.

Liber, George, 1991, "*Korenizatsiya:* Restructuring Soviet Nationality Policy in the 1920s." *Ethnic and Racial Studies* 14(1):15–23.

Linton, Ralph, 1943, "Nativistic Movements." *American Anthropologist* 45: 230–40.

Luk'iachenkho, T. V., and N. I. Novikova, 1991, "O Rabote Uchreditel'nogo S'ezda Narodnykh Deputatov ot Malochislennykh Narodov Severa, Sibiri i Dal'nego Vostoka" (On the Work of the Founding Congress of Peoples Deputies Representing the Lesser-Numbered Peoples of the North, Siberia, and the Far East). *Sovetskaia Etnografiya* 6:134–8.

Maheu, Louis, 1995, *Social Movements and Social Classes: The Future of Collective Action.* Newbury Park: Sage Publications.

Manuel, George, and Michael Posluns, 1974, *The Fourth World: An Indian Reality.* New York: Free Press.

McAdams, Doug, John McCarthy, and Mayer Zald, 1996, *Comparative Perspectives on Social Movements: Political Opportunities, Mobilizing Structures, and Cultural Framings.* New York: Cambridge University Press.

McFarlane, Peter, 1993, *Brotherhood to Nationhood: George Manuel and the Making of the Modern Indian Movement.* Toronto: Between the Lines.

Melucci, Alberto, 1989, *Nomads of the Present: Social Movements and Individual Needs in Contemporary Society.* Philadelphia, PA: Temple University Press.

Menovshchikov, G. A., 1977, *Na Chukotskoi Zemle. Iz Zapisok Uchitelia. Putevye Zametki.* (In the Land of Chukotka. From the Memoirs of a Teacher. Travel Notes.). Magadan: Magadanskoe Knizhnoe Izd-vo.

―――, 1988, *Materialy i Issledovaniya po Iazyku i Fol'kloru Chaplinskikh Eskimosov* (Materials and Research on the Languages and Folklore of the Chaplino Eskimos). Leningrad: Nauka.

―――, 1990, "Contemporary Studies of the Eskimo-Aleut Languages and Dialects: A Progress Report." In *Arctic Languages: An Awakening.* D. R. F. Collis, ed. Pp. 69–76. Paris: UNESCO.

Meyer, Alfred G., 1965, *The Soviet Political System: An Interpretation.* New York: Random House.

Mikhailova, Elena, 1977, "Zametki o Iazykovoi Situatsii u Aziiatskikh Eskimosov" (Notes on the Language Situation Among the Asiatic Eskimos). *Polevye Issledovaniya Instituta Etnografii* 1977:164–7.

Miller, John H., 1992, "Cadres Policy in Nationality Areas: Recruitment of CPSU First and Second Secretaries in Non-Russian Republics of the USSR." In *The Soviet Nationality Reader: The Disintegration in Context.* R. Denber, ed. Pp. 183–209. Boulder, CO: Westview Press.

Minority Rights Group, 1994, *Polar Peoples: Self-Determination and Development*. London: Minority Rights Group.

Mongo, M. I., 1989, speech made at the first Congress of People's Deputies. In *Pervyi S"ezd Narodnykh Deputatov S.S.S.R., 25 Maia–9 Iiunia 1989 g., Stenograficheskii Otchet*, Tom II. Pp. 417–23. Moscow: Verkhovnyi Sovet SSSR.

Mouffe, Chantal, 1984, "Towards a Theoretical Interpretation of New Social Movements." In *Rethinking Marx*. S. Hanninen and L. Paldan, eds. Pp. 139–43. Berlin: Argument-Sonderband AS 109.

Nash, J., 1993, *We Eat the Mines, and the Mines Eat Us: Dependency and Exploitation in Bolivian Tin Mines*. New York: Columbia University Press.

Nemtushkin, Alitet, 1988, "Bol' Moia, Evenkiya!" (My Pain, Evenkiya!). *Sovetskaia Kul'tura*, 28 July 1988:3.

Nikolaev, S. I., 1964, *Eveny i Evenki Yugo-Vostochnoi Yakutii* (The Evens and Evenks of Southeast Yakutia). Yakutsk: Yakutskoe Knizhnoe Izdatel'stvo.

Novikova, Natalia, 2002, "Self-Government of the Indigenous Minority Peoples of West Siberia: Analysis of Law and Practice." In *People and the Land: Pathways to reform in Post-Soviet Siberia*. E. Kasten, ed. Pp. 75–92. Berlin: Dietrich Reimer Verlag.

Nuttall, Mark, 1998, *Protecting the Arctic: Indigenous Peoples and Cultural Survival*. Amsterdam: Hardwood Academic Publishers.

Obruchev, S. V., 1957, *Po Goram i Tundram Chukotka: Ekspeditsiya 1934–1935 gg* (Through the Mountains and Tundras of Chukotka: Expedition 1934–35). Moscow: Gosudarstvennoe Izdatel'stvo Geograficheskoi Literatury.

Odulok, T., 1954[1934], *Snow People (Chukchee)*. New Haven, CT: Behavior Science Translations, Human Research Area Files.

Ong, Aihwa, 1987, *Spirits of Resistance and Capitalist Discipline*. New York: SUNY Press.

Ortner, Sherry, 1995, "Resistance and the Problem of Ethnographic Refusal." *Comparative Studies in Society and History* 137 (1):173–93.

Peoples, James, and Garrick Bailey, 2003, *Humanity: An Introduction to Cultural Anthropology*, 6th ed. Belmont, CA: Wadsworth.

Petrenko, Eduard Petrovich, 1998, *Zdorov'e Naseleniya i Deiatel'nost' Uchrezhdenii Zdravokhraneniya Chukotskogo Avtonomnogo Okruga v 1997 Godu (Statisticheskii Sbornik)* (The Health of the Population and Activity of Institutions for Public Health of the Chukotka Autonomous Region in 1997 [Statistical Collection]). Anadyr': Departament Zdravokhraneniya ChAO/Chukotskii Filial SVKNII DVO RAN.

Pika, A. I., 1993, "The Spatial-Temporal Dynamic of Violent Death Among the Native Peoples of Northern Russia." *Arctic Anthropology* 30(2):61–76.

Pika, A. I., ed., 1999, *Neotraditionalism in the Russian North: Indigenous Peoples and the Legacy of Perestroika*. Seattle, WA: University of Washington Press.

Pika, A. I., and D. Bogoyavlensky, 1995, "Yamal Peninsula: Oil and Gas Development and Problems of Demography and Health Among Indigenous
Populations." *Arctic Anthropology* 32(2):61–74.

Pika, A. I., and B. B. Prokhorov, 1988, "Bolshie Problemy Malykh Narodov"
(The Big Problems of Small Peoples). *Kommunist* 16 (November):76–
83.

————, 1994, *Neotraditionalizm na Rossiiskom Severe (Etnicheskoe Vozrozh-
denie Malochisloennykh Narodov Severa i Gosudarstvennaya Regional'naya
Politika)* (Neotraditionalism in the Russian North [Ethnic Revival of the
Lesser-Numbered Peoples of the North and State Regional Politics]).
Moscow: Institut Narodnokhoziaistvennogo Prognozirovaniya, Tsentr De-
mografii i Ekologii Cheloveka Rossiiskoi Akademii Nauk, Mezhdunarodnaya
Rabochaya Gruppa po Delam Korennogo Naseleniya.

Pipes, Richard, 1964, *The Formation of the Soviet Union: Communism and
Nationalism 1917–1923*. Cambridge, MA: Harvard University Press.

Poelzer, Greg, 1995, "Devolution, Constitutional Development, and the Russian North." *Post-Soviet Geography* 36(4):204–14.

Popova, U. G., 1981, *Eveny Magadanskoi Oblasti: Ocherki Istorii, Khoziaistva i
Kul'tury Evenov Okhotskogo Poberezh'ia 1917–1977 gg* (The Evens of Magadan
Province: Sketches on History, Economy, and Culture of the Evens of the
Okhotsk Coast 1917–77). Moscow: Nauka.

Postnikov, Aleksandr E., 1996, "Legislation on Local Government in Russia." In
Democratization in Russia: The Development of Legislative Institutions. J. W.
Hahn, ed. Pp. 276–81. Armonk, NY: M. E. Sharpe.

Rakowska-Harmstone, Teresa, 1975, "The Study of Ethnic Politics in the
U.S.S.R." In *Nationalism in the U.S.S.R. and Eastern Europe in the Era of
Brezhnev and Kosygin*. G. W. Simmonds, ed. Pp. 20–36. Detroit, MI: Univer-
sity of Detroit Press.

Rethmann, Petra, 2001, *Tundra Passages: History and Gender in the Russian Far
East*. University Park, PA: Pennsylvania State University Press.

Rosaldo, Renato, 1989, *Culture and Truth: The Remaking of Social Analysis*.
Boston, MA: Beacon Press.

Rosenberg, Tina, 1996, *The Haunted Land: Facing Europe's Ghosts After Communism*. New York: Vintage Books.

Roulet, Florencia, 1999, *Human Rights and Indigenous Peoples: A Handbook on
the U.N. System*. IWGIA Document No. 92. Copenhagen: International Work
Group for Indigenous Affairs.

Rytkheu, Iurii, 1956, *Stories from Chukotka*. David Fry, trans. London:
Lawrence and Wishart.

————, 1988a, "Lozungi i Amulety: O Proshlom i Budushchem Narodov Severa
Razmyshliaet Pisatel' Iurii Rytkheu" (Slogans and Amulets: Iurii Rytkheu
Muses on the Past and the Future of the Peoples of the North). *Komso-
mol'skaya Pravda*, 19 May 1988:2.

————, 1988b, "Svet Zvezd–Bol'shikh i Malikh" (The Light of Stars – Big and Small). *Pravda,* 31 December 1988:3.

————, 1989, "Beloe Bezmovlie?" (White Silence?). *Ogonek* 17:20–1.

Sakwa, Richard, 1993, *Russian Politics and Society.* New York: Routledge.

Sanders, Douglas, 1980, *The Formation of the World Council of Indigenous Peoples.* IWGIA Document No. 29. Copenhagen: International Work Group for Indigenous Affairs.

Sangi, Vladimir, 1988, "Otchuzhdenie" (Alienation). *Sovetskaia Rossiya,* 11 September 1988:2.

Savoskul, S. S., 1989, "Urbanization and the Minority Peoples of the Soviet North." In *The Development of Siberia: People and Resources.* A. Wood and R. A. French, eds. Pp. 96–123. New York: St. Martin's Press.

Schindler, Debra, 1990, "The Political Economy of Ethnic Discourse in the Soviet Union." Dissertation, University of Massachusetts.

————, 1992, "Russian Hegemony and Indigenous Rights in Chukotka." *Etudes/Inuit/Studies* 16(1–2):51–74.

————, 1997, "Redefining Tradition and Renegotiating Ethnicity in Native Russia." *Arctic Anthropology* 34 (1):194–211.

Schultz, Emily A., and Robert H. Lavenda, 2001, *Cultural Anthropology: A Perspective on the Human Condition,* 5th ed. Mountain View, CA: Mayfield Publishing.

Schweitzer, Peter, 1990, "Kreuzungspunkt am Rande der Welt. Kontaktgeschichte und Soziale Verhaltnisse der Sibirischen Eskimo zwischen 1650 und 1920" (Crossing Point at the Edge of the World: Contact History and Social Conditions of the Siberian Eskimo Between 1650 and 1920). Dissertation, University of Vienna.

————, 1993, "Yanrakynnot – History and Ethnosocial Trends of a Chukchi Village." In *Questions Siberiennes. Sibérie III: Les Peuples du Kamtchatka et de la Tchoukotka* (Siberian Questions. Siberia III: The Peoples of Kamchatka and Chukotka). B. Chichlo, ed. Pp. 129–47. Paris: Institut d'Études Slaves.

Schweitzer, Peter, and Evgeniy Golovko, 1995, "Traveling Between Continents: The Social Organization of Interethnic Contacts Across Bering Strait." *Anthropology of East Europe Review* 13(2):50–5.

Scott, Colin, ed., 2001, *Aboriginal Autonomy and Development in Northern Quebec and Labrador.* Vancouver, BC: UBC Press.

Scott, James, 1986, "Resistance Without Protest: Peasant Opposition to the Zakat in Malaysia and to the Tithe in France." Fourth James C. Jackson Memorial Lecture: Malaysian Society of the Asian Studies Association of Australia.

————, 1990, *Domination and the Arts of Resistance: Hidden Transcripts.* New Haven, CT: Yale University Press.

Sedaitis, Judith B., and Jim Butterfield, 1991, *Perestroika from Below: Social Movements in the Soviet Union.* San Francisco, CA: Westview Press.

Segal, Bernard, 1998, "Drinking and Drinking-Related Problems Among Alaska Natives." *Alcohol Health and Research World* 22(4):276–80.

Segal, Bernard, et al., 1991, "Alaskan and Siberian Studies on Alcoholic Behavior and Genetic Predisposition." In *Circumpolar Health 90: Proceedings of the 8th International Congress on Circumpolar Health 1991.* Pp. 474–7. Winnipeg, Manitoba: University of Manitoba Press.

———, 1994, "Biobehavioral Factors and Drinking Among Alaskan and Siberian Natives: Cross Cultural Collaborative Research." *Arctic Medical Research* 53(Suppl. 2):568–72.

Semushkin, Tikhon, ca. 1934, *Children of the Soviet Arctic.* London: Hutchinson.

———, 1952, *Alitet Goes to the Hills.* Moscow: Foreign Languages Publishing House.

———, 1954, *Chukotka.* Moscow: Sovetskii Pisatel'.

Sharlet, Robert, 1993, "Russian Constitutional Crisis: Law and Politics Under Yeltsin." *Post-Soviet Affairs* 9(4):314–36.

Sharp, John, 1996, "Ethnogenesis and Ethnic Mobilization: A Comparative Perspective on a South African Dilemma." In *The Politics of Difference: Ethnic Premises in a World of Power.* E. N. Wilmsen and P. McAllister, eds. Pp. 85–103. Chicago, IL: University of Chicago Press.

Sheldon, Jerome F., 1989, "Across the Ice Curtain: Alaska–Siberia Visits, 1988." *Polar Record* 25(154):219–22.

Shimkin, Demitri B., and Edith M. Shimkin, 1975, "Population Dynamics in Northeastern Siberia, 1650/1700." *Musk-Ox* 16:7–23.

Sikkink, Kathryn, and Margaret Keck, 1998, *Activists Beyond Borders: Transnational Advocacy Networks in International Politics.* Ithaca, NY: Cornell University Press.

Sirina, A. A., 1999, "Rodovye Obshchiny Malochislennykh Narodov Severa v Respublike Sakha (Iakutiia): Shag k Samoopredeleniiu?" (Clan-Based Communities of the Less-Numerous Peoples of the North in the Republic of Sakha [Yakutia]: A Step Towards Self-Determination? *Issledovaniia po Prikladnoi i Neotlozhnoi Etnologii* (Research on Applied and Urgent Ethnology), Vol. 126. Moscow: Russian Academy of Sciences, Institute of Ethnology and Anthropology.

Slezkine, Yuri, 1991, "The Fall of Soviet Ethnography, 1928–38." *Current Anthropology* 32(4):476–84.

———, 1992, "From Savages to Citizens: The Cultural Revolution in the Soviet Far North, 1928–1938." *Slavic Review* 51(1):52–76.

———, 1994, *Arctic Mirrors: Russia and the Small Peoples of the North.* Ithaca, NY: Cornell University Press.

Sokolova, Z. P., N. I. Novikova, and N. V. Ssorin-Chaikov, 1995, "Etnografy Pishut Zakon: Kontekst i Problemy/Zakon Rossiiskoi Federatsii: Osnovy Pravovogo Statusa Korennykh Narodov Severa Rossii (Proekt)" (Ethnographers Writing a Law: Context and Problems/Law of the Russian Federation: Foundations of the Legal Status of Indigenous Peoples of the Russian North [Draft]). *Etnograficheskoe Obozrenie* 1995(1):74–88.

Stalin, I. V., 1967, *Sochineniya*. 3 vols. Stanford, CA: Hoover Institution.

Stavrakis, Peter J., Joan DeBardeleben, and Larry Black, 1997, *Beyond the Monolith: The Emergence of Regionalism in Post-Soviet Russia*. Washington, DC: Woodrow Wilson Center Press.

Stephan, John J., 1994, *The Russian Far East: A History*. Stanford, CA: Stanford University Press.

Suliandziga, P. V., and O. A. Murashko, eds., 2000, *Severnye Narody Rossii na Puti v Novoe Tysiacheletie* (Northern Peoples of Russia on the Path to a New Millennium). Moscow: Assotsiatsiya Korennykh Malochislennykh Narodov Severa, Sibiri i Dal'nego Vostoka Rossiiskoi Federatsii.

Sverdrup, Harald Ulrik, 1978, *Among the Tundra People*. San Diego, CA: University of California.

Taracouzio, T. A., 1938, *Soviets in the Arctic: An Historical, Economic and Political Study of the Soviet Advance into the Arctic*. New York: Macmillan.

Tarrow, Sidney, 1994, *Power in Movement: Social Movements, Collective Action and Politics*. New York: Cambridge University Press.

Timchenko, E., 1995, "A Vot u Nas v 'Iarange' . . . " (Here's What We're Up to in the "Iaranga" . . .). *Vestnik Kul'tury Dal'nego Vostoka* 1995:40–2.

Tkachenko, A. A., and A. V. Koriukhina, 1995, "K Probleme Ratifikatsii Rossiiskoi Federatsiei Konventsii MOT No. 169 'O Korennykh Narodakh i Narodakh, Vedushchikh Plemennoi Obraz Zhizni v Nezavisimykh Stranakh" (Toward the Problem of Ratification by the Russian Federation of ILO Convention No. 169 "Convention Concerning Indigenous and Tribal Populations in independent countries"). *Etnograficheskoe Obozrenie* 3: 122–32.

Touraine, Alain, 1992, "Beyond Social Movements?" *Theory, Culture and Society* 9:125–45.

Tugolukov, V. A., 1979, *Kto Vy, Yukagiry?* (Who Are You, Yukagirs?). Moscow: Nauka.

———, 1985, *Tungusy: Evenki i Eveny Srednoi i Zapadnoi Sibiri* (The Tungus: Evenks and Evens of Central and Western Siberia). Moscow: Nauka.

Tymnetuvge, O. D., 1990, "Bol' i Nadezhda Moego Naroda" (The Pain and Hope of My Peoples). *Magadanskii Olenevod* 42:3–9.

Udalova, I. V., 1989, "Izmenenie Chislennosti i Sostava Intelligentsii Narodnostei Severa (Na Primere Nanaitsev)" (Change in the Number and Composition of the Intelligentsia of the Peoples of the North [on the Example of the Nanais]). In *Narody Sibiri na Sovremennom Etape: Natsional'nye i Regional'nye Osobennosti Razvitiya. Sbornik Nauchnykh Trudov* (The Peoples of the North in the Contemporary Stage: National and

Regional Particularities of Development. Collection of Scientific Works). V. S. Shmakov, ed. Pp. 100–13. Novosibirsk: Nauka Sibirskoe Otedelenie.

Ustinov, V., 1956, *Olenevodstvo na Chukotke* (Reindeer Herding in Chakotka). Magadan: Magadanskoe Knizhnoe Izdatel'stvo.

Uvachan, Vasilii N., 1960, *Peoples of the Soviet North*. Moscow: Foreign Languages Publishing House.

———, 1963, speech made at the Supreme Soviet of the USSR, 18 December 1963. In *Zasedaniia Verkhovnogo Soveta SSSR: Stenograficheskii Otchet*. Shestoi Sozyv, Tret'e Sessiya (Conference of the Supreme Soviet of the USSR: Stenographic Report. Sixth Convocation, Third Session). Pp. 415–22. Moscow: Izdatel'stvo Verkhovnogo Soveta SSSR.

———, 1982, "K Istorii Obrazovaniya Sovetskoi Avtonomii Narodnostei Severa" (Toward the History of the Formation of Soviet Autonomy of the Peoples of the North). *Letopis' Severa* 10:22–9.

———, 1990, "Socio-Economic and Cultural Development of the Peoples of the Soviet North." In *Arctic Languages: An Awakening*. D. R. F. Collis, ed. Pp. 39–48. Paris: UNESCO.

Uvarovskaya, Liubov' Petrovna, 1992, *Skazaniya Sela Snezhnoe* (Stories of the Village of Snezhnoe). Anadyr': Chukotskii Okruzhnoi Tsentr Narodnogo Tvorchestva.

Vakhtin, Nikolai, 1993, *Korennoe Naselenie Krainego Severa Rossiskoi Federatsii* (The Indigenous Population of the Far North of the Russian Federation). St. Petersburg: Izdatel'stvo Evropeiskogo Doma.

———, 1994, "Native Peoples of the Russian Far North." In *Polar Peoples: Self-Determination and Development*. M. R. Group, ed. Pp. 29–80. London: Minority Rights Group.

Van Deusen, Kira, 1999, *Raven and the Rock: Storytelling in Chukotka*. Seattle, WA: University of Washington Press.

Vdovin, I. S., 1965, *Ocherki Istorii i Etnografii Chukchei* (Sketches of the History of Chukotka). Moscow and Leningrad: Nauka.

Venne, Sharon Helen, 1998, *Our Elders Understand Our Rights: Evolving International Law Regarding Indigenous Peoples*. Penticton, BC: Theytus Books.

Verkhovnyi Sovet SSSR, 1954, *Deputaty Verkhovnogo Soveta S.S.S.R., Chetvertyi Sozyv* (Deputies of the Supreme Soviet of the USSR, Fourth Convocation). Moscow: Izdanie Verkhovnogo Soveta SSSR.

———, 1959, *Deputaty Verkhovnogo Soveta S.S.S.R., Piatii Sozyv* (Deputies of the Supreme Soviet of the USSR, Fifth Convocation). Moscow: Izdanie Verkhovnogo Soveta SSSR.

———, 1962, *Deputaty Verkhovnogo Soveta S.S.S.R., Shestoi Sozyv* (Deputies of the Supreme Soviet of the USSR, Sixth Convocation). Moscow: Izdanie Verkhovnogo Soveta SSSR.

————, 1966, *Deputaty Verkhovnogo Soveta S.S.S.R., Sed'moi Sozyv* (Deputies of the Supreme Soviet of the USSR, Seventh Convocation). Moscow: Izdanie Verkhovnogo Soveta SSSR.

————, 1970, *Deputaty Verkhovnogo Soveta S.S.S.R., Vos'moi Sozyv* (Deputies of the Supreme Soviet of the USSR, Eighth Convocation). Moscow: Izdanie Verkhovnogo Soveta SSSR.

————, 1974, *Deputaty Verkhovnogo Soveta S.S.S.R., Deviatyi Sozyv* (Deputies of the Supreme Soviet of the USSR, Ninth Convocation). Moscow: Izdanie Verkhovnogo Soveta SSSR.

————, 1979, *Deputaty Verkhovnogo Soveta S.S.S.R., Desiatyi Sozyv* (Deputies of the Supreme Soviet of the USSR, Tenth Convocation). Moscow: Izdanie Verkhovnogo Soveta.

————, 1984, *Deputaty Verkhovnogo Soveta S.S.S.R., Odinnadtsatyi Sozyv* (Deputies of the Supreme Soviet of the USSR, Eleventh Convocation). Moscow: Izdanie Verkhovnogo Soveta.

————, 1991, Spisok Narodnykh Deputatov S.S.S.R. (List of People's Deputies of the SSSR). Moscow: Vneshtorgizdat.

Viola, Lynne, 1996, *Peasant Rebels Under Stalin: Collectivization and the Culture of Peasant Resistance.* New York: Oxford University Press.

Vitebsky, Piers, 1992, "Landscape and Self-Determination Among the Eveny: The Political Environment of Siberian Reindeer Herders Today." In *Bush Base: Forest Farm. Culture, Environment and Development.* E. Croll and D. Parkin, eds. Pp. 223–46. London: Routledge.

Walicki, Andrej, 1979, *A History of Russian Thought from the Enlightenment to Marxism.* Stanford, CA: Stanford University Press.

Wallace, A. F. C., 1956, "Revitalization Movements." *American Anthropologist* 58:264–81.

Wedel, Janine R., 1998, *Collision and Collusion: The Strange Case of Western Aid to Eastern Europe 1989–1998.* New York: St. Martin's Press.

Wegren, Stephen K., 1998, *Agriculture and the State in Soviet and Post-Soviet Russia.* Pittsburgh, PA: University of Pittsburgh Press.

Yavlinsky, Grigory, 1998, "Russia's Phony Capitalism." *Foreign Affairs* May–June:67–79.

Young, Oran, 1992, *Arctic Politics: Conflict and Cooperation in the Circumpolar North.* Hanover, NH: University Press of New England.

Zaslavsky, Victor, 1993, "Success and Collapse: Traditional Soviet Nationality Policy." In *Nations and Politics in the Soviet Successor States.* I. Bremmer and R. Taras, eds. Pp. 29–42. Cambridge, UK: Cambridge University Press.

Zhikharev, N. A., 1961, *Ocherki Istorii Severo-Vostoka R.S.F.S.R.* (Sketches of the History of Northeast RSFSR). Magadan: Magadanskoe Knizhnoe Izdatel'stvo.

Index

Abramovich, Roman Arkadevich. *See also* governor of Chukotka, head of administration, xv–xviii, 210, 217–18, 246
Abriutina, Larisa, 75, 215–16
Achirgina, Tatiana, 21–4, 42
activism, indigenous
 in Alaska, 6
 in Chukotka, 6, 35, 61, 64, 68, 76, 83, 96, 219
 in Russia, 4, 29, 31, 34, 218
 international, 26, 30, 33, 213
activism, Soviet era, 39–42
activists, indigenous
 in Chukotka, 10, 12, 15, 21, 26, 34–5, 40, 42, 120, 216–18
 in Russia, 33, 69, 112, 182
 international, 33
administration, Anadyr' city, 133, 135, 152, 196, 200

administration, Chukotka regional. *See also* Executive Committee, xvi, 146, 195
 alleged corruption in, 75
 closing of native-language newspaper, 15–16, 19
 control of mass media, 80, 175
 indigenous peoples employed in, 21, 25, 38
 indigenous protest against, 17, 64, 66–7, 140
 international relations, 174, 177–80
 political changes in, 168, 172, 217
 relations with indigenous association, 37, 43–6, 172
 treatment of indigenous population, 10, 11–12, 25–7, 44, 49, 69–71, 73–4, 80, 149–52, 188, 201, 206–8, 216, 218
Ainana, Liudmila, 44, 215–16, 218